In the World Interior of Capital

In the World Interior of Capital

For a Philosophical Theory of Globalization

Peter Sloterdijk

Translated by Wieland Hoban

polity

First published in German as *Im Weltinnenraum des Kapitals* © Suhrkamp Verlag Frankfurt am Main 2005

This English edition © Polity Press, 2013

Polity Press
65 Bridge Street
Cambridge CB2 1UR, UK

Polity Press
350 Main Street
Malden, MA 02148, USA

ISBN-13: 978-0-7456-4768-5
ISBN-13: 978-0-7456-4769-2 (pb)

A catalogue record for this book is available from the British Library.

Typeset in 10.5 on 12 pt Sabon
by Toppan Best-set Premedia Limited
Printed and bound in Great Britain by Clays Ltd, St Ives plc

The publisher has used its best endeavours to ensure that the URLs for external websites referred to in this book are correct and active at the time of going to press. However, the publisher has no responsibility for the websites and can make no guarantee that a site will remain live or that the content is or will remain appropriate.

Every effort has been made to trace all copyright holders, but if any have been inadvertently overlooked the publisher will be pleased to include any necessary credits in any subsequent reprint or edition.

For further information on Polity, visit our website: www.politybooks.com

In memoriam

Siegfried Unseld

Contents

First Part

On the Emergence
of the World System

. . . and the pirate globe drifts
in the stormy ether.

Henri Michaux, *Inexpressible Places*

1

Of Grand Narratives

The present essay is devoted to an undertaking of which it is unclear whether one should call it untimely or impossible. In recapitulating the history of terrestrial globalization, it seeks to provide outlines for a theory of the present using the means of a philosophically inspired grand narrative. Whoever finds this ambition outlandish should consider that while it is certainly provocative to assert it, it would be an act of intellectual defeatism to abandon it. Philosophical thought has always tried to tell us who we are and what we should do; for over two hundred years, this has also included information about how to date ourselves in 'history'. The penetration of the philosophical thought of Old Europe by time, however, has so far caused only a partial revision of the body of tradition. Now that the era of one-sided time-idolization seems to have ended, however, the lived space is also demanding its due. Kant, at least, already knew that reason itself had its model in spatial orientation.[1] Whoever follows this clue far enough should logically arrive at a changed view of the task of philosophical activity: philosophy is its place comprehended in thoughts. In the moments when it knows what it does, it shows the characteristics of a conference in which many disciplines all have their own bit to say. To elucidate the situation, grand narratives are necessary.

Such an attempt appears untimely in the light of the consensus that has been predominant among intellectuals for a generation, namely that precisely such narratives, the 'grand' ones, have had their day once and for all. This opinion certainly does not come from nowhere. It is supported by the plausible conviction that the known narratives of this type, despite seeking to construct the course of 'history' on a large and general scale, had irredeemably provincial aspects; that, controlled by deterministic prejudices, they smuggled projected goals of shameless linearity into the course of events; that, because of their incorrigible Eurocentrism, they were in conspiracy with the colonialist looting of the world; that they, because they taught salvation history openly or covertly, helped bring down profane disaster on a grand scale; and that now, a very different form of thought would have to emerge – a way of speaking about historical matters that would be discreet, polyvalent, non-totalizing, and, above all, aware of its own perspectival conditionality.

Everything about this view is correct – except for the conclusion, which is almost always pulled in the wrong direction, that of resignation. It is true that the historian of ideas, looking back on the master texts of philosophical narration and the classical exegeses of the historically animated world with the sensibility of today, must have the impression of dealing with a bundle of rhapsodic exaggerations. What was previously called philosophy of history amounted without exception to delusional systems of prematurity. They always led to hasty montages of their material onto violently drawn straight lines, as if the thinkers had been seized by an overactivity syndrome that chased them towards the wrong goals. Fortunately, the times have passed in which doctrines could appear attractive while promising their adepts access to the engine room of world history – or even the administrative floor of the Tower of Babel – with the help of a handful of simplifying concepts. Today, the vanitas of all past historico-philosophical constructs is obvious even to the layperson; every first-year student or gallery owner meanwhile understands enough about these fabrications to show a faint smile at such terms as 'world spirit', 'historical goal' or 'general progress'.

Satisfaction over these clarifications does not last long, for the customary talk of the end of the grand narratives overshoots the mark as soon as it is no longer content to reject their intolerable simplifications. Has it not already hardened into a comfortable meta-grand narrative itself? Is this new intellectual myth not allied unmistakably with an acerbic sluggishness that sees in the extensive only the burdensome, and in the great only the suggestion of mania? Were the post-dialectical and post-structuralist scepticisms not followed, in fact, by a partial paralysis in thought of which the idea-hostile focus on detailed histories from obscure archives that is currently making the rounds in the humanities constitutes the mildest form?

If the grand narratives known so far – the Christian, the liberal-progressive, the Hegelian, the Marxist, the fascist – have been seen through as unsuitable attempts to seize power over the world's complexity, this critical realization neither delegitimizes the narration of things past nor exempts thought from striving to cast an intense light on the comprehensible details of the elusive whole. Has thinking not always meant taking on the challenge that the excessive would appear concretely before us? And is this excessiveness that challenges us to act conceptually not inherently irreconcilable with the tranquillizing nature of the mediocre? The wretchedness of the conventional forms of grand narrative by no means lies in the fact that they were too great, but that they were not great enough. The meaning of 'great', of course, remains arguable. For us, 'great enough' means 'closer to the pole of excess'. '[A]nd what would *thinking* be if it did not constantly confront chaos?'[2]

The sketches presented here form a side wing of the *Sphären* project, which constitutes a more extensive attempt to configure the narrative and the philosophical with each other in a partly neo-sceptical, partly neo-morphological fashion.[3] In the process of carrying out my intentions – the final volume was published in 2004 – I discussed the development of the orb motif in the philosophical cosmology and theology of Old Europe, examining its psychodynamic implications in some detail and testing its powers of anthropological shaping. This brought to light, among other things, the high psycho-semantic or religious utility value of the classical orb speculations. In the encompassing orbs, the ancients discovered a geometry of security; in this geometry there developed, as was to be shown, the strong motive of metaphysically or totalistically producing worldviews. The narrative of divine spheres and universe orbs laid out in *Sphären II, Globen* revealed why these sublime imaginary constructs of wholeness were doomed to vanish with the beginning of the Modern Age,[4] while the human location, the planet Terra, took on increasingly explicit contours. In a dawn that took centuries, the earth rose as the only and true orb, the basis of all contexts of life, while almost everything that had previously been considered the partnered, meaning-filled sky was emptied. This fatalization of the earth, brought about by human practices and taking place at the same time as the loss of reality among the once-vital numinous spheres, does not merely provide the background to these events; it is itself the drama of globalization. Its core lies in the observation that the conditions of human immunity fundamentally change on the discovered, interconnected and singularized earth.

If the present characterization, unlike many other attempts to address the matter, emphasizes its philosophical aspect, this is based on the frequently overlooked fact that the historical object, the terrestrial globe, is a thing full of metaphysical quirks that like to hide beneath the veneer of the ordinary. It constitutes a geographical-philosophical bastard whose logical and physical peculiarities are not so simple to comprehend. On the one hand, the printed blue orb with the savannah-coloured patches initially seems no more than one thing among many things, a small body among many bodies, that statesmen and schoolchildren set in rotation with a single hand movement; at the same time, it is supposed to represent the singular totality or the geological monad that serves as the foundation for all life, thought and invention. It is this terrestrial question of location that becomes ever more binding in the course of modernization: while the ancient conception of the cosmos paradoxically made the earth the marginal centre of a universe that humans could only observe from within, the moderns perceived it as an eccentric orb whose roundness we could verify ourselves through external viewing. This would have unforeseeable consequences for the generations after Mercator. For us, monogeism – the conviction that this planet is unique – transpires as a fact that is rejuvenated daily, while monotheism can never again be more than an age-worn religious thesis that cannot really be brought up to date, not even with the aid of pious bombs from the Near East. The proofs of God's existence must bear the blemish of their failure, while those of the globe's existence have an unstoppable influx of evidence on their side. In the following, we shall concern ourselves with the circumstances under which such extensive proof of the unity of the equally massive and sublime object we inhabit was able to accumulate.

These intimations have taken us into the heartland of philosophy – assuming we accept the supposition that the pursuit of philosophy is not, as one has often heard in recent times, merely an activity with no object, a modus vivendi, but also possesses an objectivity in its own right, not to mention a focus of its own. Philosophy can and should be conducted artfully as a quasi-science of totalizations and their metaphors, as a narrative theory of the genesis of the general, and finally as a meditation on being-in-situations – also known as being-in-the-world; I call this the 'theory of immersion' or general theory of being together, and use it to explain the kinship between recent philosophy and the art of the installation.[5]

One of the main characteristics of conventional views about globalization is, to be frank, a discreet comic element. It manifests itself in a wild philosophical activity that clearly feels most at ease as long as members of the profession do not interfere in the discussion. As a result, the most philosophical of all the contemporary topoi of politics and cultural theory travels the world with virtually no perceptible involvement of the philosophical field. The most effective totalization, the unification of the world through money in all its transformations – as commodity, text, number, image and celebrity – took place through its own momentum, without the members of the faculty for world wisdom having, initially, more to say than any newspaper reader in a country with a vaguely free press. Where contemporary philosophers commented on the subject with the skills of their profession, this usually occurred in marginal publications, without any notable effects on the larger flow of words – with the possible exception of Negri and Hardt's *Empire*, which received worldwide attention.

The irony of the situation is increased by the fact that one could believe this levelling-out of the philosophical vote into the general muddle of opinions to indicate a desirable state. One could convincingly argue that integration into non-hierarchical everyday communications was the best thing that could have happened to philosophy, which claimed until recently to dream of becoming practical. It could even be claimed that an explicit sentiment in philosophical utterances of not wanting to be anything special proved one was dealing with a form of thought that was at the necessary level for our times – and the levels of today have renounced the bad habit of standing too high. Consequently, the spokesmanship of non-philosophers in the matter of globalization could be taken as an indication that 'society' – or whatever else one wishes to call the coexisting and politicized multiplicities – has become immune to dangerous philosophically induced enthusiasms and imperiously generalized mottos about the state of the world. So why lament the marginalization of philosophy?

Far be it from me to deny the productive aspects of such a view. The monopolization of the discourse on globalization by political scientists and sociologists, to whom we owe the continuation of journalism by morose means, would be quite bearable on the whole – were it not for the fact that the basic concepts of these debates are almost all unrecognized philosophical terms whose amateurish use leads to insinuations and distortions of meaning. Ultimately, anyone who conducts philosophy without regard for the state of the art is always propagating a myth, openly or covertly, and not infrequently with dangerous consequences. One of the most notable side effects of the current para-philosophical wave is the proliferation of unverified statements that no longer stop at the borders of nation-states. Pirated copies of cluelessness circulate freely in the whole world. They provide a powerful demonstration of the thesis that today, anything seeking customers will sell on all markets or none. Curiously enough, it is often liberal minds, those declared enemies of the grand theological and philosophical narratives, that plunge into politically virulent hypotheses with underived concepts of globality and totality, of space, time and situation, of unity, multiplicity, interaction, inclusion and exclusion, along with other words that add up to an editorial when strung together.

For the time being, the only way to combat the undesired side effects of such precipitations is to recall the philosophical origin of the globe motif. This could begin with the frugal note that 'globe' is a noun representing a simple idea, the cosmos thesis, and a twofold cartographical object, the sky of the ancients and the earth of the moderns; it is on this noun that the usual adjectival derivations about 'global' facts depend, which were only recently re-elevated to nominal status via the English verb 'to globalize' – which resulted in the hybrid figure of 'globalization'. This term does, at least, have the virtue of emphasizing the active quality of the current world event: when globalization occurs, it is always through operations with long-distance effects.

The next step would be to show that the notion of an orb which serves as a vessel or carrier for biological and reflexive life was constitutive for the philosophical interpretation of the universe among the Greeks. The cosmology of Western antiquity, that of Plato and the later Hellenistic scholars, had devoted itself to the idea of representing the totality of what exists in the stimulating image of an all-encompassing sphere. The name of this construct is still present in the European memory, whatever nostalgic taints it may have accrued, for since ancient academic times, the great round body of the existent world has been known as the *cosmos* – a name that calls to mind the ornamental and beautiful character of the universe. The same object was simultaneously addressed as *uranos*, the sky. The titanic name expressed the notion that the world reached its limits in a final ethereal vault – a view one could equally have called a hope. The ancients wanted to conceive of the sky as a wide vase that held the fixed stars and calmed the human fear of falling. To Aristotle, the sky was the outermost shell of the orb that contains everything, but is contained by nothing.[6] Measuring this sky in thought meant carrying out the first globalization. In the process, the good news of philosophy emerged: that humans, as much as the disorder they experience might depress them, cannot fall out of space.

The true beginnings of globalization, therefore, lie in the rationalization of the world's structure by the ancient cosmologists, who were the first to construct with conceptual, or rather morphological seriousness the totality of the existent in a spherical form, and presented this edifying construct of order to the intellect for viewing. Classical ontology was a spherology, as a doctrine both of the world and of God – it offered a theory of the absolute globe in both forms.[7] It gained a reputation for itself as a sublime geometry that placed the well-formed, the circular, that which runs back into itself, at the centre: it acquired sympathies as the logic, ethics and aesthetics of round things. Among the thinkers of the European tradition, it was an established fact that the good and the round amount to the same thing; that is why the spherical form could become effective as a cosmic immune system. Theories of the unround came into play as a far later achievement – they heralded the victorious experiential sciences, the death of God, chaos calculations and the end of the Old Europe.

Recalling these circumstances means exposing why 'globalization' as a whole is a far more logically and historically powerful process than what it is taken to mean in current journalism and among its economic, sociological and police informants. The relevant political speeches, whether given during the week or on Sundays, deal exclusively with the most recent episode, which is marked by a greatly accelerated exchange of commodities, signs and microbes – to say nothing, for now, of the financial markets and their phantoms. Whoever wishes to envision the ontological gravity of the events we discuss as globalization – the encounter between being and form in a sovereign body – must highlight widely overlooked differences between periods in the notion itself. For this reason, the term 'globalization' is augmented here by the adjective 'terrestrial'. It is intended to show that we are dealing with a chapter in a longer story whose intellectually arousing dimensions the contributors to the current debate, in most cases, do not adequately comprehend.

Terrestrial globalization (realized practically through Christian-capitalist seafaring and politically implanted through the colonialism of the Old European nation-states) constitutes, as we will show, the fully comprehensible middle part of a three-phase process whose beginnings I have discussed at greater length elsewhere.[8] This five-hundred-year middle section of the sequence went down in history as the 'age of European expansion'. Most historians find it easy to view the time between 1492 and 1945 as a completed complex of events: it is the period in which the current world system took form. It is preceded, as noted above, by cosmic-uranian globalization, that powerful first stage of spheric thought that – acknowledging the preference for spherical figures in classical ontology – one could call morphological (or rather onto-morphological) globalization. It is followed by electronic globalization, which will be dealt with by those alive today and their descendants. What distinguishes the three great stages of globalization, then, are primarily their symbolic and technical media: it makes an epochal difference whether one measures an idealized orb with lines and cuts, sails around a real orb with ships, or lets aeroplanes and radio signals circulate around the atmospheric casing of a planet. It makes an ontological difference whether one envisages the one cosmos, which fully encloses the world of essences, or the one earth, which serves as the bearer of various world-formations.

The climax of spheric metaphysics – Dante and Nicholas of Cusa are its eminent witnesses – is at once the turning point towards its dissolution. The decline phase of the sphere-cosmological interpretation of the existent set in with the cultural caesura that we, following the trail of Jacob Burckhardt, call the Renaissance. The great historian and morphologist had suggested the formula of the 'discovery of the world and man' for this departure to the Modern Age – which, as we shall see, is identical to terrestrial realism's phase of ascent. If we look at the oceans, it begins with the great voyages of the Portuguese; if we look up to the sky, it begins with the 'revolutions' of Copernicus and with Kepler's abandonment of the dogma of ideal circular motion in planetary orbits. By removing the foundation of the idealism of the round, this renunciation had to bring about the collapse of the consoling ethereal firmament. From those days on, a very new turn towards the planet earth took place in an inexorable sequence of logical and empirical chapters – perhaps it will one day be grasped that the discovery and mapping of the neurological moons, human brains, are still part of that same turn. It is through this that the monogeistic faith of the Modern Age is empirically underpinned; the turn initiates the age of earth acquisition whose saturation phase we entered barely half a century ago.

In the present context, the term 'saturation' has an action-theoretical meaning: after the satisfaction of the aggressive hunger for the world that manifested itself in the excursions and occupations of European agents, an era began in 1945 – at the latest – whose mode of world-making differs clearly from that of the preceding time. Its hallmark is the increasing priority of inhibitions over initiatives. After terrestrial globalization had taken place over centuries as one-sidedness in action, people have now been looking back on the deeds and mentalities of that era with an obligatory contrition for the last few decades – they bear the cautionary label 'Eurocentrism', as if to convey that one has renounced the works of this formerly so arrogant centre. We will characterize this epoch as the time of the crime of unilateralism – the asymmetrical taking of the world whose points of departure lay in the ports, royal courts and ambitions of Europe. It will be shown how and why the complex of these rash, heroic and pitiful deeds had to go down in history under the name of 'world history' – and why world history in this sense of the term is definitely over. If history means the successful phase of unilateralism – and we will defend this definition further below – then the earth's inhabitants are unmistakably living in a post-historical regime. How far this can be reconciled with the claim of the USA, as the 'indispensable nation', to be the heir of the unilateral conception of the world will be examined later in a section of its own.

Globalization has been saturated in the moral sense since the victims began reporting the consequences of the perpetrators' deeds back to them from all over the world – this is the essence of the post-unilateral, post-imperial, post-colonial situation. It has been saturated in the technological sense too since fast goods vehicles and over-fast media outdid the sluggish world traffic of the seafaring age (which does not, incidentally, change the fact that there is more disenchanted drifting on the sea today than at any earlier time: 95 per cent of material world trade currently takes place by sea). One can now return from an aerial tour around the globe virtually the same day one leaves, and one usually learns of great political events, serious crimes and tidal waves on the other side of the world a few minutes or hours later. It has been saturated in the systemic sense since the carriers of this reaching out into open space were forced to acknowledge that all initiatives are subject to the principle of reciprocity, and most offensives are connected back to the source after a certain processing time. These repercussions now take place within intervals scarcely longer than a human life, and often even shorter than their actors' terms of office, such that the perpetrators themselves are increasingly confronted with the consequences of their actions – one must therefore acknowledge the trials of criminal heads of state such as Pinochet, Milošević, Saddam Hussein and other unfortunate unilateralists as moral world firsts. As immanent justice gains ground, the forced ideas of retribution in the hereafter – once an indispensable ingredient in advanced-civilized morality – can lose significance for us. The law of increasing density gives the idealistic thesis that world history includes the Last Judgement new meaning: in the compacted world, all actors who have ventured far out are indeed subject to uninterrupted assessment by their supervisors and opponents; the expectability of resistances and countermeasures gives the concept of reality its current hue. When there is dense event traffic, the individual initiatives follow the law of increasingly reciprocal obstruction – until the sum of all simultaneous undertakings stabilizes in a hyperactive, vibrating jelly: that is what the phrase 'post-historical civilization',

correctly understood, means. Word is getting around that the terms
'co-operation' and 'mutual obstruction' mean the same thing.

The process of terrestrial globalization can be considered to have
reached its completion with the establishment of the gold-based
world monetary system by Bretton Woods in 1944;[9] at the latest,
however, it ended with the installation of an electronic atmosphere
and a satellite environment in the earth's orbit in the 1960s and
1970s. The same movement encompasses the founding, however
hesitant, of the international courts of law, those havens of justice in
which atrocities that have travelled around the world are brought
back to their perpetrators.

It is at this level that the manifestations of the current *third* globalization come into view. These will primarily be discussed in the second
part of this attempt, which deals with the establishment and arrangement of the capitalist 'world interior'. To describe the globalized
world, which could equally be termed a 'synchronous world', we
shall invoke the image of the Crystal Palace from Fyodor Dostoyevsky's
novel *Notes from Underground* (1864) – a metaphor that refers to
the famous large-scale enclosure for the Great Exhibition of 1851 in
London. The Russian writer believed that it held the essence of
Western civilization, as if in a final concentrate. He recognized the
monstrous edifice as a man-eating structure, in fact a modern Baal
– a cult container in which humans pay homage to the demons of
the West: the power of money and pure movement, along with volup-
tuous and intoxicating pleasures. The hallmarks of the Baal cult, for
which modern economists offer the world 'consumer society', are still
encapsulated most convincingly in Dostoyevsky's palace metaphor,
even if we prefer to keep our distance from the author's religious
suggestions – as well as Walter Benjamin's brilliant and obscure intimations about 'capitalism as religion'. The 'Crystal Palace' houses
the world interior of capital, the site of the virtual encounter between
Rainer Maria Rilke and Adam Smith; we will hand over to these
authors at the appropriate time. We have taken up the term 'crystal
palace' once more in order, first and foremost, to express the sentiment that the current talk of the 'global market' is ill-suited to
describing the constitution of life under the spell of obtrusive monetary circumstances. The world interior of capital is not an agora or
a trade fair beneath the open sky, but rather a hothouse that has
drawn inwards everything that was once on the outside. The bracing
climate of an integral inner world of commodity can be formulated
in the notion of a planetary palace of consumption. In this horizontal
Babylon, being human becomes a question of spending power, and

the meaning of freedom is exposed in the ability to choose between products for the market – or to create such products oneself.

In terms of general spatial feelings, it is characteristic of the third wave of globalization that it de-spatializes the real globe, replacing the curved earth with an almost extensionless point, or a network of intersection points and lines that amount to nothing other than connections between two computers any given distance apart. While the second wave, at low and medium speeds, had raised the immense extension of the planet to human observation, the third, at high speeds, made the Modern Age's sense of expansiveness disappear once more. The response to this today is a nebulous unease at the over-communicative constitution of the world system – a justified sentiment, we would argue, for what is celebrated today as the boon of telecommunications is experienced by countless people as a dubious achievement with whose aid we can now make one another as unhappy from afar as was once possible only among next-door neighbours. Where the dignity of distances is negated, the earth – along with its local ecstasies – shrinks to an almost-nothing, until nothing remains of its royal extension but a worn-out logo.

After these preliminary remarks concerning the title of the book, we must still answer the question of how seriously the heading of the final part of *Sphären II*,[10] which has been incorporated into the present study in a modified form, was really meant. The author asks the reader to believe him that he finds the endism and ultimatism of the apocalyptic features pages no less ridiculous than do their weariest readers. A 'last orb' was not discussed out of any intention to perform a philosophically distorted western. The grand narrative of the encounter between being and the circle, however, was intended to provide the background for an elucidation of why terrestrial globalization does not merely constitute one story among many. It is, as I mean to show, the only period play in the life of reciprocally discovering peoples – also known as 'mankind' – that deserves to be called 'history' or 'world history' in a philosophically relevant sense.

World history was the working-out of the earth as a bearer of cultures and ecstasies; its political character was a triumphant onesidedness of expansive European nations; its logical style is the indifferent view of all things in terms of homogeneous space, homogeneous time and homogeneous value; its operative mode is compaction; its economic result is the establishment of the world system; its energetic basis is the still copiously available fossil fuels; its primary aesthetic gestures are the hysterical expression of emotion and the cult of explosion; its psychosocial result is the coercion to become cognizant of distant misery; its vital chance is the possibility to compare the sources of happiness and the strategies of risk management intercul-turally; its moral crux is the transition of the ethos of conquest to the ethos of letting oneself be tamed by the conquered; its civilizatory tendency expresses itself in a dense complex of reliefs, assurances and guarantees of comfort; its anthropological challenge is the mass pro-duction of 'last human beings'; its philosophical consequence is the opportunity to see the one world rise in countless brains.

It should not be difficult to admit that the compression of the many previously separate worlds into one global context is a subject in which the concerns of philosophy and historiography converge. Anyone who looks back through the logbook of the last half-millennium, which bore the widely aggravating, but materially correct title 'World History of Europe',[11] will understand in what sense the orb navigated by Magellan and his successors can be called the last, or even the only one.

2

The Wandering Star

When Greek philosophers and geometricians began to measure the universe mathematically two and a half thousand years ago, they were following a strong formal intuition: that all things ultimately moved in circles. Their interest in the totality of the world was kindled by the easy constructibility and symmetrical perfection of the spherical form. For them, the simplest form was at once the most integral, complete and beautiful. The cosmologists who gathered in the ancient Academy and other places of learned quarrelling were now considered not only the greatest rationalists, but also the most distinguished of aesthetes. Anyone who was not a geometrician or an ontologist was no longer of any use as a connoisseur of beautiful things. For what was the most beautiful thing – the sky – if not the material realization of the best, namely the whole? The Greek prejudice in favour of rounded totality would survive until the days of German Idealism: 'Do you know its name? The name of that which is one and is all? Its name is Beauty' (Hölderlin, *Hyperion*).[1]

From that point on, then, the name for the perfectly beautiful – *sphaira* – was formulated geometrically. This rise of the world form over the world material was guided by an aesthetics of completion that remained in force until modern Europe implemented a different set of rules concerning the beautiful and the un-beautiful. If the subtle and the massive cosmos were ever to be integrated into a single conception, it had – as was thought at the time – to be in the notional shape of the orb. It was in the sublime nature of this super-object to remain unrecognizable to ordinary eyes: there is an orb that is too large for trivial perception and too sublime for sensory comprehension. This is hardly surprising; since philosophy started its war against the sensuality of the people's opinion, invisibility has always been presented as the foremost hallmark of deeper realities.[2] What reveals itself to the senses is, according to the philosophers, mere illusion and example, while the enduringly essential appears only in conceptual thought. Regardless of whether it is an ideal construct or a manifest phenomenon, however, no object since has succeeded in satisfying and humbling its contemplators like the all-encompassing orb, which continues to shine from afar, bearing its dual name of *cosmos* and *uranos*, long after disappearing into the archive of disused ideas.

As soon as the concern was to formulate a concept – or rather an image – of the planet's globalization, however, it was the aesthetic of the ugly that had to assert its jurisdiction. The decisive aspect of this process was not that the spherical form of the earth had been ascertained, and that it was permissible – even before clerics – to speak of the earth's curves; it was the fact that the particularities of the earth's form, its edges and corners, were now in the foreground. These alone are informative for science, for only the non-perfect – which cannot be constructed geometrically – permits and requires empirical research. The beautiful in its pure form can safely be left to the idealists, while the half-beautiful and the ugly occupy empiricists. While perfection can be designed without recourse to experience, facts and imperfections cannot be deduced without it. That is why uranian-cosmic and morphological globalization had primarily been a matter for philosophers and geometricians; terrestrial globalization, by contrast, would become a problem for cartographers and a nautical adventure, and later also a matter for economic politicians, climatologists, ecologists, terror specialists and other experts in the uneven and entangled.

It is easy to explain why this could not be any other way: in the metaphysical age, it was impossible and impermissible for the planet to present itself in a more distinguished light than its position in the cosmos allowed. In the Aristotelian-Catholic plan of the spheres, the earth, being most distant from the encompassing firmament, had the humblest status. Its placement at the centre of the cosmos thus entailed, as paradoxical as it may sound, a relegation to the lower extreme of the cosmic hierarchy.[3] Its encasement in a layered system of ethereal domes did provide security within a dense totality, but also shut it off from the upper regions where perfection resided. Hence the metaphysical references to the 'earthly' and its haughty condescension towards the non-perfect down here, on the dimly lit fringe of the heavens. One must concede that the metaphysicists knew what they were talking about: what is one to think about a place where it is night half the time, and where death and decay await all that lives? The ancients were so impressed by the contrast between form and mortality that they had to separate off a deathless world on high from the death-affected depths. Thus they became increasingly infused with a dualistic nation of the cosmos: whatever happens beneath the moon will always remain marked by failure and dissolution, for this domain is ruled by the linear, finite and exhaustible movements that, in the view of antiquity, could never lead to any good. The indestructible forms and rotations of the eternal ether, on the other hand, are at home in the spaces above the moon. The strangeness of the human situation stems from the fact that mortals, despite their condemnation to heaviness, exist as denizens of both spaces. Each individual consciousness bears the faultlines of those old tremors of separation after which the intact supra-lunar spheres broke away from the corrupt zones beneath the moon. This banishment from perfection left every sub-lunar object with cracks, scars and irregularities. Humans feel the crack in their souls as a homesickness for the better state. It reminds them of brighter, rounder, ethereal days.

What contributed to the attractiveness of the metaphysical regime despite the cosmic demotion of the earth was the circumstance that above and below were clearly separated within it; it offered the inestimable advantage of a clarity that can only be provided by hierarchy. While the lower realm was naturally unable to move upwards under its own power, it remained the privilege of the upper to pervade the lower at will. That is why in ancient times, to think always meant to think from the position of the sky, as if one could get away from earth with the aid of logic. In the old days, a thinker was someone who transcended and looked down – as Dante illustrated on his ascent to paradise. Even Eichendorff's lines from the poem 'Mondnacht' – 'It seemed as if heaven / Had quietly kissed the earth' – still read like a swan song for a schema that had moulded the habitus of being-in-the-world among Europeans for an entire age, which included the confidence that unworldliness could be learned. The poet, admittedly, already lived in a time when heaven only had pretend kisses for the earth, and in which the soul flew through silent lands as if the vehicle of the metaphor could enable it to find the way home from a beautiful foreign place.

In reality, the weakened world of the living in Eichendorff's time had not exercised its *droit du seigneur* with the earth for a long time. Centuries had passed since modern physics discovered empty space and did away with the mythical enclosure of the firmament. Not everyone found it so easy to renounce completion from above, however; one can sense the sorrow over a world without heaven until Heidegger – an earth that, it was said, was 'being-historically the wandering star'. We recall that this phrase, which sounds rather distinctive and sombre today, refers not to any given planet, but rather to the one on which the question of truth and the meaning of being arose. The wandering state of Heidegger's earth-dwellers and their star is the last trace of the lost chance to be encompassed by a heaven.

Even while the earth was still lying in the ethereal domes, however, long before its nautical circumnavigation and its cosmic dis-mantling, it presented itself in thanatological terms as the star on which people died scientifically. Its vague roundness was not an immune barrier that repelled death; it delineated the site on which the fall into time had taken place, that event after which everything that came into being owed its origins a death. That is why, on earth, everything that was made to exist must end – without exception; here clocks tick irreversibly, fuses burn towards ignition points (which is significant for the 'historical consciousness' as soon as one understands that the thought figure of the 'bang' is more suitable for endings than beginnings). Anyone on earth who understands their situation faces the fact that no one leaves this place alive. People on this gloomy orb must practise – which, in the jargon of later philosophy, meant running ahead into one's death. That is why, since then, it has been better not to call humans mortals, as was customary among the ancients, but rather the provisional ones. If a historian were asked to say from the perspective of an imagined evolutionary end what human collectives, viewed as a whole, did with their respective times, they would have to respond that humans organized free-for-all runs to their death: as humble processions, Dionysian hunts, progress projects, cynical-naturalistic elimination battles, or ecological reconciliation exercises. The surface of a body in the cosmos on which humans spend their days with futile precautions against the inescapable, then, cannot be a regular one. Perfect smoothness is only possible in idealizations, while the rough and the real converge.

It is scarcely a coincidence that the first systematic utterance concerning an 'aesthetics of ugliness' – in the book of the same name by Hegel's student Karl Rosenkranz, written in 1853 – addressed the real earth as an uneven surface at the very beginning of its argumentation. In this new, non-idealistic theory of perception, the home of humans was afforded the privilege of serving as an example leading towards a theory of natural ugliness.

Mere raw mass, in so far as it is dominated only by the law of gravity, presents us with what one could call a neutral state. It is not necessarily beautiful, but neither is it necessarily ugly; it is coincidental. If we take our earth, for example, it would have to be a perfect sphere in order to be beautiful as a mass; but it is not. It is flattened at the poles and swollen at the equator, and its surface is of the greatest irregularity in its elevation. A profile of the earth's crust, viewed purely stereometrically, shows the most coincidental muddle of elevations and depressions with the most unpredictable outlines.[4]

If one follows this thought to its conclusion, the central principle of a post-idealistic aesthetics of the earth can be formulated thus: as a real body, the geographically quantified globe is not beautiful, but rather interesting – and an interesting thing is halfway to ugliness. A momentary unease returns about the sub-lunar humiliation, known in our time by the watchword 'the human condition'. Then, however, the tide turns: the irregular becomes newly attractive for observation. The modern aesthetics of the interesting and the ugly not only ally themselves aggressively with empirical research, which is by nature concerned with things coincidentally grown together – literally the *concrete* – and with the asymmetrical; they also make disappointment palatable, thus releasing forces for the counterattack. In this way, they assist disinhibition, known in its heyday as 'praxis'. The concept of disinhibition, without which no convincing theory of modernity is possible, gathers together the motives that drive us to intervene in the imperfect and disagreeable.

If one grasps the local disadvantages of existence on the earth's surface soberly enough, one can shake off the restraints that had previously curbed the anger of mortals at the impositions of existence in the unpleasant. As a result, the advent of modernity saw outrage acquire its licence as a basic stance – *on a raison de se révolter* [it is right to rebel]; Prometheus now became the titan of the hour, and Philoctetes his secretary.[5] Now that the avoidance of the coincidental, the thinking away of the burdensome and the mental adjustment of the disturbing – all advisable in the metaphysical regime – were rapidly losing their orientation by the orderly world above, it was necessary to remain in the unpleasant, to rest among the grotesque and amorphous, to hold out beside the base and adverse. Describing it turns the object of description against itself: the new aesthetics absorbs the cracks, turbulences, ruptures and irregularities into the picture – it even competes with the real for repulsive effects.

In aesthetic terms, terrestrial globalization brings the victory of the interesting over the ideal. Its result, the now-known earth, is the orb, which disappoints as a form but attracts attention as an interesting body. To expect everything of it – and of the remaining bodies on this one – would constitute the wisdom of our age. As far as the history of aesthetics is concerned, the modern experience of art is tied to the attempt to open the eye, numbed for too long by geometrical simplifications, to the perceptual charms of the irregular.

3

Return to Earth

Accordingly, in the Modern Age, the task of designing the new image of the world no longer fell to the metaphysicists, but rather to the geographers and seafarers. It was their mission to present the last orb in pictorial form. Of all large round bodies, only shell-less humanity's own planet would henceforth have any meaning. The world-navigators, cartographers, conquistadors, world traders, even the Christian missionaries and their following of aid workers who exported goodwill and tourists who spent money on experiences at remote locations – they all behaved as if they had understood that, after the destruction of heaven, it was the earth itself that had to take over its function as the last vault. This physically real earth, as an irregularly layered, chaotically folded, storm-eroded body, now had to be circumnavigated and quantified. Thus the new image of the earth, the terrestrial globe, rose to become the central icon of the modern world picture. Beginning with the Behaim Globe from Nuremberg, made in 1492 – the oldest surviving example of its kind – and continuing up until NASA's photograms of the earth and pictures taken from the space station Mir, the cosmological process of modernity is characterized by the changes of shape and refinements in the earth's image in its diverse technical media. At no time, however – not even in the age of space travel – could the project of visualizing the earth deny its semi-metaphysical quality. Anyone who wished to attempt a portrait of the whole earth following the downfall of heaven stood, knowingly or not, in the tradition of sublime cosmography. In order to implement the new procedures for providing a conception of the world, however, gravity had to be overcome no longer only in the imagination, but also technologically.

It is symptomatic of this that Alexander von Humboldt could still dare to give his magnum opus, which was published in five volumes between 1845 and 1862 (the last ones posthumously) and became the foremost scientific bestseller of its century, the openly anachronistic title *Cosmos*. It was, as one realizes in retrospect, the historically conditioned chance for this monumentally holistic 'physical description of the world' to compensate with the resources of aesthetic education for what modern Europeans had endured through the loss of the firmament and cosmic *clôture* [(en)closure]. Humboldt had wagered that he could present this metaphysical loss as a cultural gain – and he seems to have been successful, at least with the audience of his time. In panoramic nature paintings, the aesthetic observation of the whole replaced its lost safety in the vaulted universe. The beauty of physics made the tableau of the holy circles dispensable. It is telling that in his world fresco, Humboldt, who has perhaps rightly been called the last cosmographer, no longer chose the earth as the vantage point from which to look out into the expansive space. Instead, in keeping with the spirit of his time and ours, he took up an arbitrary position in the external space from which to approach the earth like a visitor from a foreign planet.

> I propose to begin with the depths of space and the remotest nebulae, and thence gradually to descend through the starry region to which our solar system belongs, to the consideration of the terrestrial spheroid with its aerial and liquid coverings, its form, its temperature and magnetic tension, and the fullness of organic life expanding and moving over its surface under the vivifying influence of light.[1]

> Here, therefore, we do not proceed from the subjective point of view of human interest: the terrestrial is treated only as a part of the whole, and in its due subordination. The view of nature should be general, grand, and free; not narrowed by proximity, sympathy, or relative utility. A physical cosmography, or picture of the universe, should begin, therefore, not with the earth, but with the regions of space. But as the sphere of contemplation contracts in dimension, our perceptions and knowledge of the richness of details, of the fullness of physical phenomena, and of the qualitative heterogeneity of substances, augment. From the regions in which we recognize only the dominion of the laws of gravitation, we descend to our own planet, and to the intricate play of terrestrial forces.[2]

What counts here is the descending motion: it no longer belongs to the metaphysical regime, which had taught a methodical condescension towards earthly things. Instead, it already presents an astronautical perspective. It becomes clear from his way of returning to earth that, despite his holistic and consolatory habitus, the world-connoisseur Alexander von Humboldt sides with the Modern Age in the decisive point, deciding against the enchantment of earth-dwellers in the illusory casings of the sense of proximity. Like all globe-makers and cosmographers since Behaim, Schöner, Waldseemüller, Apian and Mercator senior and junior, he imposes the view of their planet on them from without, refusing to admit that the outer spaces are merely extensions of a regionally confined, herd-like, domestic and socio-uterine imagination.

This opening up into the infinite heightens the risk of modern localizations. Humans know, albeit only in a confused and indirect fashion at first, that they are contained or lost – which now amounts to virtually the same thing – somewhere in the boundless. They understand that they can no longer rely on anything except the indifference of the homogeneous infinite space. The outside expands, ignoring the postulate of proximity in the humane spheres, as a foreign entity in its own right; its first and only principle seems to be its lack of interest in humanity. The delusions of mortals that they must seek something outside – recall the space travel ideologies of the Americans and the Russians – necessarily remain very unstable, shakeable, auto-hypnotic projects against a background of futility. What is certainly true is that the externalized, neutralized and homogenized space is the primal condition of the modern natural sciences. The principle of the primacy of the outside provides the axiom for the human sciences.

This is the starting point for the development of a radically altered sense of human localization. The earth now becomes the star to which one returns – no matter how distant from it one has become. The outside is the general From-where of all possible returns. It was in the cosmographic field that thought concerning the outside was first elevated to the norm. The space from which the new and inevitable encounter-from-outside with the earth occurs is no longer the naïve vault of heaven from the age before Thomas Digges and Giordano Bruno. It is that eternally silent space, the infinity of physicists – of which Pascal, warning of the new atheistic physics, admitted that it put him in a state of terror. When Dante, looking down on the earth from the heaven of fixed stars on his journey through the spheres of paradise, had to smile involuntarily at its tiny form (*vil semblante*), this emotion was very different from the amazement that accompanied Humboldt's descent from the bleak outer spaces to an earth teeming with life. The Modern Age gained the vertical in a completely different way from the metaphysical age. Notions of flying replaced the ancient and medieval ones of 'ascending'; the airport earth, where one starts and lands, replaced the ascension earth, from which one propels oneself and which at some point, after a final flight, is left for good. The view from outside results not from a transcendence of the noetic soul into the extra- and supra-terrestrial, but rather from the development of the physical-technical, aero- and astronautical imagination – whose literary and cartographical manifestations, furthermore, were always ahead of the technological ones.

When Humboldt's *Cosmos* was published, of course, there had not been any talk of the planetary domes or the all-encompassing heaven of fixed stars for centuries. That old medium of edifying astronomy, the uranian globe – a common learning tool in traditional cosmology from Alcuin to Hegel – had already been out of use for a generation by the time of Humboldt's later years, and stargazing had long since developed into an independent discipline in the spectrum of the triumphant natural sciences. With the consolidation of astrophysics, the science of the outermost spaces and the bodies contained in them, that knowledge of the mythical constellations which had made the heavenly landscapes legible since antiquity went into rapid decline. Anyone still wishing to pursue astronomy had to do so in the knowledge that they were looking up to an anthropo-fugal space in whose emptiness our hopes and projections go astray without any echo.

Just as the earth retained its special status as the star to which one returns, however, European 'humanity' – especially after its cosmo-logical, ethnological and psychological enlightenments – preserved its distinction as the intelligent nerve cell in the cosmos that must be a point of reference under all circumstances and in all situations. Alexander von Humboldt had been given the mission of formulating the return from cosmic exteriority to the self-reflexive world of humans in exemplary fashion. A generation earlier, Immanuel Kant had characterized the human mind's capacity to return to itself from the enormous, the utmost and the most foreign as the sense of the sublime – what he considered sublime was the human consciousness of one's own dignity, resisting all temptations to abandon oneself in the overwhelming.[3] By enacting the return from the terrible expanse of nature, the astral and oceanic dimensions, into the educated salons with edifying thoroughness, Humboldt's picture of the world offered his contemporaries a final initiation into the cosmologically sublime. A view of the world on the largest possible scale here became an emergency of aesthetic life.[4] This meant the continuation of the *vita contemplativa* by bourgeois, and thus ultimately consumptive means. If humans wanted to be 'moved' and 'deeply feel the monstrous', they now had to seek this in their own interiors. It was Walter Benjamin who summed up the meaning of bourgeois solitudes: 'For the private individual, the private environment represents the universe. In it he gathers remote places and the past. His drawing room is a box in the world theatre.'[5]

Where cosmic safety has become unattainable, humans are left to reflect on their situation in a space in which they must come back to themselves from any distant place – preferably without leaving their own 'four walls'. Hence the exemplary human of modernity is *Homo habitans*, with the accompanying bodily extensions and touristic extensions. Even if the essential transcendence and the dream of a true home in the world above were irretrievably lost for Modern Age humans, the transcendental, on the other hand, the self-reference of thinking and dwelling subjects as the condition of possibility for a return from the external to the own, emerges all the more distinctly in nineteenth-century thought. The transcendental turn – the turn of the cognizer towards their own cognitive apparatus and the local cognitive situation – is the heart of Humboldt's description of the world, as well as the designs for philosophical systems among idealistic and post-idealistic thinkers. It is the figure that shaped all further anthropological thought by following on from the precepts from the founding days of the human sciences in the late eighteenth century.

The natural scientist is also confronted with a concept of the earth with a discreet philosophical shading: it is now the transcendental star that comes into play as the locational condition for all self-reflections.[6] It is the exemplary hybrid in which the empirical is unified with the transcendental – on the one hand, an ordinary object of ordinary research, and on the other hand, the singular carrier of singular intelligences. As the star on which the theory of stars appeared, the earth shines with self-generated phosphorescence. When its strange, knowing inhabitants cast their thoughts into the homogeneous emptiness, it is not least to return to their place from far outside. Modernized dwelling is the condition of possibility for modern cognition. When Humboldt brings the term 'spheres' into play, then, he is naturally no longer speaking of the imaginary celestial domes of the Aristotelian bimillennium, but rather the transcendental 'spheres of perception', which refer not to cosmic realities but to the schemata, auxiliary concepts and radii of space-imagining reason.

In the twentieth century, what had been a thought figure in Humboldt's century would become concrete as a movement in the physically real space: the astronaut Edwin Aldrin, who became the second human to set foot on the moon on 21 July 1969, shortly after Neil Armstrong, took stock of his life as an astronaut in a book with the title *Return to Earth*.[7]

4

Globe Time, World Picture Time

Hence the same thing that had been true for the earth since Columbus's voyage was confirmed for the extra-terrestrial dimensions too: in the earth's circumnavigated space, all points are of equal value. This neutralization subjected the spatial thought of the Modern Age to a radical change of meaning. The traditional 'living, weaving and being' of humans in regional orientations, markings and attractions is outdone by a system for localizing any point in a homogeneous, arbitrarily divisible representational space.[1] Where modern, position-spatial thought gains the upper hand, humans can no longer remain at home in their traditional world interiors and the phantasmal extensions and roundings-off of those interiors.[2] They no longer dwell exclusively beneath their home-centred sky. In so far as they take part enterprisingly in the great departure, sharing in its ideas, discoveries and gains, they have given up their provinces of birth; they have left their local language-houses and their terrestrially fastened firmaments to move for all time within an insuperably antecedent outside – albeit an increasingly furnished outside in which social policy and interior design converge.

These new entrepreneurs from the pilot nations of European expansion are no longer rooted in their native country; they no longer float amid its voices and smells; they no longer obey, as in the past, its historical markers or magical poles of attraction. They have forgotten what enchanted springs were, what pilgrimage churches and places of power meant, and what curses lay upon twilight corners. For them, the poetics of the natal space is no longer decisive. They no longer live forever in the landscapes they were born into, they no longer breathe beneath the indigenous skies of their canopy poems; instead, they have learned to carry out their projects in the other place, the outermost and abstract place. In future, their location will be the map, on whose points and lines they localize themselves without reservations. It is the knowledgeably painted paper, the *map-pamundo*, that tells them where they are. The map absorbs the land, and for imagining spatial thought, the image of the globe gradually makes the real extensions disappear.

For the terrestrial globe, the typographical marvel that informs modern humans of their location more than any other image, this marks the start of an illustrious success story extending over a span of more than five hundred years. Its monopoly on complete views of the earth's surface, shared with the great maps and planispheres, was only broken in the final quarter of the twentieth century by satellite photography.[3] In the epoch of its dominance, the globe not only became the central medium of the new homogenizing approach to location, an indispensable worldview instrument in the hands of all who had come to power and knowledge in the Old World and its branches. In addition, through constant amendments to the maps, it documents the permanent offensive of discoveries, conquests, openings and namings with which the advancing Europeans established themselves at sea and on land in the universal outside. From each decade to the next, European globes and maps published the state of the process whose formula was supplied after the event by Martin Heidegger when he wrote: 'The fundamental event of modernity is the conquest of the world as picture. From now on the word "picture" means: the collective image of representing production [*vorstellendes Herstellen*].'[4] What is advertised and decried as 'globalization' in the late twentieth and early twenty-first centuries – as if it were a new phenomenon that had only recently befallen us – constitutes, from these perspectives, a late and dishonest moment in an event whose true scale becomes visible when one understands the Modern Age consistently as a transition from meditative speculation on an orb to the practical acquisition of facts about it. One should emphasize, admittedly, that continental Europeans did not put an end to the agony of the inherited Ptolemaic worldview until the twentieth century. Now they must catch up, almost at the last minute, with the realization which the vast majority of them refused to accept regarding themselves: that virtually every point on a circumnavigated orb can be affected by the transactions of opponents, even from the greatest distance.

The meaning of terrestrial globalization reveals itself when one recognizes in it the history of a space-political externalization that is seemingly indispensable for the winners and unbearable for the losers, but inevitable for both. The latent metaphysical information of the earth to all its users had always been that all beings populating its surface are outside in an absolute sense, even if they still attempt to shelter themselves in pairings, dwellings and collective symbolic shells – systemicists would say in communications. As long as thinking people, considering the open sky, meditated on the cosmos as a vault – immeasurable, but closed – they remained protected from the danger of catching cold from their externality. Their world was still the house that lost nothing. Since they circumnavigated the planet, however, the wandering star that carries flora, fauna and cultures, an abyss has opened up above them; when they look up, they peer through it into a fathomless outside. A second abyss opens up in the foreign cultures that, after the ethnological enlightenment, demonstrate to everyone that practically everything can be different elsewhere. What we took to be the eternal order of things is no more than a local context of immanence that carries us – leave it, and you will see that there are quite differently built rafts of order floating on the chaos. The two abysses, the cosmological and the ethnological, confront the observers with the fortuity of their existence and thusness. Together, they make it clear that the immunological catastrophe of the Modern Age is not the 'loss of the centre', but rather the loss of the periphery. The final boundaries are no longer what they once seemed; the support they offered was an illusion, its authors we ourselves: this notice of loss (in technical terms: the de-ontologization of fixed edges) is the dysangelium of the Modern Age, which disseminates itself at the same times as the gospel of the discovery of new opportunity spaces. It is one of the hallmarks of the epoch that the good news rides upon the bad.

It was in the Iberian ports that the plague ships of knowledge first landed. Back from India, returned from the antipodes, the first eyewitnesses of the round earth gazed with transformed eyes at a world that would henceforth be called the Old. Whoever sailed into their home port after circumnavigating the world – like the eighteen emaciated survivors of Magellan's 1519–22 expedition, who had barely disembarked before staggering into a church to sing the *Te Deum* – set foot on land once more in a place that could never again be idealized as the domestic-native world-cave. In this sense, Seville was the first location-city in world history; its port, or more precisely that of San Lucar de Barrameda, was the first in the Old World to receive homecoming witnesses to a voyage around the globe. Locations are former homes that present themselves to the disenchanted and sentimental gaze of the returned. In such places, the spatial law of the

Modern Age is in effect, namely that one can no longer interpret one's own place of origin as the hub of the existent and the world as its concentrically arranged environment. Anyone living today, after Magellan and after Armstrong, is forced to project even their home town as a point perceived from without. The transformation of the Old World into an aggregate of locations reflects the new reality of the globe after the circumnavigation of the earth. The location is the point in the imagined world at which the natives grasp themselves as grasped from the outside; it is what enables the circumnavigated return to themselves.

The strangest thing about this process is the way countless native Europeans have managed to ignore and falsify it for almost an entire age, and to delay their participation in it for so long that, in the late twentieth century, they suddenly acted as if they had entirely new reasons to examine that unheard-of phenomenon, globalization. What arguments would they put forward if one reminded them, as a precaution, that the state of the world around 1900 – before the nationalist regressions of the twentieth century – was in many ways more open and global than it was in 2000? Certainly: the quicker and more routine the circumnavigations become, the more generally the transformation of 'lifeworlds' into locations spreads – which is why it was only in the age of fast transportation and super-fast information transmissions that the disenchantment of local immune structures became epidemically palpable.

In the course of its development, globalization bursts open the dream shells of grounded, housed, internally oriented and autonomously salvific collective life – that life which had previously rarely been anywhere except with itself and amid its native landscapes (Heidegger's *Gegnet* gives these outstripped spaces a belated and futile name). That older life knew no other constitution of the world than the self-harbouring, vernacular, microspherically animated and macrospherically walled one – it viewed the world as a strong-walled socio-cosmological extension of a locally earthed, self-centred, monolingual, group-uterine power of imagination. The premodern space, each part in its own way, was a volume stretched out by enlivened qualities. Now, however, globalization, which carries the screened outside everywhere, tears the freely trading cities – and ultimately even the introverted villages – out into the public space, which reduces all local particularities to the common denominator: money and geometry.[5] It breaks open the independently growing endospheres and takes them to the mesh grid. Once caught in it, the settlements of the grounded mortals lose their immemorial privilege of being the respective centre of the world.

Viewed from this perspective, the history of the Modern Age, as we have stated, is initially nothing other than the history of a spatial 'revolution' into the homogeneous outside. It carries out the explication of the earth, in so far as the latter's inhabitants are shown bit by bit that the categories of direct neighbourhood are no longer sufficient to interpret coexistence with other people and other things in the expanded space. This history brings about the catastrophe of local ontologies by doing away with the old poetry of domesticity. In the course of these clarifications, all Old European countries *de jure* become locations on the surface of an orb; numerous cities, villages and landscapes are transformed *de facto* into stations of a limitless traffic where our lively modern capital marches through in its fivefold metamorphosis as commodity, money, text, image and celebrity.[6] Every empirical place on the earth's surface becomes a potential address of capital, which regards all points in space in terms of their accessibility for technical and economical measures. While the speculative cosmic orb of the philosophers had, in former times, made a peak performance of security within the encompassing into an object of observation, the new 'earth apple' – as Behaim called his globe – announced discreetly, cruelly and interestingly to the people of Nuremberg, and via these to the Europeans, the topological message of the Modern Age: that humans are creatures which exist on the edge of an uneven round body – a body whose whole is neither a womb nor a vessel, and has no shelter to offer.

The globe may rest on a precious stand with feet of engraved rosewood, enclosed in a metal meridian ring, and it may strike the observer as a paradigm of straightforwardness and delimitation; yet it will always reproduce the image of a body that lacks an enclosing edge, the spheric outer vault. Its uppermost part already appears outside it. What philosophers of the nineteenth and twentieth centuries called 'existing' is thus explicated by every globe: whoever regards it is called upon to imagine themselves as a being on the threshold between the earth and nothingness. No circumstance characterizes the cartographical art of the Modern Age – and *eo ipso* its way of thinking – more profoundly than the fact that no globe we have ever seen shows the earth's atmosphere. Two-dimensional maps likewise provide views of airless territories. All older models of the earth neglect the atmospheric element as naturally as if there were a permanent agreement that only the solid body merits depiction. It was not until the twentieth century that the atmosphere was added once more and the objectified conditions for human milieu-connectedness made nameable. Only then can one state explicitly that existence and immersion are equally potent concepts.

Every globe adorning the libraries, studies and salons of educated Europe embodied the new doctrine of the precedence of the outside. Europeans advanced into this outside as discoverers, merchants and tourists, but they saved their souls by simultaneously withdrawing into their wallpapered interiors. What is a salon but the place where one chats about distant monstrosities? The celestial globes set up in parallel with the terrestrial globe still disputed, as long as it was possible in any way, the message revealed by the terrestrial globes;[7] they continued to promote the illusion of cosmic shelter for mortals beneath the firmament, but their function became increasingly ornamental – like the art of the astrologers, who changed from experts on stars and fate to psychologists of edification and fairground prophets. Nothing can save the physical heavens from being disenchanted as a form of semblance. What looks like a high vault is an abyss perceived through a shell of air. The rest is displaced religiosity and bad poetry.[8]

5

Turn from the East, Entrance into the Homogeneous Space

To establish the precedence of the outside, the bare fact of the first circumnavigations of the earth by Magellan and del Cano (1519–22) and by Francis Drake (1577–80) was not sufficient in itself. These two early deeds of nautical heroism nonetheless deserve a place in the history of terrestrial globalization, for their actors, in deciding to sail westwards, carried out a change of direction of world-historical significance with an inexhaustible wealth of spiritual meanings. Both Magellan and Drake were following the intuitions of Columbus, for whom the idea of a western route to India had become a prophetic obsession. And although, even after his fourth voyage (1502–4), Columbus could still not be convinced of his error in believing he had found the sea route to India – while on the Central American islands, he believed in all seriousness that he was only ten days' sail from the Ganges, and that the inhabitants of the Caribbean were subjects of the Indian 'Grand Khan' – the tendency of the time was on his side. In opting for the western course, he had set in motion the emancipation of the 'Occident' from its immemorial solar-mythological orientation towards the East; indeed, with the discovery of a western continent, he had succeeded in denying the mythical-metaphysical priority of the Orient. Since then, we have no longer been returning to the 'source' or the point of sunrise, but rather moving progressively with the sun without homesickness. Rosenstock-Huessy rightly noted: 'The ocean crossed by Christopher Columbus turned the Occident into Europe.'[1] Whatever may have happened since then in the name of globalization or universal earth documentation, it was now entirely guided by the Atlantic tendency.

After the Portuguese seafarers from the mid-fifteenth century on had broken through the magical inhibitions obstructing the westward gaze with the Pillars of Hercules, Columbus's voyage gave the final signal for the 'disorientation' of European interests. Only this 'revolutionary' de-Easting could bring about the emergence of the neo-Indian dual continent that would be called 'America'. It alone is the reason why for half a millennium, the cultural and topological meaning of globalization has always also meant 'Westing' and Westernization.[2] The inevitability of this was pinpointed by Hermann Schmitz, initiator of the New Phenomenology, with welcome conciseness in the space-philosophical expositions of his *System of Philosophy*. Regarding Columbus, he writes:

> In the West he discovered America for humanity, and thus space as locational space [*Ortsraum*]. This deliberately exaggerated formulation is intended to mean that the success of Columbus – and later the circumnavigator Magellan as the executor of his initiative – on the western route forced a shock-like change in the human notion of space that, in my opinion, marks the entrance into the specifically modern mode of consciousness more profoundly than any other transition.[3]

The westward turn induced the geometricization of European behaviour in a globalized locational space. Even the most summary description of the still widely unexplored zones of the earth must therefore follow a new methodological ideal from the outset: an even analysis of all points on the planet's surface in terms of their accessibility for European (which initially meant Iberian) methods, interests and measures – even if the actual access often took place only centuries later, or never. Even the famous white spots on maps marked as *terrae incognitae* acted as points that would have to be made known in future. They were the attractors of cognitive sadism, which took the quiet form of research. The words printed above the supposedly enormous Australian continent on some influential sixteenth-century world maps applied to all of these: *Terra australis nuper inventa nondum cognita* – recently discovered, *not yet* explored, but already marked as a space for future examination and utilization. The spirit of the not-yet speaks up, for the time being, as a matter among geographers. The Modern Age is the *nondum* age – the time of a promising becoming, emancipated as much from the stasis of eternity as from the circling time of myth.

The historical nub of Columbus's voyage lies in its sweeping effects on modern location-spatial movements. The West, formerly understood as a point on the compass and a wind direction, but even more as the zone of sunset (and hence of death for the ancient Egyptians) – a thoroughly direction-spatially defined factor – was assigned the civilization-historically far-reaching role of assisting the breakthrough of the location-spatial and geometrical imagining of the earth, and of space as such. The westward departures marked the start of movements that would one day culminate in indifferent *traffic* in all directions. Whether it is the Columbus expedition of 1492 or the penetration of the North American continent in the nineteenth century, the two greatest enactments of the imperative 'Westwards!' stimulated a spatial opening up that would later lead to the regular back-and-forth traffic between any given points in the explored zones. What the twentieth century would, with one of its most dulled-down terms, call 'circulation' (in the sense of traffic) only became possible through the triumph of location-spatial thought. For the routine mastery of the symmetry of outward and return journeys that is constitutive for the modern concept of traffic can only be established in a generalized locational space that gathers together points of equal value in a field to form timetables and images of routes. It is no coincidence that one of the most important power systems of the nineteenth century, the railway engines, were given the name '*loco-motives*' – locationally mobile units – for their introduction actually marks an exceptional stage in the evening-out of the locational space. The technicians of the nineteenth century knew that overcoming space through steam locomotion was closely connected to the 'evaporation of space' through electric telegraphy, whose wires usually followed railway lines.[4]

The precondition for what we call world traffic is that the discovery of marine conditions and terrain in geographical and hydrographical terms can be considered complete. Authentic traffic can only come about with a network that makes a given zone accessible, whether as *terra cognita* or *mare cognitum*, for routine crossings. As the epitome of traversal practices, traffic constitutes the second, routinized phrase of the process that had begun as the adventure history of global discoveries by the Europeans.

6

Jules Verne and Hegel

There is barely anyone who illustrated what globalized traffic means and achieves more accurately and entertainingly than Jules Verne, in his satirically tinged, best-selling novel *Around the World in Eighty Days* from 1874. In its galloping superficiality, the book offers a snapshot of the process of modernity as a traffic project. It demonstrates the quasi-historical-philosophical thesis that the purpose of modern conditions is to trivialize traffic on the global scale. Only in a globalized locational space can one organize the new mobility needs, which seek to provide both passenger transport and movement of goods with a foundation of quiet routines. Traffic is the epitome of reversible movements. As soon as these are expanded into a reliable institution for long distances too, it ultimately becomes meaningless in which direction a circumnavigation of the earth takes place. It is external conditions that lead the hero of Jules Verne's novel, the Englishman Phileas Fogg Esq., and his unfortunate French servant, Passepartout, to undertake the journey around the world in eighty days via the eastern route. Initially, the only reason for this was a newspaper announcement stating that the Indian subcontinent had become traversable in a mere three days through the opening of the last stretch of the Great Indian Peninsular Railway between Rothal and Allahabad. From this, a journalist at a London daily newspaper constructed the provocative article that would lead to Phileas Fogg's bet with his whist friends at the Reform Club. The issue of Fogg's bet with his partners at the club is essentially the question of whether the tourist system is capable of realizing its theoretical promises in practice. The momentous essay in the *Morning Chronicle* contained a list of times that a traveller would need to go from London around the world to London again – needless to say, the British capital was the location of all locations at the time; a large proportion of ships and commodities embarked on their voyages around the world from there. That this calculation was based on a hypothetical eastward journey was due, alongside the habitual British affinity for the Indian part of the Commonwealth, to a topos of the time: the opening of the Suez Canal in 1869 had sensitized Europeans to the subject of acceleration in world traffic and created incentives for the dramatically shortened eastern route. As the course of Fogg's journey shows, it was already a completely Wested East that, for all its Brahmans and elephants, was no different from any other curved stretch on a location-spatially represented planet that had been made accessible through traffic.

This is the calculation done by the *Morning Chronicle*:

London to Suez via the Mont Cenis Tunnel and Brindisi, by railway and steamship	7 days
Suez to Bombay, by steamship	13 "
Bombay to Calcutta, by railway	3 "
Calcutta to Hong Kong (China), by steamship	13 "
Hong Kong to Yokohama, by steamship	6 "
Yokohama to San Francisco, by steamship	22 "
San Francisco to New York, by railroad	7 "
New York to London, by steamship and railway	9 "
Total	80 days

'Possibly 80 days!' exclaimed Stuart [. . .]. 'But not allowing for unfavourable weather, headwinds, shipwrecks, derailments, etc.'
'All included,' said Fogg, continuing to play – for the discussion was no longer respecting the whist.
'Even if the Indians and Red Indians tear up the rails?' cried Stuart. 'Even if they stop the trains, plunder the carriages and scalp the passengers?'
'All included,' repeated Phileas Fogg.[1]

Jules Verne's message is that adventures no longer exist in a technically saturated civilization, only the danger of being late. That is why the author considers it important to note that his hero does not have any experiences. Mr Fogg's imperial apathy cannot be shaken by any turbulence, for, as a global traveller, he is exempt from the task of showing respect to the local. Following the creation of circumnavigability, the tourist experiences the earth – even in its furthermost corners – as a mere epitome of situations that the daily papers, travel writers and encyclopedias have long since portrayed more comprehensively. This makes it clear why the 'foreign' is barely worth a glance to the traveller. Whatever incidents may occur, be it a widow-burning in India or a Native American attack in the west, they can never really be more than events and circumstances of which a member of the London Reform club is better informed than the tourist on site. Whoever travels under such circumstances does so neither for their own amusement nor for business reasons, but rather for the sake of travel as such: _ars gratia artis; motio gratia motionis._[2]

Since the days of the Calabrian Giovanni Francesco Gemelli Careri (1651–1725), who sailed around the world between 1693 and 1697 out of frustration over family problems, the type of globetrotter without any business interests – the tourist – has been an established figure in the repertoire of modernity. His _Giro del Mondo_, published in 1699, is one of the founding documents of a literature of globalization on a pure whim. Gemelli Careri likewise adopted the habitus of the explorer who believes that the zeitgeist has given him the mandate to tell those at home of his experiences outside. His Mexican observations and description of the Pacific crossing were still considered ethno-geographically respectable achievements generations later. Even though later globetrotters turned towards a more subjective style of reporting, the liaison between travelling and writing remained untouched into the nineteenth century. As late as 1855, the Brockhaus _Conversationslexicon_ was able to define a tourist as 'a traveller who has no specific, e.g. scientific purpose for travelling, but only does so in order to have made the journey and then be able to describe it'.

In Jules Verne's tale, the globetrotter has abandoned his profession as a documentarist and become a pure passenger. He presents himself as a customer of transportation services who is paying for a voyage _without_ any experiences that could later be recounted. For him, the circumnavigation of the world is a sporting achievement rather than a philosophical lesson – no longer even part of an educational programme. Thus Phileas Fogg can remain as speechless as an athlete.

As far as the technical side of the circumnavigation of the world in eighty days was concerned, Jules Verne was no visionary by the standards of 1874. With regard to the decisive means of transportation, namely railway and propeller-driven steamboat, his hero's journey corresponded precisely to the state of the art of moving apathetic Englishmen from A to B and back. Nonetheless, the figure of Phileas Fogg has prophetic traits, in that he appears as the prototype of the generalized stowaway, whose only connection to the landscapes drifting past is his interest in traversing them. The stoic tourist prefers to travel with the windows shut; as a gentleman, he insists on his right to consider nothing worth seeing; as an apathetic, he refuses to make discoveries. These attitudes anticipate a mass phenomenon of the twentieth century: the hermetic package tourist, who changes transport means everywhere without seeing anything that differs from the brochures. Fogg is the perfect opposite of his typological precursors, the circumnavigators and geographers of the sixteenth, seventeenth and eighteenth centuries for whom every voyage was accompanied by expectations of discoveries, conquests and monetary gains. From the nineteenth century on, these experience-led travellers were followed by event travellers, who journeyed to remote places in order to enhance themselves through impressions.

Among the impressionistic travellers of the previous century, the cultural philosopher Hermann Graf Keyserling achieved a certain fame with his travel notes: in the years after the First World War, his *Reisetagebuch eines Philosophen* [Travel Diary of a Philosopher] was a fixture in any serious German private library. The author completed his great tour of the world's cultures in thirteen months as a form of Hegelian experiment – illumination through delayed return to the German provinces.[3] Phileas Fogg had a clear advantage over Keyserling, admittedly, because he no longer had to pretend that he was concerned with learning anything fundamental on his journey around the whole. Jules Verne is the better Hegelian, for he had understood that no substantial heroes are possible in the arranged world, only heroes of the secondary. It was only with the idea that came to him on the Atlantic crossing between New York and England, namely to overcome the lack of coal by burning the wooden constructions on his own ship, that the Englishman touched for a moment on the original heroism, giving the principle of self-sacrifice a twist in keeping with the spirit of the Industrial Age. Aside from that, sport and spleen describe the last horizon for male endeavours in the spatially structured world. Keyserling, on the other hand, crosses the threshold of the laughable when, like some belated personification of the world spirit, he wants to travel around the world in order to come 'to himself' – his correspondingly comical motto is: 'The shortest path to oneself leads around the world.' As his book shows, however, the travelling philosopher cannot have any experiences, only gather impressions.

7

Waterworld: On the Change of the Central Element in the Modern Age

In the decisive point, Jules Verne's schedule perfectly mirrors the original adventure of terrestrial globalization: it unmistakably shows the considerable predominance of sea voyages over those on land. Here we still find, in a time when the circumnavigation of the earth had long become an elite sport ('globetrotting', which is to say trampling on everything), the trace of Magellan's radical revision of world pictures, in whose wake the notion of a largely terran earth was replaced with that of the oceanic planet. When Columbus was proposing his project to the Catholic majesties of Spain, he was able to state that the earth was 'small' and mostly dry, with the damp element constituting only a seventh of it. The sailors of the late Middle Ages likewise declared the predominance of the terran space – for understandable reasons, as the sea is an element not usually loved by those closely familiar with it (the romanticization of the sea, like that of mountains, is an invention of modern urban sentimentality). It was not without deep-seated reasons, based on experience, that the hatred of coast-dwellers for the open water was translated into the vision in the Apocalypse of Saint John (Revelation 21:1) that the world would no longer exist after the coming of the Messiah – a statement very fittingly quoted by the ship's vicar in James Cameron's *Titanic* while the ship's stern assumes a vertical position before sinking.

All of a sudden, the Europeans of the early sixteenth century were expected to understand that in the face of the predominance of water, the planet earth had been named rather inappropriately. What they called the earth was revealed as a waterworld; three quarters of its surface belonged to the damp element. This was the fundamental globographical insight of the Modern Age, and it never became entirely clear whether it was an evangelic or a dysangelic one.

It was no easy matter for humans to abandon their immemorial terran prejudices. The oldest surviving post-Columbian globe that hints at the existence of the American continents and the West Indian island world, the small metal Lenox Globe of around 1510, depicts – like many later maps and globes – the legendary island of Zipangu, or Japan, as being very close to the western coast of North America. This mirrors the continued dramatic underestimation of the waters west of the New World, as if Columbus's cardinal error – the hope of a short western route into supposedly proximate Asia – were now to be repeated with America as the base. A little over a decade later, on the Brixen Globe of 1523 or 1524, a caravel placed in the 'peaceful sea', the *Mar del sur*, pointed to Magellan's circumnavigation of the earth; pamphlets disseminated as far as Eastern Europe had reported the return of the *Victoria* as late as the autumn of 1522, and yet the creator of this first post-Magellan globe was unable to participate in the oceanic 'revolution'. This was not an expression of any reprehensible narrow-mindedness; no European at the time could assess the implications of what the Basque captain Juan Sebastian del Cano and the Italian author of Magellan's logbook, Antonio Pigafetta, had to say when they reported that after sailing from the southwestern coast of America, they had sailed 'for three months and twenty days' – from 28 November 1520 to 16 March 1521, with consistently favourable winds – on a north-westerly course through an immeasurable, unknown sea that they named *mare pacifico*, 'for during that time we did not suffer any storm'.[1] This short note holds the oceanographic reversal that would bring geographical antiquity, the Ptolemaic belief in the predominance of landmasses, to a sensational end.

The extent to which the pre-Magellan, Ptolemaic conception of the world was terracentrically oriented is revealed by the most artful among the late medieval descriptions of the earth, dating from barely a generation before Columbus's voyage: the monumental world disc of the Venetian Camaldolese monk Fra Mauro, made in 1459. In its time, it was considered not only the most extensive, but also the most detailed representation of the earth. Naturally it still presents the medieval-Old European earth, which lies contained in the immunizing circle, and on which the damp element literally plays a marginal role. Aside from the patches of the Mediterranean shifted slightly away from the centre and the rivers, the water is only granted the outermost edges. In Fra Mauro's map, the empirical and the fantastic present themselves in a wondrous compromise, and, despite the knowledgeable and dense reproduction of terran conditions, which is in keeping with the research of the time, the picture as a whole obediently submits to the Old European dream command: to imagine a world with as few aquatic areas as possible.

Without the translation of the new Magellanic truth into the maps of the next globe generations and the generation after those, no European would have had an adequate notion of the 'revolutionary' inflation of the watery areas. This inflation was the basis of the shift from mainland thought to oceanic thought – a process whose consequences would be as unforeseeable as the Columbian-Magellanic transition from the ancient three-continent conception (which appears on maps as *orbis tripartitus*) to the modern four-continent scheme augmented by the two Americas. As for the fifth continent, the mythical *terra australis*, of which the sixteenth century began to dream as the largest and richest of all earthly spaces, the history of its discovery – by the standards of the initial hopes – was a long history of disappointment and shrinking. It would take centuries for European seafarers and globographers to reduce their Australian phantasms to a natural scale. The Britons acted on this when they turned the failing southern realm into their penal colony; now the 'irredeemable, unwanted excess population of felons' amply produced by England could be more or less permanently 'transported' to a place an optimal distance away from the motherland.[2]

To anyone familiar with the history of concepts, it seems especially bizarre, yet also revealing, that the contiguous landmasses of the earth's surface would soon bear only the name of the encompassing – *continens* – that had, into the time of Copernicus, referred to the cosmic shell or firmament of the world's final boundary. If the watery planet doggedly continues to call itself *Terra*, and if the landmasses on it adorn themselves to this day with the absurd title 'continent', this only shows how the Europeans of the Modern Age responded to the damp revolution: after the shock of circumnavigation, they withdrew to misnomers that feigned the long-familiar in the unaccustomed new. For just as the circumnavigated planet does not deserve to be named after the little mainland that protrudes from its oceans, the 'continents' have no rightful claim to their name, as they are precisely not the encompassing, but rather the – aquatically – encompassed. It is not only in lexical and semantic terms, however, that the history of the Modern Age was a drawn-out process of manoeuvring and evasion on the part of the terran conception of space and substance in the face of the sea and the flow of goods that passed over it. The hesitance to accept the oceanic truths informed the terran-conservative wing of the entire Modern Age.

The offensive sting of early globalization knowledge lay in the Magellanic views of the true extension of the oceans and their acknowledgement as the true world media. That the *oceans* are the carriers of global affairs, and thus the natural media of unrestricted capital flow, is the message of all messages in the period between Columbus, the hero of the maritime medium, and Lindberg, the pioneer of the age of the air medium – a message the grounded Europeans fought for centuries with their will to provincialism. It seemed as if the old earth would sink anew in diluvian floods – this time, however, floods that would not fall from the sky, but rather rush in from unheard-of logbooks. In the nineteenth century, Melville, the greatest writer of the maritime world, could let one of his figures exclaim: 'Yea, foolish mortals, Noah's flood is not yet subsided.'[3] Both the unity and the division of the planet earth had become subject to the maritime element, and European seafaring – in its civil, military and corsair manifestations – had to prove itself as the effective agent of globalization until the rise of aeronautics. It was via the oceans that the European world powers wanted to build their 'seaborne empires'. During that time, anyone who claimed to understand the world had to think hydrographically. Even the sardonic itinerary in the *Morning Chronicle* acknowledged this truth by featuring a total of sixty-eight days at sea alongside a mere twelve by rail to travel around the earth. Only the sea offered a foundation for universal thoughts; the ocean alone could bestow the doctorate caps of the true Modern Age. Melville rightly let the same protagonist declare: 'a whale-ship was my Yale College and my Harvard'.[4]

One of the first to draw practical conclusions from the insights of Magellan and del Cano was the young monarch Charles V, king of Spain from 1516 and ruler of the Holy Roman empire from May 1519. In the autumn of 1522, Pigafetta presented his ship's log to him at Valladolid as the most secret document of the new international situation.[5] Charles quite rightly took the information about the Pacific and the superhuman efforts involved in the circumnavigation of the earth on the western route as news that was both wondrous and frightening. After only a few failed attempts to repeat Magellan's voyage, he considered it advisable to abandon the idea of new trips to the Maluku Islands. Thus, in the Treaty of Zaragoza of 1529, he sold the asserted Spanish claims to the islands to the Portuguese crown for 350,000 ducats – which transpired as an excellent deal after improved longitude measurements on the other side of the globe a few years later showed that since the division of land agreed on in 1494 in the Treaty of Tordesillas, the sought-after Spice Islands had belonged to the Portuguese hemisphere anyway.

This inter-dynastic change of ownership of distant lands, where clearly neither the buyer nor the seller even knew their exact location, mirrors more accurately than almost any other act from that time the speculative nature of the original globalization. It is somewhat ridiculous when today's journalists presume to identify the most recent movements of speculative capital as the real cause of the world-form shock known as globalization. From the first moment on, the world system of capitalism established under the interwoven auspices of the globe and speculation.[6] Likewise, the knowledge that merchant capital has a tendency to emancipate itself from ties to a particular country is as old as the modern economic system itself. In 1776, Adam Smith was able to note down the following words as if uttering a self-evident truth:

> A merchant [. . .] is not necessarily the citizen of any particular country. It is in a great measure indifferent to him from what place he carries on his trade; and a very trifling disgust will make him remove his capital, and together with it all the industry which it supports, from one country to another.[7]

The overseas empire of Charles V had been financed with loans from Flemish and Augsburg banks, and later Genoese ones, whose owners set globes in rotation in order to gain an idea of the outward journeys of their credit and the return journeys of their interest.

From the start, the oceanic adventure entangled its actors in a race for hidden chances to access opaque distant markets. Cecil Rhodes's notorious statement already applied to them: 'Expansion is everything.'[8] What economists after Marx called original accumulation was often – as the aforementioned example suggests – more an accumulation of ownership titles, options and claims to usage than a management of production plants on the basis of invested capital. For the princely and civil clients of overseas navigation, the discovery and formal appropriation of distant territories established an expectation of future income, whether in the form of loot, tribute or regular trading transactions, where it was never forbidden to dream of fabulous profit margins.

The globalization of the earth by the early seafaring merchants and cosmographers was clearly far removed from submitting to theoretical interests; since its initiation by the Portuguese, it had followed a resolutely anti-contemplative knowledge programme. Whoever sought to gain control over the newly discovered world had to dispense with idealizations and deductions. The *experimentum maris* provided the criterion for the new understanding of world-experience. Only at sea did it become clear how the Modern Age intended to envisage the interplay of theory and practice. A hundred years before Francis Bacon, the contractees and actors of global circumnavigation knew that knowledge of the earth's surface was power – power in its most concrete and profitable form. The increasingly precise image of the earth directly took on the character of quantitative and access knowledge; new oceanographic insights amounted to arms deliveries for the battle against competitors in the open space. Geographical and hydrographical discoveries were therefore guarded like state secrets or industrial patents; the Portuguese crown forbade – on pain of death – the proliferation of nautical charts that showed the country's discoveries and descriptions of coastlines. That is why hardly any of its famous portolans, which were used like itineraries for sailing along navigable coastlines, have survived.[9] A counterpart to calculation with Arabic numerals emerged, one might say, in the form of calculation with European maps. After the introduction of the Indo-Arabic zero in the twelfth century had enabled an elegant arithmetic, the earth globe of the Europeans provided an operable round view of geopolitical and world economic affairs.

In the same way, however, that – as noted by the philosopher Alfred N. Whitehead – no one leaves the house to buy zero fish, no one sails from Portugal to Calicut or Malacca to return with zero cloves in the cargo hold. From this perspective, a group of spice islands in the South Pacific targeted and occupied by European desires is not simply a vague spot on a vague world map, but also a symbol of expected profits. In the hands of those who know how to use it, the globe is the true icon of the newly navigable earth; even more than this, it constitutes an image of monetary sources flowing from the future to the present. One could even consider it an occult clock that showed the hours of profit connected to distant islands and foreign continents. The modern globe made its fortune as an opportunity clock for a society of long-distance entrepreneurs and risk-takers who already saw the wealth of tomorrow on the coasts of other worlds today. This clock, which showed the hours in the never-before-seen, told the quick-witted agents of the new era – the conquistadors, spice merchants, gold hunters and later political realists – how things stood for their enterprises and their countries.

It is clear why the same globographers served both the princes and the civil large-scale entrepreneurs. Before the new, emperors and peddlers are equal, and Fortuna barely discriminates between noble and non-noble minions. Charles V, whose attention was drawn to these extremely useful scholars by his secretary Maximilian Transylvanus, had friendly relations with Gerhard Mercator and Philipp Apian, the outstanding globographers of their time, who simultaneously worked for the entire financial and scientific elite. Raymund Fugger, certainly no mere peddler, had a globe of his own produced by Martin Furtenbach in 1535, which was later exhibited at the Fuggerschloss in Kirchbach; like the slightly earlier Welser globe made by Christoff Schiepp, the Fugger globe was an artfully fashioned unicum. The future, however, belonged to printed globes, which reached the market in larger numbers; they provided globalization with its first mass media foundation. Whether it was a unique specimen or a serial product, however, every globe spoke to its viewers of the pleasure and necessity of gaining advantages in the borderless terrestrial space.

On 22 March 1518, after the nautical hero Magellan had turned his back on ungrateful Portugal, he and a representative of the Spanish crown cast a joint glance at one such promising globe, which located the Spice Islands somewhere near the Antipodes, and made a contract for the discovery of the same (*Capitulación sobre el descubrimiento de las Islas de la Especeria*) which already stipulated in minute detail the division of the virtual riches that would be generated by these sources. This shows with uncommon explicitness that even the concept of 'discovery' – the central epistemological and political word of the Modern Age – referred not to an autonomous theoretical category, but rather to a special case of the investment phenomenon; and investment is in turn a case of risk-taking. Where the schemata of risk-taking spread at a general level – taking up loans, investing, planning, inventing, betting, reinsuring, spreading risks, building up reserves – people emerge who want to create their own fortune and future by playing with opportunities, not simply accepting whatever God's hand grants them. In the new property and money economy, this is a type which has learned that damage makes people wise, but debts make them wiser. The key figure of the new age is the 'debtor-producer' – better known as the entrepreneur – who constantly flexibilizes their business methods, their opinions and themselves in order to access by all lawful and unlawful, tried and untried means the profits that enable them to pay off their loans on time. These debtor-producers give the idea of owed debt its radically renewing, modern meaning: a moral fault becomes an economically logical relationship of incentive. Without the positivization of debt, there can be no capitalism. It was the debtor-producers who began to turn the wheel of permanent monetary circulation in the 'age of the bourgeoisie'.[10]

The primary fact of the Modern Age was not that the earth goes around the sun, but that money goes around the earth.

8

Fortuna, or:
The Metaphysics of Chance

This economic and psychopolitical constellation saw the reappearance of the Roman goddess of luck within the horizon of European interests, as she was capable as no other figure in the ancient pantheon of making a pact with the surge of entrepreneurial religiosity among merchants and seafarers. The return of Fortuna corresponded to the world feeling of chance ontology, embodied in the opportunism of Machiavelli, the essayism of Montaigne and the experimentalism of Bacon. The neo-fatalism of late Shakespeare likewise belongs to the characteristic self-utterances of the age that, in its gloomier moments, perceives humans as competition-infected, jealousy-blinded, failure-scarred risk-takers; here the actors on the world stage appear as balls with which illusory powers, malign genies, money spirits and greed demons play their games.

Fortuna appears everywhere as the goddess of globalization par excellence: she not only produces herself as the eternally ironic equilibrist perched on her orb, but also teaches humans to consider life as a whole a game of chance in which the winners have no cause for boasting and the losers no cause for complaint. Boethius, who laid the foundations for medieval speculations about Fortuna in the sixth century in his book *The Consolation of Philosophy*, and was still a source of inspiration for the philosophies of happiness in the Renaissance, already let his goddess reveal the premises for existence on the wheel:

> The power that I wield comes naturally to me; this is my perennial sport. I turn my wheel on its whirling course, and take delight in

switching the base to the summit, and the summit to the base. So
mount upward, if you will, but on condition that you do not regard
yourself as ill-treated if you plummet down when my humour so
demands and takes its course.[1]

This was mostly taken by stability-infatuated Middle Ages as a
vanitas warning; thus they saw the temperamental goddess as a
demon of harmful changeability, while the incipient Modern Age
suspected that in the image of the revolving wheel of fate lay a metaphysics of chance which largely corresponded to its own motives. In
the four basic positions of the wheel of fortune – ascending/sitting
enthroned/sinking/lying – the new era recognized not only the basic
risks of the *vita activa*, but also the typical stages of entrepreneurial
fortune.

Fortuna was no longer only depicted with her wheel, however, but
equally with maritime emblems such as the swelling sail and especially the rudder, which was her oldest attribute along with the orb;
it shows that luck is not only coincidental, but also due to individual
diligence. Antiquity had already associated luck with seafaring, and
the Modern Age could not help reinforcing this connection. One
maritime symbol it did add was that of the dice, whose falling –
cadentia – generated the concept of risk-taking, and thus one of the
key concepts of the modern world: chance. The falling dice are
in play whenever the likelihood of success or failure is reckoned.
One can go so far as to identify, in the refreshed Fortuna idea of
the Renaissance, the approaching philosophical success of proto-
liberalism, in which the positions of the wheel of fortune would
correspond directly to the ordeals of the market. In success, selection
by coincidence comes before all subjectivity of control or method.
What is liberalism in philosophical terms if not the emancipation of
the accidental? And what is the new entrepreneurship if not a practice
for correcting one's luck?

It is one of the more profound thoughts of the sixteenth century
that alongside the hereditary nobility, which had been on top since
mythical times, and the nobility of officials, which had begun to make
itself indispensable in the service of early Modern Age states, it
already conferred the necessary qualifications on the anarchic nobility
of the future, the nobility of luck; this alone emerged from the womb
of Fortuna as the true child of the Modern Age. This chance nobility
would prove the recruiting ground for the prominent figures of the
globalization age – a society of individuals who had become rich,
famous and favoured in their sleep, and who never quite understood
what had carried them upwards. The airy children of Wotan, from

Fortunatus to Felix Krull, are, alongside the entrepreneurs and artists, the most legitimate offspring of the luck-blessed Modern Age. This was not only the age in which the wretched attempted, with varying success, to work their way up from their misery; it was also the great time of fortunate natures who sit with light heads and light hands with the sibyls and queens, devoting themselves to integral consumption, including the flight of birds and the lands of the stars. What else should they do, the effortless winners, but dine without remorse at the *'table d'hôte* of chance'?[2]

It was Nietzsche who would go on to coin the formula for this release of the accidental: ' "Lord Chance" – that is the oldest nobility in the world.'[3] The gesture of counting oneself among this nobility and wearing the die on one's coat of arms brings forth a new justification for life that Nietzsche, in *The Birth of Tragedy*, called aesthetic theodicy. In the Modern Age, emancipated luck gazes up at a sky unknown to the neediness of old. 'Over all things stands the Heaven Accident'[4] – a post-metaphysically enlightened elite audience is supposed to hear this as the improved Good News. The concern was a sky that vaulted a liberated immanence, far removed from any retribution in the hereafter. The sky of the Modern Age was the playing field for chance's throws of the dice. Would Nietzsche have resented a reminder that in imperial Rome, Fortuna was primarily the goddess of slaves and unemployed plebeians who depended entirely on chance alms and the generous moods of the rich?

9

Risk-Taking

Taking calculated risks within the horizon of uncertainty: this concept is the pragmatic foundation of the modern culture of attack and reaching out. The aggressiveness of European expansionist practices was not rooted in a regional psychodynamic disposition; it was not any species-specific sadism that propelled their extroversion into the global terrestrial space. It was rather the adjustment of European practices and mentalities to generalized risk-taking that resulted in the surprising, almost mysteriously successful offensive force of the first generation of discoverers. The willingness to take risks among the new global actors is *ultima ratione* driven by the urge to generate profits in order to repay debts from investment loans. Europeans before 1500 were not greedier or crueller or more diligent than any other race before them; they were more willing to take risks – which means more loan-inclined in relation to creditors and more loan-dependent in relation to debtors, in keeping with the economic paradigm shift from the ancient and medieval exploitation of resources to modern investing economies. Through such economic activity, mindfulness of deadlines for the payment of interest is translated into practical ventures and technological inventions. Enterprise is the poetry of money.[1] If necessity is the mother of invention, then credit is the mother of enterprise.

Merely because the outside was simultaneously the future, and because the future *post mundum novum inventum* could be imagined as the space from which spoils, wealth and idealization originated, the early seafarers and eccentric merchant-entrepreneurs unleashed the storm of investments in the outside that would develop in the course of half a millennium into the current capitalist-informatic ecumene. From the time of Columbus on, globalization meant the general futurization of state, entrepreneurial and epistemic action. It is the subjugation of the globe to the form of yield. Now 'profit' meant only the hazardous money that returned multiplied to its account of origin after its great loop across the oceans. In this respect, terrestrial globalization transpired as the mint of entrepreneurship in the narrower modern sense. The fact that this entrepreneurship did not, in its adventuring early days, always differ clearly from pseudo-seriously mystified project-making – Daniel Defoe, himself a luckless speculator and dealer in wine, tobacco and hosiery, examined it critically[2] – or from therapeutic and political charlatanry, as well as occasional and organized crime, lent the practices of global expansion the ambiguity associated with them to this day.

The pragmatic heart of the Modern Age was located in the new science of risk-taking. The globe is the monitor on which the field of generalized investment activities can be viewed. At the same time, it is already the gambling table at which the adventurer-investors place their bets. Its emergence, rapid success and chronic updating began the era of the global players, in whose world a great many ships sink, but the sun never goes down. They are gamblers who take a globe in hand in order to outdo their rivals in long-distance vision, long-distance speculation and long-distance winning. The imperial motto under which the fleet of Charles V sailed the oceans, *Plus oultre* [Further beyond], stimulated a form of thought concerned with seeing and proceeding not simply far, but fundamentally *ever further*. Schumpeter was right when he identified *plus ultra* as the code-word of entrepreneurship in the Modern Age.

The principle of television, then, did not make its first appearance in the age of moving images; it was *de facto* given as soon as entrepreneurial foresight and far-sight employed the medium of the globe – a medium that insisted of its own accord on constant updates. The moving images of the twentieth century were preceded by the revisable images in the great age of globes and maps. The seller of the Maluku Islands – Charles V – and their buyer – John III – were exemplary actors in this far-sighted culture of risk. Their transaction of 1529 shows that from that point on, princes were not so much God's first regional servants on earth as the first entrepreneurs of the money-dependent state. Under their chairmanship, European peoples developed into modern investment collectives that, from the eighteenth century on at the latest, distinguished themselves under the name of 'nations' as self-appointed *chargés d'affaires*.[3] And when economized nations democratically restructured themselves from the American Revolution on, it was brought about by the realization that kings had become unproductive factors on the supervisory boards of these political investment collectives. Modern history is characterized by the structural long-term unemployment of kings.

10

Delusion and Time:
On Capitalism and Telepathy

The history of discoveries has been written countless times as an adventure novel of seafaring, a success and crime story of conquests, a history of jealousy among major imperial powers, as well as a neo-apostolic ecclesiastical history (which was in turn the history of jealousy among the missionary orders and confessions). 'European expansion' served as an object of every kind of glorification and condemnation; in the Old World, it became a field on which self-doubt gleaned the remains of its harvest.[1]

As far as we know, a philosophically thought-out history of discoveries, terrestrial and maritime alike, has never been considered, let alone attempted or carried out – probably mainly because the indispensable central concepts that would form part of a philosophical résumé of globalization processes only play a secondary part in the philosophical vocabulary, and most are missing altogether: distance, extension, externality, canopies, barbarians, becoming-image, density, one-sidedness, disinhibition, dispatchability, capture, inhibition, investment, capital, mapping, medium, mission, ecumene, risk, feedback, debt, obscurity, crime, traffic, interconnection, delusional system, world system, wishful thinking, cynicism. Even as eminent a word as 'discovery' is not so much as mentioned in the *Historisches Wörterbuch der Philosophie* [Historical Dictionary of Philosophy], edited by Joachim Ritter and Karlfried Gründer, the highest intercultural yardstick for the terminology of the trade.[2] We shall touch on the significance of these gaps in the vocabulary of academic philosophy, and the dispositions of which they are symptoms, further below. First of all, however, we will make a sketch showing how a discovery-philosophical theory of globalization should approach its theme, and what problems face a theory of the discovery-dependently globalized commune, also known as mankind. It will hopefully not be considered unseemly if we begin by considering the deliriums of the discoverers.

It seems a trivial observation that the practice of geographical discovery was connected to a very hazardous departure to an un-homelike externality. Upon closer inspection, however, it becomes clear to what extent non-trivial forces drove these enterprises. The Portuguese and Spanish expeditions could never have been under-taken without motivating systems of delusions to justify these leaps into the unclear and unknown as sensible acts. It is in the nature of a well-systematized delusion to be capable of presenting itself to others as a plausible project; a delusion that is not contagious does not adequately understand itself.[3] Columbus himself, at any rate, was no longer content in later years to view himself only as the seaman, the conquistador of a new world and its cartographer; rather, he had become convinced that he was an apostle called by the will of God to bring salvation across the water. Encouraged by his incomparable success, he made his first name Christophorus, 'Christ-bearer', into his religion, and turned his Hispanicized paternal name Colón, 'settler', into his existential maxim – a success-psychological styliza-tion phenomenon that still casts light on the modern entrepreneurial world and its autogenous religions as a whole. In *The Book of Prophecies* of 1502, he interpreted himself as a nautical messiah whose coming had been foretold since ancient times.[4] No project without delusions of success; and without a project, no chance of infecting others with one's own fever. In this, Columbus was an agent of a pan-European willingness to embrace delusion – though it was only psychotechnically perfected by the USA in the twentieth century (and re-imported to Europe through the consultancy industry) – that became workable worldwide through the principle: seek your own salvation by bringing it to others.

This ideal synthesis of selflessness and self-service sums up the Modern Age-enabling psychotechnical figure of 'self-enthusiasm' or 'autogenic mania' – in due course, German philosophers would mystify it as 'self-determination' and generalize it beyond all recogni-tion. If self-enthusiasm has to take on smaller forms, it appears as self-counselling and self-persuasion – those two pragmatic expres-sions of the new effort of being a subject. Because most actors in the Modern Age were only partly successful in their self-motivation, however, they became dependent on advisers who supported them in their attempt to believe in their mission and their luck. For projectprompters and astrologers, overseas traffic in capital marked the start of the Golden Age – which was still in progress at the threshold of the twenty-first century. With its compulsion to act into the distance, the Modern Age became a paradise for soothsayers and consultants. The concern for capital that was intended for realization on journeys around the world bestows a sixth sense. It would indeed be amazing if people for whom reality is the flow of money and goods did not also believe in subtler forms of inflow and outflow. Flux-based thought (in telepathic, astrophysical, magnetic and monetary forms) broke the hegemony of substance-oriented scholasticism – though it would take everyday Euro-American life four centuries to complete the adjustment.

Anton Fugger, who had become a secret master of the world as a financier of the imperial Spanish colonization of South America, was ensnared during his final years in the nets of an attractive healer, Anna Megerler, who was notorious for sleeping with a priest. She had to appear before the judges of the Augsburg town council in 1564, accused of witchcraft; she was acquitted, however, because the great man's name acted as a legal talisman in her favour after his death. Anton Fugger himself, who harboured parapsychological ambitions, claimed that he had acquired, with Anna's help, the ability to observe his distant agents in a crystal ball. To his displeasure, however, this far-seeing ball showed his employees better dressed than he was – a discovery that, in a time when clothing customs indicated rank and class, inevitably called for sanctions.[5]

In the years before his murder by terrorists of the Red Army Faction, Alfred Herrhausen, chairman of Deutsche Bank, had, under the influence of the trained Germanist and business consultant Gertrud Höhler, introduced group-dynamic exercises in self-experience for his employees in order to motivate higher performance. His brilliant adviser had recognized the signs of the time, which demanded flexible, emotionally intelligent, team-suited and self-driving (more Protestant, one could say) staff, before many others.[6]

A continuum that shaped the Modern Age spans the time between these two dates: that of the search for ways to transfer salvific knowledge to unholy practices. What characterizes a substantial part of the current consultancy industry is the adoption of spiritual traditions which are then filtered into realistic business – a paradigmatic example being the adaptation of Zen Buddhism to a decidedly non-meditative clientele.

It cannot be emphasized enough, then, that what was termed European expansion was *not* originally rooted in the Christian mission idea; rather, expansion and systematized colonial and mercantile risk-taking over great distances triggered proselytization, transmission and bringing as a type of activity in its own right. This type also encompasses general salvific transfer, exportation of advanced civilization, consultation and all procedures for the transference of success and advantage. In this sense, we can say that the Modern Age as a whole is the object of a secular missionary science. The Christian missionaries simply recognized their historical chance early on by jumping aboard the departing ship.[7]

The group of advantage-bringers in the Modern Age includes conquerors, discoverers, researchers, priests, entrepreneurs, politicians, artists, teachers, designers, journalists – all of them supported by their own advisers and outfitters. Without exception, these factions dress their practices in manic assignments, that is to say secular missions. They constantly attempt to close their depressive gaps and clear away their doubts by insuring themselves through the services of paid motivators. These are meant to show them ways to become a modern subject, that is to say a rationally motivated perpetrator.

11

The Invention of Subjectivity –
Primary Disinhibition and Its Advisers

Being-'subject' means taking up a position from which an actor can make the transition from theory to practice. This transition usually takes place once an actor has found the motive that liberates them from hesitation and disinhibits them for action. Since time immemorial, the most powerful agent of disinhibition has always been compulsion through command – whether of an inner and affective or an external and social nature. As the activity culture of modernity constitutes itself against heteronomy, however, it will seek and find methods to place the commanding authority inside the hearer of the command themselves, so that they seem only to be obeying their inner voice when they submit. In this way, the fact of 'subjectivity' is demanded, created and fulfilled. What is meant, then, is the individual's co-determination of the authority that can give them commands. This organization of disinhibition usually makes itself invisible by claiming that in the moment when the actors make the transition to action, they are not following rousing passions or inescapable compulsions, but rather obeying sound self-understood reasons and sensible interests.

Correctly understood subjectivity, then, always implies the capacity to act, but not in the sense of an irrational rapture or a submission to unresolved drives – which French psychoanalysis noted in the term *passage à l'acte*. And contrary to what Lacanians and crypto-Catholics believe, not everyone who stands under the symbolic order of some 'great Other', of God or the fatherland, is a subject, but rather one who takes part in the experiments of modernity in the psychological formatting of entrepreneurial energies. This task always has to be borne in mind when one speaks of being a subject as 'acting of one's own accord' or thinking for oneself. An entrepreneur is constantly in transition to acting 'from within themselves', and the bridge to action erected by them or someone else is constructed from interests – which could certainly also include reasonable interests. Whoever knows how to interpret their interests is obeying, in the parlance of modern philosophy, none other than the 'voice of reason'. It is thus sufficient to declare reason entirely one's own in order to remove any suspicion of heteronomy from one's actions. Admittedly, the advanced Enlightenment found it increasingly problematic to say whether that voice can fully become the intimate property of its listener, as its demands led not infrequently to conflicts with the other *intimissimum* of the subject, namely its own feelings. Romanticism escaped this dilemma by giving priority to emotion, crediting it with being 'more reasonable than reason alone'.

Revealing the figure of self-obedience at the core of Modern Age subjectivity means showing how 'subjects' upgrade themselves to action-capable agents by advising themselves, persuading themselves and giving themselves the sign to shed inhibitions and act – or acquiring it from third parties. Subjectification is thus inseparable from authorizations and corresponding forms of training. In noting this, we reject critical theory's misconception of modern subjectivity as an agency for self-control – an obsessional neurosis, psychoanalytically speaking. The true meaning of becoming a subject can only be understood in terms of the arming and self-disinhibition of the actor – their hystericization, in a sense. A modern actor cannot get into shape without support from a specific training of auto-consultation and auto-persuasion. The aim of drawing on such capacities is not usually theoretical insight as such, but rather the application of insights in order to achieve practical goals. Then self-advice and self-convincing will ultimately result in self-disinhibition.

It is the transition from theory to practice, then, that defines the nature of subjectivity. One can never, of course, be certain where this might lead the actors. An agent who might take some action for inner reasons more or less opaque to the outside observer, at any rate, displays the primary characteristic of the subject: unpredictability.[1] Moral philosophy processes this state of affairs into freedom, or indeterminacy of action. Anyone who desires the empowerment of the subject on account of its freedom, however, must thus find a way to bring this activated power point in the world under effective control. Hence reason is meant to ensure this power control from within. But what if it remains unclear to what extent reason is at the helm within the interior of the released power points or subjects? It is thus advisable for anyone who deals with subjects to be fundamentally suspicious towards them. We can go further: only those whom one suspects of being up to some mischief can effectively become notable as a subject. Because subjectivity implies indeterminate offensivity, one can only do it justice with the attitude of a suspended distrust.[2] One factor in the fundamental dubiousness of the construct we call the 'subject' is the difficulty of establishing whether the suspect carries out their potential and present deeds 'from within themselves',[3] or is rather a possessed person or an automaton, subordinated to anonymous forces – be they mechanical or demonic. The subject is a non-trivial complex of ambition and reflection, or of energy and insidiousness.

The first subjects of the Modern Age in the precise sense of the word were, as we shall hint in the following, the Jesuits, who established themselves in the sixteenth century as a special intervention group of the Counter-Reformation – with the unmistakable intention of helping the Catholic party to catch up on the lead of the motivationally superior Protestants. As an explicit attempt at psychotechnical and medial modification, Jesuit subjectivity was driven by the longing to understand the successes of the Protestants better than the Protestants themselves. This passing manoeuvre revealed the unique disinhibiting value of the confession: whoever expresses their creed in actions undeniably has the force of vigour on their side. In the era of religious wars, this observation resulted in a psychosemantic arms race in the course of which confession was used not only as a motive, but also as a weapon. But while the Protestants appeared as primary fundamentalists, the Jesuit position was based on the parodying of their opponents' fundamentalism. The Jesuit theatre, with its large repertoire, essentially derives from the Jesuit position: it dictates a role to each actor in which orthodoxy becomes performance. On this path, obedience likewise had to become an overbearing exercise. The secret of the order lay in the fact that it knew how to create a Catholic equivalent to Protestant psychodynamics: its aim was to exploit the new combination of an enthusiastic motivation system with an ascetic executive system for the Catholic party in the global civil war of faith.

These radically available activists could not, therefore, leave it at the *humilitas–castitas–paupertas* vow that had applied to Christian monastic life since the days of the great rule-makers. With their notorious fourth vow, they placed themselves – in a rather modern way – under the pope's supreme command. They conceived themselves, one might say, as exquisitely weak-willed precision instruments that placed themselves entirely in the hands of their user. To set them going, therefore, no less than the will of the highest possible earthly motivational authority in Catholicism was used. With fanatical irony, the Jesuits offered themselves up as marionettes of the most modern construction whose strings were to be pulled by a single puppeteer, the Roman commander of counter-modernity. (Note: whoever wants power must serve the powerful to the point of indispensability.) To become such puppets, they developed a far-reaching combination of exercises and study – the first to crucify their own will and make themselves usable as pure tools, and the second to enter the battleground equipped with the newest state of the art. The metaphor of Jesuit 'cadaver obedience' refers to the classical implementation of subjectivity as the combination of maximum motivation and pure availability.[4] The exaggeration of obedience on the Jesuit path to subjectivity highlights the fact that the incentive to act here comes entirely from an external authority; this factor would taint the model for non-Catholics and anti-authoritarians until the twentieth century. From the start, it was impossible to doubt the efficiency of the construction. The power of the intelligent instrument was so great that even its master could not but become suspicious – a suspicion that, after long intra-Catholic quarrelling, would lead to the dissolution of the order in 1773.

In its design for the Catholic subject of the post-Tridentine era, the Ignatian turn unifies four traditional motifs of self-moulding practices: athleticism, monasticism, soldierdom and scholardom.[5] All of them are cultural manifestations of the ability to suffer and cultivations of *pónos* (effort, exertion), of which the Greeks of the classical age had already taught that without it, no *paideía*, no instance of the human-shaping practice known as education, will produce the desired results. The medium in which the unification of older exertion techniques was able to succeed was initially provided by late medieval passion piety, whose significance for the emergence of the culture of subjectivity cannot be overestimated. The controlled inward turn, furthermore, had been prepared through the decree that annual confession was compulsory for all Christians after 1215. Thanks to a broad religious trend towards the awakening of a taste for the passion among the middle classes of early modern cities – the keyword for this was *imitatio Christi,* and its liturgical mark the establishment of the feast of Corpus Christi in the thirteenth century – there emerged that inclination towards an active appropriation of one's own passivity without which the modern-subjectivist stylization of the human condition would have been inconceivable. When a sequence of adverse events can be experienced as a passion, suffering is converted into ability. Only through this transformation can the subject appear as the bearer of all mental 'representations' [*Vorstellungen*], which then also include all modifications of passive sensuality and all motives that dispose the subject to become active. This means that only someone capable of learning how to master and possess their own suffering can be a subject. In this sense, subjectivity constitutes an apparatus comparable to an automobile; in the latter, a propulsion system of passion-like (and later also interest-like) motives is combined with a control system of reason-like orientations. If modern subjectivity often presents itself as a passionate one, it is because modern 'passions' wish to be the ability-form of subjugation by powers from within oneself.

Later generations of subjects naturally drew on more modern means than the Jesuits to organize their disinhibitions. In keeping with the changed spirit of the age, they drew on inner authorities such as evidence, moral principle, genius or decision, as well as the influences of allied external elements that made themselves useful as lawyers, secretaries, advisers and therapists. Regarding the inner factors, which were later unified with the term 'faith', William James noted in his 1896 essay 'The Will to Believe' with constructive irony that even empirically minded people often behave like 'infallible popes' when formulating their central hypotheses on life.[6] This *bon mot* tells us that modern individuals are generally quite successful in the establishment of a 'final authority' that is personally binding for them. The liberal American psychologist had realized that 'papacy' is not an exclusively Roman speciality, but rather a ubiquitously valid mental function that must be explicitly activated whenever individualistic life forms begin to dominate. The inner pope has the task of stopping the endless regression of doubt in order to establish the psychosemantics of dogma, namely resting on a secure foundation and being able to take it as a point of departure, at an individual level. It is due to the actions of this authority that the 'subjects', though usually equipped with ample inhibitions (viewed more as neuroses by psychoanalysis) thanks to their typically modern pedagogical grooming, find their way through the uncertainties of the 'society of opportunities'. This enables them to make the transition from hesitation to action whenever inner and outer circumstances invite it. Only a minority fixed in endless reflection emphasizes, in agreement with Hamlet, that it is out of the question to be truly convinced of anything – which inevitably results in a chronic inhibition to act and a possible compensation for this in the form of disinhibition procedures, especially the collection of the subject for a 'leap' first examined by Kierkegaard.[7]

The dominant figure of modernity is thus by no means the excess of reflective inwardness, as some authors have suggested, or the continuous state of inhibition that results from it; rather, it reveals itself in a pragmatic hesitation whose conclusion usually succeeds within limited time spans – whether alone or with the help of others. What becomes manifest in the process is that the task of reflection is to prepare the desired disinhibition. Only in the most exceptional cases does modern thought gain a fundamentally procrastinating function – from which one can conclude, furthermore, that nothing is less likely in modern times than the stance of an observing philosophy. This is unaltered by the fact that the early twentieth-century phenomenologists after Husserl, with their theory of *epochè*, were able to show how one can adopt this stance proficiently; the philosophy-enabling 'step back' was made explicit at the moment when everything else was focused on the steps forwards. For political holists and military actors, the principle of service and duty, in which morality and excuses merge in a premodern or timeless fashion, remained available well into the twentieth century.

According to Descartes, Kant, Fichte and Marx, the subject-to-be no longer progresses from mortification to practice, but rather from theory to practice – though 'theory', of course, no longer means the quiet gazing of thinkers before the icons of being; what is now meant is the active establishment of sufficient reasons for successful deeds – an undertaking that is only productive until the point of disinhibition or action is reached. Kant suggests anchoring the highest authority of self-advice, the categorical imperative, in the discriminating subject so as to equip it with the measure of all justified practice – which would, incidentally, have resulted in immediate paralysis if any individual had ever decided to assess their own actions in detail by this standard. (This means that the utility of the categorical imperative lies in its sublimity, which ensures its inapplicability.) The weak surplus of theoretical thought not leading into disinhibition gains an intrinsic value as scientified philosophy; it does not lead into an external practice, but rather establishes itself as its own realization. As the quiet voice of reason rarely issues such clear directives as the Roman pope, however, and as those called upon to act are often unaware, almost until the time of action, if they have heard a clear command in their inner forum or not, they surround themselves (as noted earlier) with advisers and motivators who have no other task than to assist the actors with their leap into action. Hence the auto-persuasive form of subjectivity ('I took counsel with myself') actually calls for a division of labour in the production of disinhibition – a fact mystified by later idealism as a turn towards intersubjectivity (as if several people all unaware of what they had to do would be stronger together). In reality, this is how the modernization of consultation takes place.

For people with plans, the immeasurable advantage of viewing oneself as a subject is clearly that one can mentally remove the external master – taken as the epitome of inhibiting power – and the master's resistance must indeed be removed as soon as we claim freedom of expression and enterprise for ourselves. If the master shows no sign of opening the way in reality, then the first undertaking of the united expressive-expansive 'subjects' will be to dethrone him through a 'revolution'. Thus 'revolution' is not only a type of political event, but even more a philosophical motto: it stands for the phantasm of disabling the oppressive, obstructive and depressing qualities of the real as such. That is why, since 1789, political coups have usually included a delegation of liberation philosophers.

Memories of the great days when the first interferer in the state was disposed of constitute the happy moments in subject history; liberal parties process them into the authentic New Mythology. National holidays are thus always independence days – they call to mind the animated scenes when the people removed their external master and elevated the entrepreneurial and expressive freedom of the offensive middle classes to the starting point for a new legislation. The naïve happiness of such special days flows from the allegation that the entire resistance of the real is concentrated in the master, and must dissolve with his removal. Post-revolutionary times are those in which the 'subjects' outgrow this naïveté. The great disadvantage of being a subject reveals itself in the fact that the function of the master, namely the authorization – granted by managerial powers – of disinhibition among the subalterns, cannot be adopted one to one when I apply it to myself. Autocracy may be a task inevitably faced by the moderns on account of their historical screenplay; that same script tells us that we chronically fail in this task and why.

The quandary of being a subject creates markets for intellectuals who offer their support for needy, under-informed and under-motivated subjectivity. The gaps left by the master's removal were filled between 1793 and 1968 by the ideologues, until their more discreet successors, the consultants, appeared and took up residence in the hollows of lordlessness. The ideologues (whose functional predecessors in the sixteenth century were the Italian *secretarii* and the father confessors of the princes) usually disinhibited themselves and their clients in the name of 'history' and its iron laws – hence the inevitable task for these advisors of presenting their not infrequently violent promptings as products of a 'science of history'. As 'history', alongside 'nature', was viewed for a time as the highest client of action, invocation of its assignments held the greatest disinhibiting value. Needless to say, historicism of this type was the legally cloaked form of opportunism. Obedience to the 'law of history' (and its application to the opportunities) provided the most discreet method of participating in supposedly unavoidable acts of violence – although most intellectuals were careful not to contribute personally to the crimes they advised or considered acceptable. With their willingness to provide the keywords that would trigger attacks, left and right extremists proved close relatives, as embarrassing as both parties may find this proximity.

The most embarrassing constellation is simultaneously the clearest: the notes of the young Lukács on the meta-humanitarian duty of the revolutionary to commit criminal acts of violence (1922) would be mirrored in Himmler's Poznan speech in October 1943 about SS troops retaining their decency while committing mass murder. However great the distance between the sketches of a Hegelianizing legitimizer of Bolshevist exterminism and the murderous commands of a Kantianizing agent of National Socialist conquest and elimination policy may seem, both authors provide closely related samples of that same assiduousness in the service of the grand narrative which conveys its 'commands' through the mouths of clear-sighted amoralists. Both make it clear how one's own act of taking action as a voluntary self-obligation against one's better judgement only becomes possible through explicit disinhibition figures.[8] As the intellectual activists describe the world as a war zone between irreconcilable parties – progress and reaction, work and capital, rooted and rootless – their discourse, with varying openness, takes on the character of an issue of orders in the generalized word war; consequently, the prevailing tone among radicals in the field is exterministic.[9] The moderates among the advisers retreat to the terrain of philosophical scepticism and cultivate indecision as the life form of small freedom. Where scepticism is intensified, it specializes in a generalized dissuasion.

The consultants, on the other hand, whose good fortunes began when those of the ideologues ended, disinhibit their clientele and themselves within a less martial framework, as their conception of the world has rivals, but not enemies. They do this in the name of market freedom and the human right to success – but this is no picnic either, to be sure. Their profession is based on the decision to portray economic success and its factors – leadership skills, intuition, charisma and so on – as something that can be learned using varyingly reliable methods. They must create the fiction that one can establish a controllable connection between project and luck.[10]

The replacement of the ideologues with the consultants took place mainly after 1968, after neo-Marxism had raised itself in a great pose once more, boosted by an illusory Freudian rejuvenation and little challenged by the suspicion that it might have more in common with what Thomas Mann, in a well-known formulation from the 1940s, had called 'intellectual fascism' than merely its radical demeanour.[11] Since then, the victims of the imposition of being a subject, that is to say an actor on an inevitably oversized stage with little evidence and insufficiently supplied with keywords for disinhibition, have been at the mercy of vague professional advice rarely willing or able to say more than that real action always retains a remainder of experimentation in the dark, as the notion of complete control over the basic conditions of the experiment is utopian. The later wave of advisers works with the correct assumption that agents who cannot do very much are best supported by consultants who know that they do not know very much. Through this development, Socrates is in our midst once again. Leading indecision-makers today are prepared to pay almost any sum for advice of this kind: it is not only the top managers who spare no expense to receive absolution through consultation. In recent years, numerous German government ministries have purchased consultative bluff on a grand scale under the name 'commission of inquiry' – for sums in the billions, such that the notoriously waste-tolerant federal audit office even requested an explanation at the start of 2004.

The only strong keyword for disinhibition that can enable the transition to practice after the fading of ideologies all over the world is, quite simply, 'innovation'. Only a few people are aware that this represents a stage of attrition in the erstwhile 'laws of history'. Ever since the new human being was taken off the market in a major product recall, technical novelties, procedural novelties and design novelties have constituted the strongest attractors for all those who are still condemned to ask what they can do to reach the top. Whoever innovates can be sure that the maxim of their actions could become the principle of a general legislation at any time.

With the rise of fun as a disinhibition agent from the 1980s on, even the pretext of innovation became dispensable. As vulgar sovereignists, the actors of the fun culture frolic in their superficial feel-good zones and consider wilfully letting themselves go an adequate motivation. They could dispense with consultants, as they address their seducers directly; if anything, they confide in their entertainer, trainer or gag-writer. Sovereignty means deciding oneself what to fall for.

12

Irreflexive Energies:
The Ontology of the Headstart

With the turn towards the oceans, with nautical risk-taking and with the new techniques of luck, the agents of the European Modern Age inaugurated an interest in subjectivity that differed fundamentally from all earlier stylizations of human being-in-the-world and letting-oneself-be-led. The human being that describes itself in humanism as the sculptor and inventor of itself, and defines itself in idealism as the subject of all its inner representations, is – to an extent unknown in earlier epochs – a perpetrator of *new* deeds, an author of *new* effects, a carrier of *new* imaginings. The firm link between subjectivity and offensivity reveals that the inner stabilization of a perpetrator culture is at stake here. Nonetheless, the future actors are chronically over-taxed by their own offensivity and originality, as they can never convincingly manage to explain the nature of their perpetratordom and their leap ahead into the unknown. The notorious stammering about genius and creatordom that has pervaded the European art scenes since the end of the fifteenth century is a proof of the inability of the moderns to take a meaningful stand on their own powers of initiative. If one invokes a *genius* and derives works and actions from it, one is implicitly declaring the actor possessed, albeit in a sense that demands respect; the deed is consequently shifted from the per-petrator to a supra-personal authority that reaches through them and places them in a state of sublime irresponsibility. The same thing happens when one claims that the actors were not inspired by heathen geniuses of art and war, but rather sought to participate in divine plans for salvation: in this way too, one removes the perpetrator from the 'middle of the deed' and makes them a medial, sublimely irresponsible factor. Whoever speaks directly of creatordom retreats to tautology, attributing the effect to an authorial spirit that wanted to bring it about because it could.

In both cases, edifying observation wins out over the precise perception of mobilized and released forces, preventing the development of a language that is at the level of the action culture attained. This effect characterizes the overall situation of European philosophy in the Modern Age, which remained resolutely silent in almost all quarters about the central event of its time: the taking of the world by the mercantile and imperial forces, and the disinhibition of the perpetrators to carry out acts of pure aggression. This deficit may have been due to the prejudice that there could be biographies of captains and conquistadors, but no theory. The truth is that one readily finds the theory of captains as soon as one seeks it in the languages of non-academic literatures. From the logbook of Columbus's ship to Melville's observations on Captain Ahab, the Euro-American archive holds an entire encyclopedia of offensive knowledge that still awaits an adequate edition. Needless to say, this is a rejected archive from today's perspective, as the policy changed from attack to co-operation after the period of world history shaped by Europe came to an end – and the new moral philosophies were correspondingly no longer interested in discoveries or deeds, which glowed with the sinister aura of one-sidedness, but in reciprocity, responsibility, fairness, lack of side effects and compatibility with locally grown sensibilities.

In order to better understand the dynamic of the Modern Age, one must accept the uncomfortable thought that 'spirit' and 'deed' must not be noted down in two separate accounting books. The authors of the philosophical tradition have only admitted this extremely rarely – but one who did was Hegel, whose cursory remarks on Napoleon indicate the consequences of a synthetic examination of intellect and energy. For Hegel, the victor of Jena was a manifestation of the 'world soul', and *eo ipso* the highest incarnation of the Old European action culture. The spirit of the offensive is interpreted here through a stern personalism: when it was a matter of concentrating the dynamic ideas of 1789 and the need for order in the civil state of law in the figure of a leader, Napoleon had to emerge. There is no deeper praise for spirited offensivity than Hegel's aphoristic justification of the Bonaparte phenomenon – perhaps one can even see in it a hidden theory of the captain, in that Napoleon's militarily inspired politics, always based on the necessary precedence of movement, left the safe haven of the status quo in a fundamental state of restlessness to undertake expanded reachings-out. The ironic variant of the same pattern is found in Marx's theory of character masks: capital, too, always chooses the right time to produce those people by whom it feels represented sympathetically, and co-criminally if need be. As a mentality of unconditional disrespect towards anything that obstructs profit (just as nobility obliges, so too does the disenchantment of the world), it is embodied in the class of capital owners and entrepreneurs, who, with devastatingly progressive energy, blow to pieces all stationary conditions and cause all solid states to evaporate.

Nonetheless, little is gained through such phrases as 'world soul' or 'synthesis of spirit and vigour' (any more than the Marxian concept of the character mask), as they do not teach us anything more precise about the mode of interconnection between the energetic and intelligible elements in this new culture of perpetrators. In the light of this difficulty, it might prove useful to seek insights in literature that feels its way towards the riddle of intelligent energetics with its own specific means.

We shall here content ourselves with a single example: Heinrich Mann's essay collection *Geist und Tat* [Spirit and Deed] contains a remark on Napoleon that, in our view, proves how poetic expression can occasionally achieve almost in passing what is still beyond the reach of concepts. He discusses the exile on St Helena, who wrote his memoirs in the third person, as if the world-historical actor had carried the narrator of his deeds around with him from the start: 'The great man whom this writer knew entered the world as a bullet enters the battle: that is how the revolution sent him. In his life, he was one with an idea, he had the same body and the same path [. . .].'[1] Going out into the world like a bullet into battle: Heinrich Mann put this characterization of the unconditionally offensive mode of existence in the context of a neo-liberal Napoleonic cult on paper in 1925 – at the same time as Heidegger's breakthrough to his epoch-making analyses in *Being and Time*, published in 1927. These marked the first time that the being-thrown-into-the-world of existence was brought up in a way that allowed the primal prejudice of all prior philosophy, the subordination of knowledge to the theoretical ideal, to be done away with. Heidegger's 'thrownness' [*Geworfenheit*] conceptualized a mode of pre-theoretical world-disclosure in which 'understanding' forms an uncircumventable aspect of active existence – just as if Fichte's erratic 'activity into which an eye is inserted' had clarified itself into a thrownness with an inherent knowledge of its surroundings. Heinrich Mann's occasional note on the great man of action and Heidegger's violent hermeneutics of existence converge in the articulation of a 'projectile existentialism' in which existence takes on qualities of intelligent ammunition. The constitutive interconnection of power and sight results in a bright motion that is always already pulling forwards – not by following a heteronomous order to attack, but by gleaning the necessary information about its own situation, however unclear, from the attack that it always constitutes from the start. Launched existence, then, has nothing whatsoever in common with a mechanical projectile; it resembles a cruise missile that is sent into the unknown and autonomously chooses its own direction en route.

Anyone who shoots into the world like a bullet into battle requires the appropriate weaponry to fire them. Heinrich Mann had no difficulty naming the artillery responsible for propelling Napoleon: he succinctly called it 'the revolution', referring to that epitome of offensive missions which messianic radicals since 1789 had seen as positioning them in their categorical Forwards. Heidegger increased the calibre of the weapon by explaining it as Being, which launches 'existences' on their route into the world. But while the novelist's Napoleon projectile was given its route through the 'idea' of the revolution (and its purported aim, the United States of Europe), Heidegger's projectiles, thrown into existence, must first project and programme themselves in flight – they lack any built-in sight picture; they are, in a sense, ontological duds, stray bullets that keep flying after the war has been lost.

What is decisive about this self-projection in mid-throw is that the responsibility for it cannot lie with a self-reflexive consciousness, in so far as one understands reflection as the returning of thought to a prior fact of consciousness. The existential projectile does not refer back to itself in the reflexive mode, but rather carries its prelogical élan into its cognitive orientations; this is precisely what is meant in the fundamental ontologist's strong statement on the simultaneously thrown and projecting quality of existing. If projecting is revealed as the primary activity of existence, however, a mode of intelligent energetics comes to light in which thought is not subsequent to being, but rather its equal. Existing is not a dark movement forced to wait until the light of an 'enlightenment' shows the way; it is a self-lit offensive, though the light is usually only of low intensity and moderate reach. The existential philosophies of the early twentieth century were of epochal significance, as they explicitly carried out the switch from reflection to projection. They cleared a view of the dynamics within originally bright, pre-reflexive and pre-inhibited motion. Herein lies their key role in the shift from the primacy of the past to that of the future, a process in which several contemporary authors – systemicists and futurologists – see, with good reason, the central mental event in Western civilization during the twentieth century.

The existential philosophies, admittedly, were themselves merely the rearguard of a literature that had advanced the exploration of being a perpetrator further than any book-learning, even Heidegger's audacious academicism, could ever dream of doing. The great probings in the space of perpetrator subjectivity – from Shakespeare to Joseph Conrad, from Camões to Gabriel García Márquez, from Machiavelli to Dostoyevsky – all operate on the same level, and make the philosophical theories of active life, whether they deal with work, politics or communicative action, seem second-rate not only in their depictions, but also in their concepts; Fichte and Nietzsche, and possibly Bergson, are the only exceptions. We can assume that one habitual reason for the powerlessness of philosophers in the face of eminent action is that, owing to their bias towards the reflexive attitude, they virtually always gave precedence to inhibition over offensive. This prevented them from seeing more in active energy than the wild horse of affects, waiting to be ridden by reason.

One can gain insight into the deeper reasons for the hesitation of the culture of reflection to study the world of action as soon as one considers how much the moral shadow cast by energy in its reachings-out into the real grows with each radical examination of action. If one takes the informed power of action in its insurmountable twilight as a basic factor, one encounters an authority in which the differentiation between legitimate and criminal energy has not yet taken place. Anyone who would, in all earnest, place the 'deed' at the beginning like Goethe's Faust would initially lack any criteria to separate economic undertakings, political expeditions, religious missions and artistic creations with sufficient clarity from what is usually closely connected to such operations: crime. Separating the deeds is usually the business of historiography, as much as some perpetrators might attempt to bring the evaluation of their actions under their own control. No one who truly acts – be it Columbus, Pizarro, Napoleon or Lenin – can know before the deed whether they might not stand as a fool or a criminal after carrying it out. Goethe's well-known remark that someone who acts is always without conscience puts this situation in a nutshell. The more serious among the doers of deeds took this as indicating the tragic nature of all true action – not without requesting their own acquittal due to supra-legal circumstances. They were joined early on by a category of perpetrators who communicated quite frankly how little they worried about such uncertainties; they were called 'blasphemers' in the language of the eighteenth century, or 'adventurers' in a slightly more timeless manner of speaking. Understandably, their 'practice' is ignored by practical philosophy, even though it is obvious that this group frequently includes those agents who turn the wheel of modernization most energetically.

The reason for this disregard deserves to be pointed out: the philosophy of the Modern Age could never be persuaded, despite Hegel's Sunday dictum, to formulate its time in thought – it would be better described as the predominant missing of the point. If it had provided what Hegel demanded of it, it would have constituted itself between 1500 and 1900, in its practical part, as a faculty of adventurism, or at least as a moderator of colonialism and a consultant for coming revolutions – in its more daring forms, it would even have undertaken blasphemer counselling (which, to our knowledge, only occurred once, in the subterranean œuvre of the Marquis de Sade). It would have provided a conceptual formulation of the three primary manifestations of modernized and modernizing élan – European expansion, mechanical engineering and the war of movement – instead of evading them through inner emigration. From a civil perspective, it is to the credit of philosophy that it was never prepared to offer such services; the price it paid was a form of voluntary castration. The consequences of this castration manifest themselves atmospherically: one senses them as an unease at the self-inflicted harmlessness of the philosophical text. The ordained philosophers save their souls in exchange for the licence not to understand what it would have been their business to understand. Their state of awareness is comparable to that of the educated, sensitive daughters of Mafiosi, whose happiness in life depends on remaining enclosed in a world of blissful ignorance as to the sources of their fathers' wealth.[2] The few thinkers who deviated from the norm – whether Bacon, Hobbes, de Sade, Nietzsche, Spengler or Bergson – paid for their proximity to the spirit of action with marginalization or banishment from the canon; not without reason are they termed the 'dark authors of the bourgeoisie'. As far as Hegel is concerned, it is at least permissible to ask whether we should not consider him a wolf in sheep's clothing, as his pragmatic 'world spirit' expresses nothing other than a higher form of crime that always manages to return home in the nick of time, slipping under the roof of legally fostered necessity.

The only thing that prevented Europe's dangerous talent for producing the necessary teams for its colonizing or 'civilizatory' projects from disappearing under the inhibiting effect of Christian-bourgeois obedience training was the maintenance, throughout the entire era of expansion, of a state of consciousness in which even Christians and bourgeois individuals could make an exception to their own norms if circumstances permitted or demanded it. This applied whenever the actors found themselves confronted with foreign peoples whose foreignness could, it seemed, be interpreted as inferiority. The most favourable starting situation for the disinhibition of perpetrators against a Christian background was undoubtedly one in which expansive movement could present itself as missionary work – even if missionaries generally let soldiers and merchants proceed first. The second best was in effect when knightly or military customs justified a temporary suspension of the inhibiting norms, to which one would return after the completion of the un-Christian acts as if nothing happened. This combination of motifs proved its effectiveness most unmistakably during the Spanish conquest of Central and South America and the great migrations to the North American West. Modern perpetrator consciousness presupposes a well-functioning auto-persuasive agency that constantly unlocks actors for deeds by arranging a combination of special permission, promises of gain and the prospect of later absolution.

No one has illuminated the way in which the disinhibiting auto-persuasion of future perpetrator subjects works in individual cases with greater precision than Fyodor Dostoyevsky in his novel *Crime and Punishment*, written in 1868 – a psychological-moral study that can be read, especially its first half, as a handbook of practical philosophy with particular reference to special permission for crimes. Though the novel is focused, in its general tendency, on proving the necessary failure of the Westernization of the Russian soul – 'Westernization' here means the adoption of the Napoleonic ideal by a young utilitarian in St Petersburg – its pragmatic aspect deals primarily with asking under what circumstances an intellectual can cross over to the ranks of the people of action. It is precisely because Raskolnikov's complete lack of criminal energy is never in doubt – why else would he fall into a guilt-induced delirium for three days after committing the murder? – that he is the perfect specimen for an examination of the preconditions that make even the most inhibited capable of disinhibition with the bloodiest of consequences. The answer can be found in the sophistic construction of a prerogative to make exceptions to the moral law. Raskolnikov quotes to the prosecutor Porfiry from his own article 'On Crime', in which he believes he has shown the unbreakable connection between innovation and delinquency:

> In short, I argued that all people – not only the great, but even those who deviate only marginally from the common rut, that's to say who are only marginally capable of saying something new, are bound, by their very nature, to be criminals – to a greater or lesser degree, of

course. Otherwise they would find it hard to get out of the rut, and it goes without saying that, again because of their nature, they could not possibly agree to remain in it.[3]

According to Raskolnikov's reasoning, belonging to the group of extraordinary or innovative people is sufficient in order to have the right and duty to commit crimes – which, in the present case, simply means removing the obstacles to the new posed by ordinary people. The term 'crime' thus stands for 'the destruction of the present reality in the name of one that is better'.[4] The intellectual's self-persuasion leads to success from the moment when they manage to take themselves, with sufficient evidence, for a member of the extraordinary category – needless to say, this is where Dostoyevsky will come in and characterize his hero as the victim of a demonic (one would later call it narcissistic) fallacy. One can tell from the experimental set-up of the novel that the structure of the modern disinhibition to action can generally be found in the synthesis of exceptionalism, innovationism and evolutionism – and it does no harm to include a supplement of democratic-messianic motives too. This forms the matrix for countless crimes of modernization against Christian and humanistic backgrounds.[5]

The full implications of these reflections can be grasped if one examines the process-theoretical content of Raskolnikov's seemingly naïve distinction between ordinary and extraordinary people (leaving aside, for now, the fact that in the further course of the novel, motivated by anti-modern *ressentiment*, Dostoyevsky seeks to neutralize this difference 'before God' or 'before love'). The concept of the 'extraordinary people' holds a reference to a division of humanity on the basis of different speeds, differing intensities and different paths of becoming. The result of this division is that individuals who live in the midst of accelerated research, more daring expeditions and more refined methods of production will gain access to particular truths, realities or techniques earlier than others. Through this temporal privilege of access to the new truths, new realities and new techniques, they gain a headstart that forces the rest to respond whether they like it or not, either by deciding to follow or by refusing to do so – arguing, for example, that those headstarts lack any normative power. If one dispels the pseudo-anthropological aura surrounding Raskolnikov's talk of 'extraordinary people', what remains is a resilient process-theoretical core: what is addressed here as exceptionality is nothing other than the inclusion of individuals and groups on courses of being that could be termed advanced 'developments', assuming it is possible to use this word without implicitly making a statement about the duty of the others to catch up with these 'developments' sooner or later. When Dostoyevsky's hero emphasizes the gulf between those people who can speak the 'new word' and those who repeat the old and familiar, he adopts one of the basic assumptions of progressism, which stipulates a duty for ordinary people to catch up; the alternative is consenting to be cleared out of the way. His conception of the world shows him a humanity of two speeds – and its division into the overtakers and the overtaken. Two generations after Raskolnikov, Joseph Schumpeter would state in his theory of economic development that in economic life, functionally speaking, there are ultimately only innovators and imitators.

Such assumptions urge towards a naïve ontology of progress in which the distance between the vanguard and the main body can consistently be interpreted as the pilot function of those at the forefront: it shows the sluggish majority where the journey as a whole is heading. Although Raskolnikov does not deny the conservative rights of the average humans, he even claims to believe in a constant conflict between movement and preservation. In this schema, the headstart of the extraordinary is made possible by a vocation to disinhibition that forges ahead solely through active contempt for the restrictive power of morality and convention – hence the thesis of the inevitable criminality of the innovators. Here Dostoyevsky unmistakably places words in the modernist Raskolnikov's mouth that remain coloured, down to their basic terminology, by the anti-innovatory stance of classical metaphysics: in truth, within a metaphysics of the completed world (and neither the Christian Platonism of the East nor the post-Tridentine Catholic-Aristotelian church of the West was able to conceive of any other), any innovation arouses suspicions of diabolical originality; every innovator is thus in need of a merciful return to the consensus. For Christians, the event of God's love for humans (the only substantial supplement to the work of the creation) is innovation enough.

Even after Dostoyevsky's contribution, then, the decisive elements for the theory of the first world-taking and an understanding of the headstart of the more intense perpetrator have not yet been gained: so far, the acquittal of the active human from the primacy of inhibition and the release of pure offensivity have not proved sufficiently articulable. Even Raskolnikov's 'extraordinary people' remain bowed under the metaphysical prejudice of the innovators' guilt; they merit not only the admiration of their contemporaries, but equally also the disapproval of the well-meaning, for instead of integrating themselves into the community of love or communication between finite creatures, they break through the unity of the human race and transform it into an ensemble of competitors consisting, due to the effect of real headstarts and arrears, of real winners and losers.

It was only Nietzsche, in his central work *Thus Spoke Zarathustra*, who sketched the outlines for a doctrine of fundamentally acquitted offensivity. In its basic tendency, one could call the book a work of Dionysian pragmatism. The acquittal of those who feel the spark of action in themselves wants to be more than a mere theorem: the transformation of the philosophical text into a hymn offers itself as an example for the emancipation of the offensive. In its language form, this poeticized philosophy demonstrates *in actu* what purely thetical energy can achieve. With the vigour of an autogenic evangelic message addressed to all and none, the hubristic Zarathustran speech act repeats the Atlantic crossing: only from that point on could one say that Columbus's deed had arrived in thought. The key philosophical passages of *Zarathustra* are those in which the singer calls upon the élan of his own song – he calls it chance, whose banality does not contradict its divinity. This singing knows that it is a coincidental bright force which overexerts itself and affirms the overexertion – however much the heroically sun-like act of giving brings sorrow to the giver who is reimbursed by none. 'Over all things stands the Heaven Accident, the Heaven Innocence, the Heaven Contingency, the Heaven Exuberance. "Lord Contingency" – that is the oldest nobility in the world, which I restored to all things [. . .].'[6] This includes the laments in which the prophet articulates his loneliness: as he embodies the transition from a past-based to a future-based state, he must bear its consequence – to become lonely amid the unaccelerated lives of the rest. A human of his type exists not from their origin, but rather from their headstart.[7] Their speaking élan marks the transition from the headstart one person has to the headstart that truly is one. Whoever lives in this headstart will always be too early.

The existential path of the radically headstarting human summarizes the spirit of movement in Old Europe, to which only four statements scattered over previous centuries bear witness. One comes from Oliver Cromwell, who is reported to have said: 'No one rises so high as he who knows not whither he is going.' Another was made by Napoleon on his flight from Russia, according to Colencourt, when he repeated in a monotone after the loss of his army: 'From the sublime to the ridiculous is but a step.'[8] The most profound words of European movement wisdom, however, were written by Hölderlin in his poem 'The Poet's Courage' [*Dichtermut*] (which, in a later version, bears the title 'Blödigkeit' [Weakness]): 'So then wander defenceless / through life and fear nothing!'[9]

Needless to say, after the debacle of Old Europe, Nietzsche's insights have only antiquarian value; and all the more needless to add that with the transference of the realm of action to the USA, the game of 'world history' is essentially over for us – we shall explain below why America too, in grasping for a 'history' to be made, came away empty-handed. The golden age of European one-sidedness was long ago; reviews of daring opera productions or films of legendary mail robberies inform us what can become of the remaining one-sidednesses that have survived from the days of unobstructed action. Viewed as a whole, an added time appended to 'history' proper has begun whose rules are still largely unknown – except for the fact that since the appearance of rapid feedbacks, a different style of 'fate' is controlling the stage.

13

Nautical Ecstasies

On the subjective side of things, early transatlantic seafaring can be described as an informal technique of ecstasy whereby discoverers, like shamans of an undefined religion, acquired information from a significant realm beyond. This was no longer to be envisaged as a heavenly 'above', but rather as a terrestrial 'yonder'. Like all former transcendences or quasi-transcendences, this modern hazardous beyond came at a price. Early intercontinental travellers not infrequently had to pay for access to distant shores by enduring bitter asceticisms. These included involuntary fasts and passages drawn out by weather conditions, or the torture of boredom from calm at sea and sluggish sailing. Frequent sleep deprivation as a result of heat, cold, stench, cramped conditions, noise and fear on a heavy swell also wore away at the irritable and delirium-prone crews. Every ship on the high seas placed the travellers in constant connection to what one could here, more fittingly than anywhere else, call the last things. The alternative of port or death was the formula for mediating at sea on the precariously goal-directed nature of human action. As an examination of the end, Ignatian exercises could not be any more explicit than an Atlantic crossing. No group of ascetics on the seas, admittedly, bore the brunt of the maritime law 'port or death' more harshly than those who searched for the most difficult passages on earth, the Northern Sea Route between the Norwegian Sea and East Siberia and the Northwest Passage between Greenland and Alaska. By the turn of the twentieth century, the delusional systems and idealized fantasies of numerous researchers and adventurer-merchants had foundered on these nigh-impossible routes. In both of these northern passages, the Modern Age's campaign against the notion of 'impossible' claimed its exemplary victims.

If one characterizes the current civil world, in terms of its mentality conditions and immune constitutions since the eighteenth century, as a therapy and insurance 'society' – a formation that differs clearly from the preceding 'society' of religion – one usually overlooks the fact that an intermediate world had grown between the religious and therapeutic regimes which was involved in both systems, yet based on practices of its own. Seafaring constituted an autonomous third force between religion and therapeutics until the nineteenth century. Countless people sought healing from the frustrations of the mainland at sea. Perhaps the *Nautilus* of Captain Nemo was the last ship of fools on which a great, lonely misanthrope could act out his rejection of the disappointing land-dwelling humans in a sovereign fashion. For Herman Melville, it was quite self-evident that the open sea is the most reliable remedy for both melancholy and manic moods. Thus he was able to make the narrator of *Moby Dick* – published in 1851, barely twenty-five years before Jules Verne's literary forays into terran and subterranean, marine and submarine globalization – begin his tale with these words:

> Call me Ishmael. Some years ago – never mind how long precisely – having little or no money in my purse, and nothing particular to interest me on shore, I thought I would sail about a little and see the watery part of the world. It is a way I have of driving off the spleen, and regulating the circulation. Whenever I find myself growing grim about the mouth; whenever it is a damp, drizzly November in my soul; whenever I find myself involuntarily pausing before coffin warehouses, and bringing up the rear of every funeral I meet; and especially whenever my hypos get such an upper hand of me, that it requires a strong moral principle to prevent me from deliberately stepping into the street, and methodically knocking people's hats off – then, I account it high time to get to sea as soon as I can. This is my substitute for pistol and ball. With a philosophical flourish Cato throws himself upon his sword; I quietly take to the ship.[1]

The message is easy to decipher: next to the monastery and suicide, seafaring offers itself as the third option for throwing away a life that has become unliveable on land. In nautical globalization, everything undertaken by restless Europeans to tear away from their older spheric anchorings and local inhibitions would flow together for an entire age. What we here term restlessness (the keyword of older emigration research) encompasses entrepreneurial spirit, frustration, vague expectation and criminal uprooting without any distinctions between them. The unrest of money mingles with the unrest of 'uprooted existences'.[2] Like a different kind of purgatory, the sea now offered a chance to escape the disappointing inhabitants of the homeland and the mainland. In this group, people aged quickly beneath the wind and hopelessness. An observation by Victor Hugo about Gilliatt, the hero of his third great novel *The Toilers of the Sea* (1866), was true of them all: 'He wore the sombre mask of the wind and the sea.'[3]

The new entrepreneurial-nautical yonder was constituted as an experiential beyond open only to those who ventured out with total commitment. One cannot go halfway to sea, any more than one can be halfway in God. Whoever steps on deck has laid aside their attachment to the terran concepts of death and life. One does not know, however, how many of these men who died in advance would have been able to follow the words of the commander Pescara, the victor of Pavia, who explained the secret of his cold-bloodedness in battle thus: 'My guardian God has stilled the storm that tossed about my helm.'[4]

But regardless of whether the new restless ones board ships or travel in their imaginations to distant worlds from a fixed business location, glancing up from a travel account, the desire of the Europeans who learn to listen aims at a wondrous transatlantic transcendence. The European dream of the good and better life is caught up in the maelstrom of a totally other overseas. These notions have nothing in common with the panic-stricken legends and superstitions of sailors and fishermen; the yonder is no longer the edge of a cosmic shell but another coast – the Caribbean, which would later be the American.

It was only this displacement of transcendence to the horizontal plane that made *utopia* possible – as a school of thought, a mode of writing and a mould for wish plasmas and immanentized religions. The literary genre of utopia that suddenly appeared in the sixteenth century organized a wish culture geared towards progressive explication, and later the matching politics, where alternative worlds could be constructed without the need for a context – according to the taste of the terrestrially discontent, but always based on the primal fact of the Modern Age, namely the real-life discovery of the New World in the inexhaustible diversity of its insular and continental manifestations (not least in the countless Pacific islands, where it was supposed that the *experimentum mundi* could be undertaken once more from scratch). As any glance at the relevant documents shows, the empirical and the fantastic were inextricably intertwined in the early Age of Discovery. By means of its rapidly effective new media – whether chapbooks, travel accounts, novels and utopias or broadsheets, globes

and world maps – thoughts of the genuine New World and its imaginary variants produced a post-metaphysical wish regime which
believed that its fulfilments were perhaps not within reach, but at
least in the not-too-distant future. This set in motion a form of self-
fulfilling wishful thinking that learned to steer a course, both in
fantasy and in reality, towards distant worlds and their fortunes in
happiness, as if their supposed appearance at some distant point
already held the promise of their imminent appropriation.

14

'Corporate Identity' on the High Seas, Parting of Minds

Outside, of course, only those who knew how to wish and sail in the sworn team made their fortune. The crews on the discovery ships were the first objects of naïve and effective group modelling processes that were re-described in the present day as 'corporate identity' techniques. On the ships, the advancing pioneers learned to want the impossible in a team whose members were all dreaming in the same direction. In psychohistorical terms, the central New European principles of constant progress and general enrichment, which became amenable to politicization from the nineteenth century onwards, are essentially projections of team visions from the early days of nautical globalization back onto a national and social horizon. They constitute attempts to transfer the categorical Forwards of seafaring back onto the circumstances of settled life. One can read Ernst Bloch's writings – to name an eminent example of generalized progressivism – as if he had reformulated socialism from the position of the seaside and recommended it as a dream of emigration to New Worlds filtered through reason. Progress is emigration in time: as if it were wisdom to make people to believe that, with the aid of productive forces freed from greed for property, one could turn the entire world into a South Pacific paradise. For this reason, the party of objectively fulfillable wishes must always be right.[1]

But the dream of the main prize that comes to us outside will, at least, help the new globonauts to look the horror of exteriority in the face. That is why the seafarers and their crews are not simply psychotics whose loss of touch with reality at home makes them suitable to discover new worlds in the unknown; often enough, they genuinely have one foot on the ground of untrodden paths, and undoubtedly it is often well-suited to reality, especially on the high seas, to postulate the imminent miracle. The mightiest captains are those who commit their crews most effectively to the pure Forwards, particularly when it seems sheer insanity not to turn around. Without a constant, strict spell of optimism on board, most of the early expeditions would have been thwarted by demoralization. The leaders kept their crews mentally on course with visions of fame and riches for the discoverers; but draconian punishments were also among their techniques for success. Had the Portuguese Magellan, after the mutiny of his captains off St Julian on the Patagonian coast of South America on 1 April 1520, not overruled the objections of the next men in command, marooning and executing Spanish nobles along with the other rebels, he would not have made it unmistakably clear to his people what it means to be on an unconditional outward voyage. And had he not, as Pigafetta recounts, forbidden on pain of death any talk of a return home or the lack of provisions, then the westward journey to the Spice Islands – which would become the first circumnavigation of the world – would probably have been over in its first fifth.[2] On his first crossing, Columbus, as he recorded in the logbook of the *Santa Maria*, falsified his information about the distance they had covered 'so that the men would not be frightened if the voyage were long'.[3] Facing a nascent mutiny during a storm off the East African coast, Vasco da Gama had the compasses, maps and measuring instruments of his captains thrown into the sea to eliminate any future thoughts of turning back among his crew. Experiments of this kind gave rise to a veritable expedition psychology on board these delusionally bold ships, driven by the constant, acute coercion to part the optimistic minds from the despondent.

Only when these naval insights returned to the people on land would the thing known in later times as the progressive mentality become possible – a commitment to a resolute *Forwards*. Géricault's *The Raft of the Medusa* – the classic disaster seascape of the empire – painted in 1818/19, highlights the maritime origin of the difference between progressive and regressive psychology. One can immediately distinguish the depressive group on the left part of the raft from the hopeful group on the right; the former stare into their own misery, while the latter espy the saving ship on the horizon. Faced with extreme conditions, these shipwrecked men wage a conflict that was constitutive of the Modern Age: that between hopes and discouragements.[4] Since the mutiny of Vasco da Gama's captains and its suppression, the globalization campaign has been a constant war of moods and a battle for group-hypnotic means of orientation – and more recently, programming power in the mass media and consultation power in businesses. On the progressive side, it was not infrequently the courage of desperation – allied with an inextinguishable physiological optimism – that kept the world 'revolution' of the non-turners going. The pessimists on board would later be the potential and actual mutineers against the project of modernity, including the rediscoverers of the tragic consciousness. They tend, with eminently sensible pretexts, to abandon undertakings in which they do not see themselves and those close to them as the winners. The history of these abandonists has yet to be written. Its motto, latently or manifestly, is the call of 'Stop history!' that makes allies of apocalypticists, tragedians, defeatists and pensioners.[5] And yet the combined gravity of the calm-keepers, the losers, the off-putters and their literary tribunes achieved little against the unleashed visionary energy of the project-makers and entrepreneur-charlatans. Today, as yesterday, all of these live off their productive errors and the followings spawned by those errors. Through their auto-hypnotic talents, practical natures manage time and again to build up empires around themselves from self-deceptions that succeed in the medium term.

Because the practices of the captains were based not on delusion and motivational spells alone, however, but also on incontestable geographical competencies and actually worked-out nautical routines, the insane New European wish projects occasionally gained the chance to make themselves a reality. Only thus can fear be converted into ecstasy on the oceans; only thus do records of ecstasies become logbooks; and only thus are the cargo holds filled with treasures. Every ship on the open sea embodies a psychosis that has set sail, and each is also real floating capital. As such, it participates in the great work of modernity: developing substance as a flow.

15

The Basic Movement: Money Returns

With every ship that is launched, capital begins the movement that characterizes the spatial 'revolution' of the Modern Age: the circuiting of the earth by the money employed, and its successful return to its starting account. Return of investment – this is the movement of movements that all acts of risk-taking obey. It lends all operations of capital, even those that do not cross the open sea, a nautical aspect, as every sum invested multiplies itself through a metamorphosis from the commodity form to the monetary form and back – from the booking form to the travel form, one could also say. As a commodity, money plunges into the open sea of the markets, and, like the ships, must hope for a happy return to its home port, the owner's account; the circumnavigation of the globe is implicitly envisaged in the commodity metamorphosis. It becomes explicit when the goods for which the money is exchanged have to be sought on the distant markets, in the chemist's shops of the Orient.

The return of floating capital from its long-distance journey turns the madness of expansion into the reason of profit. The fleet of Columbus and his successors comprises ships of fools that are converted into ships of reason. The most reasonable ship is the one that returns most reliably – saved up by a new *Fortuna Redux* for regular, happy journeys home.[1] And because the money invested in speculative undertakings is expected to bring the investor a substantial gain, the true name for such yields is 'revenues' – returns of itinerant monies whose multiplication constitutes the premium for the investors' property, which is burdened with changes of form and nautical risks.[2]

As far as the reasonable-insane overseas merchants in the ports is concerned – all these new risk-nationalists: the Portuguese, Italians,

Spanish, English, Dutch, French and Germans who hoisted their flags on the oceans – they had learned by 1600 at the latest how to make their risks calculable through diversification. The new insurances seemed suitable to outwit the sea and its cliffs economically. Humans and property can be in what one calls danger; 'a commodity at sea' (Condorcet), on the other hand, is subject to a risk, that is to say a mathematically describable probability of failure, and calculating solidary communities can be formed to combat this probability. Here the risk society comes about as the alliance of well-insured profit-seekers. It unifies the insane who have thought everything through beforehand.

In business undertakings, unlike in everlasting philosophy, someone who bets everything on one outcome is a fool. The wise man thinks far ahead and relies, like every bourgeois who can count, on diversification. One can entirely understand how Antonio, Shakespeare's merchant of Venice, could explain so convincingly why his sadness did not come from his enterprises:

> My ventures are not in one bottom trusted,
> Nor to one place; nor is my whole estate
> Upon the fortune of this present year;
> Therefore, my merchandise makes me not sad.[3]

Antonio's merchant intelligence mirrors the average wisdom of an age in which floating capital had already spent a while thinking about the art of reducing risks to a reasonably acceptable level. It is no coincidence that the beginnings of the European insurance system, for example its mathematical foundations, extend back to the early seventeenth century.[4] The blooming of the insurance idea in the middle of the first adventure period of globalized seafaring shows that the great risk-takers were willing to pay a price in order to be taken seriously as reasonable subjects. For them, everything depended on establishing a sufficiently deep divide between themselves and ordinary madmen. Such insurance systems as Modern Age philosophy drew their justifications from the imperative to separate reason and madness clearly and unambiguously. Their kinship therefore extends deeper than the history of ideas has thus far been able to show. Both deal with techniques for security and certainty; both are interested in controlling fluctuating processes (flows of commodities and money, states of consciousness and streams of signs), and hence synonymous with the disciplinary systems of the absolutistic and bourgeois 'society' examined by Michel Foucault in his histories of order.

16

Between Justifications and Assurances: On Terran and Maritime Thought

The early insurance system was one of the harbingers of systemic modernity, provided one defines modernization as a progressive replacement of vague symbolic immune structures classifiable as final religious interpretations of human living risks with exact social and technical security services. In fundamental aspects, the assurance of the mercantile professions replaces what had previously seemed to lie in God's hands alone. This applies especially to provisions for the consequences of unforeseeable twists of fate. Prayer is good, insurance is better: this insight led to the first pragmatically implanted immune technology of modernity; it was augmented in the nineteenth century by the social security system and the hygienic-medical institutions of the welfare state. The immaterial price paid by the moderns for their insurability was high, admittedly, in fact metaphysically ruinous – they increasingly dispensed with fate, that is to say with a direct connection to the absolute as an irreducible danger. They declared themselves specimens of a statistical averageness that dressed itself up individualistically. The meaning of being shrank to an entitlement to benefits in a standard damage case.

The philosophy of the Modern Age, by contrast, initially managed no more than a reorganization of symbolic immunity. This, as we know, was done in the name of 'certainty'. If there is such a thing as a characteristically modern philosophy – an assumption supported by the phenomenon of Descartes and its consequences – it is due not least to the fact that it succeeded in modernizing self-evidence. In addition, this revealed an inner basis of certainty which, as one says, could be taken as a point of 'departure' – shown by the currently and immediately clear and obvious self-observation of doubt. The cycle of civil, non-monastic philosophies in modernity probably rests on the increasing demand among the middle classes for proof of non-insanity. Their clients are no longer the clerical courts, the bishoprics, monasteries and theological faculties, but rather the project-makers in the anterooms of Western princes and the enterprising minds in the growing audience of educated private persons; this was finally accompanied also by what, with reference to the scholarly world of books, one could call the scientific public sphere. Perhaps the rationalist branch of continental philosophy that followed on from the emigrant Descartes attempted precisely that: providing a new breed of risk-citizens who take up loans, speculate on floating capital and have loan redemption dates in view with an unshakeable logical mainland on which to stand – an offer to which the seaworthy Britons proved less receptive in the long term than the other Europeans, who rarely made a secret of their hydrophobia and, furthermore, always had to reckon with a higher public spending ratio in their intellectual enterprises.[1]

It is of epoch-typical significance that the title copperplate of Bacon's *Novum organum* of 1620 depicts *returning* ships, with the legend *Multi pertransibunt & augebitur scientia*: 'Many will pass through and knowledge will be increased.'[2] Here we find a betrothal of newer experiential thought to the Atlantic fleet guided by pragmatism, just as the doge of Venice, as lord over Mediterranean seafaring, annually married the Adriatic Sea. That same Bacon, like a Pliny of rising capitalism, authored *The History of the Winds*, which opens with the statement that the winds gave humans wings with which they learned how to fly – if not through the air, then at least over the seas.[3] The totality of these winds formed what would later be called the earth's 'atmosphere' – taken literally, the orb of vapour or mist. The sailors on Magellan's voyage had been the first to see for themselves the unity of the earth's surface and that of the sea enclosed by an air breathable by humans. The seaman's breath gained the first access to real atmospheric globality: it led Europeans into the true Modern Age, in which the connection between the human condition and the atmosphere established itself as the master idea of an epochal caesura that had not yet been fully thought through.

Even if the new centres of knowledge could not be located directly on the ships, they would still have to display certain port qualities in future. Experience only reaches people via importation; its further treatment via concepts would be the business of philosophers – enlightenment begins at the docks. The true terrain of experience in the Modern Age is the ship's deck, no longer that 'earth' of which, as late as the twentieth century, the ageing Edmund Husserl had sought to reassure himself, a desperately conservative turn of phrase, as a 'primal ark' [*Urarche*] or 'primal home' [*Urheimat*]; one can speak here of a regression to the physiocratic view, which holds that all values and validities stem from agriculture and a bond with the soil. Husserl's attempt to base all insights ultimately on a general world soil, the 'ground of universal passive belief in being',[4] is still tied to a premodern form of terranism that cannot interrogate the reason for having a foundation excessively enough.[5] This happened at a time when marinism had long provided the more pragmatically astute answers, though perhaps not the better ones in absolute terms; maritime reason knows that one should be wary of running a-ground;[6] only those who navigate on the surface can operate successfully. The nautical spirit requires not foundations but terminals, foreign partners, inspiring port connections, remote destinations and a dose of civilly made criminal energy.

In its form, a philosophy that sought to follow its reputation for formulating the world-concept of the Modern Age would be destined to constitute itself as a swimming faculty, or at least as the port authority of Old Europe. It belonged to the poverty of continental philosophy, the German in particular, that it was usually bound – even in the twentieth century – to the atmospheres and morals of small provincial residences, where philosophical studies could scarcely be anything other than the continuation of the lower priesthood's training by other means. Not even the Tübingen dreams of the Aegean, which were certainly the best thing that ever touched German intelligences, could force access to the sea for idealistic thought.

Johann Gottfried Herder pinpointed the small-town spell affecting German thought into recent times in his bold early travel journal: 'On earth, one is fixed to a dead point and locked in the narrow circle of a situation.' He attempted to counter this claustrophobia, which touted itself as philosophy, with the leap into a different element: 'O soul, how will it be for you when you depart from this world? The narrow, fixed, restricted midpoint has vanished, you flutter through the air or swim on a sea – the world disappears for you . . . how new a way of thinking.'[7] One could read this as suggesting that the German disposition only wanted to see its chance at globalization in death.

The maritime dimension of the Modern Age world format, however, was notoriously underestimated by most continental capitals and royal seats, whether Vienna, Berlin, Dresden or Weimar. For the most part, the continental philosophies placed themselves pre-emptively in the service of a terran counter-revolution that instinctively rejected the new world situation. In the end, one does want to continue controlling the whole from the position of a secure national territory, pushing forward a firm foundation against the impositions of nautical mobility. This applies to the territorial rulers as much as the territorial thinkers. Even Immanuel Kant, who purported to be repeating the Copernican revolution in the field of thought by elevating the subject to the location of all representations, never fully realized that the Copernican revolution was actually less decisive than the Magellanic one. Like every terran mind of the past, Kant, despite living in a seaport town, remained indebted to the fixed-location mentality. What good did it do, then, to make phenomena revolve around the intellect if said intellect had no desire to travel around the world? With his insistence on the cogito owner's duty to reside, Kant was destined to misunderstand the essential features of a world of fluctuations. The well-known quasi-lyrical passage in the *Critique of Pure Reason* concerning the island of pure reason, the 'land of truth' that breasts the ocean, 'the true seat of illusion' where 'many a fog bank and rapidly melting iceberg pretend to be new lands',[8] probably reveals more about the defensive motives of the modern business of thought in its German variety than the author intended: in front of the full faculty, this passage formulates the anti-maritime oath with which the rational mind ties itself to the perspectives of deep-rooted, terran-regional self-assertion. It crosses this treacherous ocean but once, with clear disgust – or critical intent, some would say – to assure itself that there is really *nothing* of interest for reason to be found there. That is why, in 1788, the same author could publish a *Critique of Practical Reason* from which readers learned absolutely nothing about the most practical matter of his time, namely seafaring – and how could they, when the maxims for the actions of captains on the high seas were unsuitable as a guideline for any set of universal rules?

Matters were made all the worse by Heidegger's defence of provincial life, a defence whose message was this: Berlin is no good for someone who, like some location-specific grotto oracle, is the medium through which the truth of Being speaks – four hundred and fifty years after Columbus and one hundred and fifty after Kant. He too understood truth as a chthonic function – a revocable emergence from earth, mountain and cave – and granted only a temporal, not a spatial meaning to that which comes from afar. Thought concerning the whole was the last to board the ship.

And so Goethe noted in his journal from the *Italian Journey*, on 3 April 1787 in Palermo: 'No one who has never seen himself surrounded on all sides by nothing but the sea can have a true conception of the world and of his own relation to it.'[9] The great majority of

Central European scholars, almost all cowed and sustained by territorial states and their lords, preferred to be surrounded by the walls of schools and libraries, or at the utmost by urban backdrops. Even Hegel's seemingly magnanimous acknowledgement of the sea as the natural element of industry, which joins different nations, in the famous §247 of his *Philosophy of Right* – 'the greatest medium of communication', 'one of the chief means of culture'[10] – is in fact no more than an administrative note, and does not take on any significance for the conceptual culture of the habitually enthroned, non-wandering philosopher.[11] Telling the truth remains, for the time being, a sedentary activity on mainland foundations. *Romanus sedendo vincit* (Varro).[12]

Only the solitary Schopenhauer, away from the universities and regional churches, managed overdue breakthrough to a way of thinking that made a fluidified foundation its starting point: *The World as Will and Representation* is the first manifestation of an ocean of the philosophers. On this ocean, the subject navigates on the nutshell of the *principium individuationis*, kept secure by the saving illusions of space, time and I-ness. This discovery was taken up by Nietzsche and the vitalists, who declared the re-fluidification of ossified subjects the true task of a 'philosophy of the future'. In their writings, one can witness a remoulding of subject-oriented thought suitable for the high seas.

It was not a philosopher who succeeded in formulating the true concept of the subject's ambition in the age of mobilization, however, but a novelist – Jules Verne, who found the formula for the epoch in the motto of his Captain Nemo: *MOBILIS IN MOBILI*. His maxim, 'moving amid mobility', explains with unsurpassable clarity and generality what modernized subjectivity seeks to and should do. The goal of the great flexibilization is the power to navigate amid the totality of all accessible places and objects without being oneself vulnerable to the detecting instruments of others. Realizing oneself in the liquid element as a subject: this is absolute freedom of enterprise, perfect an-archy.[13] Only Schopenhauer, if anyone, had come close to this approach when he declared succinctly in his central work: 'The *subject* is the seat of all cognition but is itself not cognized by anything.'[14]

It was Schopenhauer's contemporary Ralph Waldo Emerson who, with his first series of *Essays* published in 1841, initiated the 'American evasion' and nautical reformulation of philosophy – which is why Nietzsche discovered a kindred spirit in him already as a young reader.[15] In Emerson's work, the offensive tones from the early

European period of de-restriction reappear in transatlantic translation.

Centuries earlier, in *On the Infinite Universe and Worlds*, published in Venice in 1583, Giordano Bruno, another thinker of solitary motivations within his time, celebrated the emancipation of the human spirit from the impoverishment of a nature so 'mean and niggard in her fruit' and a miserly God restricted to a single small world: 'There are no ends, boundaries, limits or walls which can defraud and deprive us of the infinite multitude of things. Therefore the earth and the ocean thereof are fecund [. . .].'[16] The Nolan described his own role as that of a Columbus of the outer spaces who had given earthlings insight into shattering the domes of illusion. Just as Columbus had returned from crossing the Atlantic with news of another shore, Bruno wanted to return from his voyage into the infinite bearing news of the absence of an upper edge. On the exterior, the world is devoid of boundaries or fortifications on all sides: this was the central space-theoretical announcement of the Brunian Modern Age, and it was not meant to sound any less evangelical than the Columbian one.[17]

A quarter-millennium later, the American sage Emerson replied to this in his pitilessly optimistic essay 'Circles' with the following words:

> Our life is an apprenticeship to the truth that around every circle another can be drawn; that there is no end in nature, but every end is a beginning [. . .]. There is no outside, no enclosing wall, no circumference to us. The man finishes his story – how good! how final! how it puts a new face on all things! He fills the sky. Lo! on the other side rises also a man and draws a circle around the circle we had just pronounced the outline of the sphere.[18]

Only from the later nineteenth century on would continental philosophy – in spite of all phenomenological, neo-idealistic and neo-Aristotelian revivals – steer towards the collapse of absolutist-territorial fortifications of evidence, a collapse that could be postponed, but not prevented. With more than a century's delay, some German professors even hinted at their willingness to consider whether the conceptual means of terran idealism were still suitable for processing the actual conditions of globalization intellectually. These too, to their own advantage, were closer in recent times to the legacy of the British common sense doctrine, which facilitates the transition from the old *inconcussum* standard to a globalized probability culture

– particularly because theoretically approaching a universe of fluctuations seems less painful from that position. This implies, admittedly, a conversion from the 'Catholic' path, which connected poverty with security bonuses, to the 'Protestant' lifestyle of the Calvinist variety, which spurringly relates wealth and risk.[19] It was Friedrich Nietzsche who, as a critic of metaphysical *ressentiment*, first realized that philosophical thought after Zarathustra must become something fundamentally other than a sensible waiting and circumspection in the idealized orb of being.

On the market of modern immunity techniques, the insurance system, with its concepts and procedures, has completely won out over philosophical techniques of certainty. The logic of controlled risk has proved far more economical and practicable than that of ultimate metaphysical justification. Faced with this choice, the large majority of modern societies made fairly unambiguous decisions. Insurance defeats evidence: this statement encapsulates the fate of all philosophy in the technical world.

The only modern country not to have chosen the path to the precautionary insurance state is the United States of America, with the result that religion, or more generally speaking the 'fundamentalist disposition', retained a significance atypical of modernity: it resisted the religion-dissolving Enlightenment as vehemently as it opposed any attempts to take away the firearms of its citizens. For the USA, immunity and security remain constructions that must come about in the imagination of each individual. (It is for similar reasons that Hollywood keeps the figure of the hero alive, despite its undeniable premodernity; heroes are still needed if statehood cannot keep the continuing moral wilderness under control.[20]) Wherever else insurance-oriented thought has established itself, however, one witnesses the change of mentality that characterizes postmodern boredom 'societies': uninsured situations become rare, and consequently the disturbance can be relished as an exception, the 'event' is positivized, and the demand for experiences of difference floods the markets. Only fully insured 'societies' have proved able to set in motion that aestheticization of insecurities and unfathomabilities which forms the criterion for postmodern life forms and their philosophies.[21]

In so-called risk 'societies', however, the spirit of the insurance system drove out the willingness to take those very actions that gave them their name: a risk 'society' is one in which anything truly hazardous is *de facto* forbidden – that is to say, it is excluded from compensation in the event of damage. One of the ironies of modern conditions is that by their standards, one would have to forbid retroactively everything that was ventured in order to realize them. It follows from this that post-history is only seemingly a historico-philosophical concept, and in reality an insurance-related one. The post-historical states are those in which historic actions (foundations of religions, crusades, revolutions, wars of liberation, class struggles and the accompanying crimes) are impermissible on account of their uninsurable risk.

17

Expedition and Truth

The centuries that followed the first strike of the adventurer-seafarers were, consistently enough, initially obedient to the impulse of making the world outside safe for Europeans to move in – whether through an entrepreneurial insurance system or through philosophical sciences that provided ultimate justifications. The European experiential sciences made their own contributions to this plan. With increasing routine and optimization of marine technology, real seafaring in particular lost a significant part of its ecstasy-inducing effects, and with the reduction of the adventurous element to residual risks, it approached routinized traffic – the game of trivialized outward and homeward journeys, albeit with a shipwreck quota that would be completely unacceptable for users of transportation services in the twentieth century. We should qualify this by noting that the perfect symmetry of outward and homeward journeys (which defines the concept of traffic in its exact sense) can only be achieved on land. It was only with the advent of railway traffic that the utopia of complete control over reversible movements was largely realized; modern air traffic also strives to attain this ideal by carrying out flights along precisely defined routes. Nonetheless, the primacy of the outward journey remains the hallmark of sea voyages in the heroic age of explorations and merchant voyages.

One characteristic of European extroversion is that its decisive advances always have exodus-like qualities, even if there are no pilgrim fathers re-enacting the escape from Egypt on the Atlantic.[1] The Modern Age has no shortage of chosen exodus peoples, and promised lands can be projected into all areas of the world with little difficulty.

The exploration that gives this era its name therefore constitutes the epistemological form of adventurism, which behaves like a service to truth. Once the primacy of the outward journey is brought up programmatically, long-distance voyages present themselves as *expeditions*. Here, the penetration of the unknown is not simply the by-product of a mercantile, missionary or military undertaking, but is carried out with direct intent. The closer we come to the hot core of typical Modern Age movements, the more obvious the expedition character of journeys to the outside becomes. And even if numerous discoveries must be attributed to Captain Nobody or Admiral Hazard, the essence of the Age of Discovery remained determined by the expedition as an entrepreneurial form – one finds because one seeks, and one seeks because one knows in what area things might be found. Until the nineteenth century, it was virtually impossible for Europeans to be 'outside' without, at least in some aspect, being on an expedition.

The expedition is the routine form of entrepreneurially directed seeking and finding. For its sake, the decisive movement of real globalization is not simply a case of spatial expansion; it is part of the core process of the history of truth in the Modern Age. Expansion could, of course, not take place were it not prefigured in truth-related terms – and thus in all terms – as a disclosure of what had previously been concealed. This is what Heidegger had in mind when, in his tremendous and violent 1938 essay 'The Age of the World Picture', he felt he could pinpoint the basic process of the Modern Age in the conquest of the world as picture:

> Whenever we have a world picture, an essential decision occurs concerning beings as a whole. The being of beings is sought and found in the representedness of beings. [. . .] The world picture does not change from an earlier medieval to a modern one; rather, that the world becomes picture at all is what distinguishes the essence of modernity.[2]

> No wonder that humanism first arises where the world becomes picture. [. . .] The name 'anthropology', here, does not refer to an investigation of humanity by natural science. [. . .] It designates, rather, that philosophical interpretation of man which explains and evaluates beings as a whole from the standpoint of, and in relation to, man.[3]
> To be 'new' belongs to a world that has become picture.[4]

The epochal keyword 'discoveries' – a plural that actually refers to a singular phenomenon, namely the authentically historical hyper-event of the earth's circumnavigation and quantification – thus denotes the epitome of methods whereby the unknown is transformed into the known, the unimagined into the imagined. With regard to the still largely unexplored, undepicted, undescribed and unexploited earth, this means that procedures and media had to be found to bring these into the picture as a whole and in detail. Hence the 'Age of Discovery' encompasses the campaign driven along by the pioneers of terrestrial globalization to replace the previous non-images with images, or chimeras with 'recordings'; consequently, all acquisitions of land, sea and world began with pictures. Each of these images brought home by the discoverers negated the externality of the external, bringing it down to a level that was satisfactory or bearable for average Europeans. At the same time, the exploring subject stands facing the pictures provided and withdraws to the threshold of the pictorial world – seeing all while itself unseen, recording everything but predetermined only by the anonymous 'point of view'.

Hence the Modern Age, interpreted along Heidegger's lines, was also an epoch of 'the truth' – an era of truth history characterized by a particular style in the production of obviousness. Once and for all, truth is now no longer understood as that which shows itself from within itself, as in the sense of the Greek *physis* (as the 'growth of the seed of emergence') or Christian revelation, where the infinitely transcendent God reveals through grace what human means of insight, left to themselves, could never have uncovered. These ancient and medieval pre-conceptions of truth were discarded in the age of research, for both understand truth as something that tends, prior to all human intervention, to step out into unconcealment in the sense of the Greek *alétheia*, which meant something along the lines of 'undisguised proclamation' – a concept that Heidegger sounded out in an attitude of cultic receptivity throughout his life. With the dawn of the Modern Age, truth itself seems to have made the transition to the age of its artificial uncoverability: from that point on, research could and had to exist as an organized theft of hiddenness. Nothing else could have been meant when the Renaissance was presented as the age of 'the discovery of the world and man'.

'Discoveries' are initially a summary name for recording procedures of a geotechnical, hydrotechnical, ethnotechnical and biotechnical kind – even if these appeared, at first, very rudimentarily and randomly. When the Spanish queen sent her emissary Columbus a handwritten letter commanding him to bring her as many specimens of unknown birds as possible from the New World, one can already see – behind the mask of a royal whim – the technical impulse and the measuring grasp in play. At the end of this history of access, the zoological and botanical gardens would open their gates and integrate the animal 'kingdom' and the plant 'kingdom' into the modern exhibition system. When trained seafarers such as Abbé Incarville brought back flowering plants from Asia and the South Pacific for European gardens, the technical element – the acts of breeding and replanting – is unmistakably involved. It has too rarely been taken into account how far directed plant migrations shaped and contributed to enabling the life forms of the Modern Age.[5] Even things that, in terms of how they developed, often present themselves as sheer adventurous turbulence and chaotic improvisation – the stormy crossing of the open seas, the hasty adoption of new coastal maps and countries, as well as the identification of unknown peoples – were in essence already technical processes. Heidegger's dictum can be applied without reservation to all of these gestures: 'Technology is a mode of revealing.'[6]

18

The Signs of the Explorers: On Cartography and Imperial Name Magic

If research is the organized working-away of concealment, then no process in the history of the expansions of human knowledge fulfils this definition more dramatically or fully than the globalization of the earth via discovery between the sixteenth and nineteenth centuries. The cultural philosopher Hans Freyer, who was temporarily attracted to the political far right but later held more sedate educated-conservative views, was not entirely mistaken when he wrote of this crude adventure: 'Whether the technology with which people set off was primitive or modern, adequate or inadequate, is the wrong question to ask. All technology is the arming of a will to the point at which it can strike out directly.'[1] The technological aspect in the mode of the early voyages of discovery comes to light most clearly when one examines how these enterprises rid themselves of the mission to create images of the traversed space. Even on the earliest expeditions, the captains and the scientists, artists, writers and astronomers on board had no doubts that it was their mission to collect and report conclusive evidence of their finds – in the form not only of commodities, samples and booty, but also of documents, maps and contracts. Crossing foreign waters can only be considered a secure achievement from the moment when a sighting is accompanied by an exploration, an observation by a record, and an appropriation by the creation of a map. The discovery of an unknown quantity – a continent, an island, a people, a plant, an animal, a bay, a sea current – presupposes the availability of the means to repeat the first encounter. What has been discovered, then, must never fall back into concealment, the antecedent Lethe, if it is to become the secure property of the lord of knowledge. To understand the phenomenon of discovery, then, it is indispensable to show the means of acquisition which guarantee that the cover concealing what was previously hidden is removed once and for all. Accordingly, whenever Europeans of the Renaissance spoke of discovery – *découverte, descumbrimiento, Entdeckung* – they meant episodes of finding and the things found, but above all the means of making them known and keeping them.

For the great majority of modern discoveries in the open terrestrial space, it was merely spatial distance that had acted as the concealing cover. The conquest of distance through the new means of transportation and the establishment of cross-oceanic traffic connections created the necessary conditions for a lifting of the 'cover' with lasting consequences. It is no language-historical coincidence that, until the sixteenth century, the word 'discover' meant nothing other than removing the covering of an object, that is to say an exposure of the known, and only later came to denote the finding of something unknown. The mediating factor between the two is traffic, which exposes the distant and is capable of taking the covering off the unfamiliar. From this perspective, one can say that the essence of this discovering traffic is the de-distancing of the world. Globalization here means nothing other than having access to the technological means for eliminating distance.

Where the successes of such reaching accumulate, the undiscovered can itself become a scarce resource. While barely half the globe was known to Europeans in its outlines in 1600, four fifths had already been explored by 1800. One of the atmospheric effects of enlightenment at the end of the twentieth century is that the earth's reserves of secrets were considered exhaustible; thus Columbus's belief that the navigable planet was 'small' attained its pragmatic goal. While the discovered world initially seemed to take on immeasurable proportions, the end of the age saw it shrink to a small ball, to a single point.

Discovery aims for acquisition: this gave cartography its world-historical function. Maps are the universal instrument for securing what has been discovered, in so far as it is meant to be recorded 'on the globe' and given as a secure find. For an entire age, two-dimensional maps of land and sea – together with the globe – provided the most important tool for localizing those points in the locational space of the earth from which the shroud of concealment had been lifted. The rise of the map at the expense of the globe is an indication that the acquisition of data soon extended to the most minute details, even for the furthest reaches.

While the globes – the main media of the Columbian age – later served ever predominantly summary and representative, and ultimately decorative functions, the increasingly precise maps took on ever greater operative significance. They alone could meet the demands of land description in detail, occasionally functioning as political land registers in the process. The new atlases brought about map collections revealing all countries and continents on interesting scales. (Since the introduction of the school subject 'geography' in the late nineteenth century, European schoolchildren were brought up to look at maps that had been presented to the princes and ministers a hundred years earlier by their returning conqueror-geographers like secret diplomatic dispatches and geopolitical gospels.) The general tendency is characterized especially by the creation of the planispheric world map – that depiction of the earth which reproduced the orb as a surface, whether in the form of the early heart-shaped maps, in the rolled-out representation of all continents and oceans (as often seen today in the backdrops of news studios), or in the classic double hemisphere, with the more land-filled Ptolemaic Old World in the right half, and the water-dominated American-Pacific New World in the left.

The irresistible pull towards the map repeats the process of conquering the world, highlighted by Heidegger, in the depictive media of globalization as an image. When the planispheric world maps push away the globe, when even the name *Atlas* no longer stands for the orb-bearer, only a bound book of maps – a transposition brought about by the most momentous map collection of the Modern Age: *Gerardi Mercatoris Atlas sive cosmographicae mediationes de fabrica mundi et fabricati figura*, Amsterdam 1608/1609[2] – the two-dimensional medium triumphs over the three-dimensional, and *ipso facto* the image over the body. Semanticists of the twentieth century would, therefore, have good reason to remind their contemporaries that the map is not the land – this warning anticipates the 'return of space' of which the history-weary thought of the closing twentieth century began to speak; it was for similar reasons that, at the start of the twenty-first, the suppressed arts of map-reading and geopolitical calculus can be recommended for rediscovery.[3] In both name and substance, the planispheres – literally meaning 'flat orbs' – sought to erase the memory of the dimension not mastered by the imagination: the third dimension, namely spatial depth. What art history has to say about the problem of perspective in Renaissance painting barely scratches the surface of the war for control of the third dimension. Where people succeeded in committing spheres to paper and simulating spatial depth on canvases, the conquest of the world as picture opened up infinite new possibilities. Imperialism is applied planimetry: the art of reproducing orbs as surfaces and worlds as charts. The master determines the scale; sovereignty belongs to the one who decides on flattening. Only that which can successfully be stripped of one dimension can be conquered.

The land acquisition enabled by seafaring and cartography, then, preceded the genesis of the world system. Carl Schmitt, who enjoyed presenting himself as the last legitimist of European power in the world, did not hesitate in his study *The Nomos of the Earth* to claim that European expansion was only allowed to invoke the legal titles provided by discovery. The fiction of 'finder's rights' was based on this, as was that of a 'communication right' that went beyond mere visiting rights (the *ius communicationis* defended by Francisco de Vitoria in his famous *relectio On the Indians*). Only as discoverers and finders of foreign arts and cultures, he argued, had the Europeans become able to be the *legitimate* masters over the majority of the world; only their willingness to be masters trained them to take on the responsibility that fell to them from their superior devotion to the open world. The responsibility of discoverers, according to Schmitt, manifests itself first of all in the duty to reclaim the new territories for the European masters, usually royal clients, with formal gestures. The legal ceremonies of these claims included, beside the erection of crosses, stone coats of arms, *padrãos*, banners and dynastic emblems, the mapping and naming of the lands.[4] In the European understanding, these could *de jure* only come under the dominion of their new lords once they had become localized, recorded, demarcated and named entities.

The coincidence of sighting, landing, appropriation, naming, mapping and certification is what constitutes the complete, legally consequential act of a discovery.[5] This, according to Schmitt, is followed by the real subjection of a country to the legal jurisdiction of the discoverer-occupier. He gives the discovered the fruits of their discoveredness, namely the privilege of being protected by this master and no other – a prerogative that simultaneously covers the risks of exploitation by the distant sovereign.

As a 'finding' of seemingly or genuinely unclaimed objects that is relevant to ownership rights, discovery could never have been consolidated into a particular mode of appropriation if motifs from nautical natural law had not also influenced it. The venerable equation of the catch and the find declared – through the transference of an old habitus – the discoverers of new lands fishermen of a sort, whose claim to rightful ownership of their prey could not so easily be contested. In his great whaling novel, Melville reminds the reader of the difference between 'fast-fish' and 'loose-fish', which was supposedly an iron rule for the hunters on the Modern Age seas: a fast-fish belonged to the party 'fast to it' (when connected with an occupied ship or boat), while a loose-fish was considered 'fair game for anybody who [could] soonest catch it'. Looting on land, as Melville noted, was subject to the same distinction:

> What was America in 1492 but a Loose-Fish, in which Columbus struck the Spanish standard by way of waifing it for his royal master and mistress? What was Poland to the Czar? What Greece to the Turk? What India to England? What at last will Mexico be to the United States? All Loose-Fish. What are the Rights of Man and the Liberties of the World but Loose-Fish? [. . .] What is the great globe itself but a Loose-Fish?[6]

It is unmistakably clear that Schmitt, a man as legally sensitive as he was morally thick-skinned, modelled his theorem of the legitimacy of European dominion through legal titles from discoveries on the Columbian mission described above, where the taker presents himself as the bringer of the more precious goods. While Columbus saw himself as the man who brought Christ's salvation to the New World, the conquistadors defended by Schmitt probably considered themselves justified as conveyers of European legal and civilizatory accomplishments.

Such justificatory fantasies were not a product of late apologetics and *post factum* applications of legal unscrupulousness, however; they were interwoven with the events themselves from the start. In the fourth canto of his epic of world-taking, *The Lusiads*, the poet Luis de Camões has the Indus and the Ganges appear to the Portuguese king Manuel in a dream, in the guise of wise old men who urge him to subjugate the people of India – whereupon the epic's king decides to prepare a fleet for the Indian voyage under the command of Vasco da Gama. Literature of the Modern Age is poetry of success.[7] It is no coincidence that Manuel I, known as 'the Fortunate', would later include the globe in his coat of arms – a pictorial image that is being taken up once more today by countless businesses in their logos and advertising. In Manuel's century, this was a privilege afforded only to one man after him: Sebastian del Cano, who brought the *Victoria* back to Spain after Magellan's death, thus completing the circumnavigation, and was rewarded with the right to wear the globe in his insignia, accompanied by the motto *primus me circumdedisti*[8] and a crown land, the royal Portuguese colony of Brazil, whose flag features Manuel's sphere to this day.

The fact that the association of globe-viewing and conquest had already become a metaphor-spawning fixed idea among European poets shortly thereafter is illustrated by some lines from Shakespeare's early dramatic poem 'The Rape of Lucrece' (1594), in which the rapist Sextus Tarquinius views the uncovered body of his sleeping victim:

> Her breasts, like ivory globes circled with blue
> A pair of maiden worlds unconquered . . .
> These worlds in Tarquin new ambition bred.

It would seem that in the Modern Age's organization of fantasies, it is already sufficient for an object to appear round, desirable and asleep in order to become describable as a conquerable 'world'.

But just as the national Portuguese epic provided the belated heroic justification for the factual conquest by declaring the expansionist Iberian people chosen from among the less worthy Christian peoples,[9] the recorded land and sea maps served in the occupation as prosaic legal means and notarial files that certified the new conditions of ownership and dominion with a degree of formality. *Cuius carta, eius regio.*[10] Whoever draws the map behaves as if they were culturally, historically, legally and politically in the right.

One of the hallmarks of European expansion was always the asymmetry between the discoverers and the inhabitants of found lands. Overseas territories were considered ownerless things as long as the discoverer-occupiers felt unhindered and unchallenged in the mapping of new areas, be they inhabited or uninhabited. Usually the inhabitants of distant lands were viewed not as their owners, but as part of the colonial lost property – its anthropic fauna, as it were, which seemed available for hunting and harvesting (though this, admittedly, also tended to apply to the vast majority of people inhabiting European territories in the feudal age). The so-called primitives initially had no concrete idea of what it meant that Europeans wanted to gain a concrete idea of them and their territories. Where the discoverers became aware of their own technological and mental superiority in their encounters with native peoples – which was slightly less often the case in Asian and Islamic realms – they generally concluded that this entitled them to take the land and subject it to the rule of European sovereigns. Even in retrospect, Carl Schmitt viewed these fateful and violence-laden events with unreserved affirmation:

> Thus, it is completely false to claim that, just as the Spaniards had discovered the Aztecs and the Incas, so the latter could have discovered Europe. The Indians lacked the scientific power of Christian-European rationality. It is a ludicrous anachronism to suggest that they could

have made cartographical surveys of Europe as accurate as those Europeans made of America. The intellectual advantage was entirely on the European side, so much so that the New World simply could be 'taken' [. . .].[11]

Discoveries were made without prior permission of the discovered. Thus, legal title to discoveries lay in a higher legitimacy. They could be made only by peoples intellectually and historically advanced enough to apprehend the discovered by superior knowledge and consciousness. To paraphrase one of Bruno Bauer's Hegelian aphorisms: a discoverer is one who knows his prey better than the prey knows himself, and is able to subjugate him by means of superior education and knowledge.[12]

This means that the maps – especially in the early history of discovery – directly documented claims to civilizatory sovereignty. 'A scientific cartographical survey was a true legal title to a *terra incognita*.'[13] One is inclined to note that it is the map sovereign who decides on a discovered world's state of emergency – which applies when the finder gives a discovered and charted land a new name along with a new master.

It would be of immeasurable epistemological value for the theory of terrestrial globalization if a detailed history of geographical naming practices during the last five hundred years were available. It would not only mirror the primal scenes of discovery and conquest, as well as the struggles between rival factions of discoverers and conquerors; it could also explain how, in the world history of names, the semantic side of a world de-distancing carried out seemingly instinctively by Europeans came about. Only a few cultural regions proved able to keep their proper names despite the discoverers' efforts; where this succeeded, it points to the resistance of sufficiently powerful empires to infiltration from without. Overall, the Europeans managed to catch the largest part of the earth's surface in their naming nets like a swarm of anonymous lost property and to project their lexica into the open world. The European discoverers unrolled *The Great Map of Mankind* – this resonant phrase goes back to Edmund Burke – and labelled it according to their naming moods. The christening of seas, currents, rivers, passages, capes, coves and shallows, of islands and archipelagos, and of coasts, mountain ranges, plains and countries grew into a century-long passion among European cartographers and their allies, the seafarers, merchants and missionaries. Wherever they appeared, a torrent of new names rained down on a world that had seemed mute until then.

Where there is naming, however, there can also be renaming. The small Bahaman island of Guanahaní, whose coast was the first in the New World to be visited by Columbus, on 12 October 1492, was given the name – a completely natural act on his premises – of *San Salvador*, a phrase that, in the ideology of the bringer, represented the highest value the conquerors could carry with them. The early discoverers barely ever went on land without believing, however vaguely, that the God of Europe was revealing Himself to these areas through their presence. In keeping with this habitus, any Buddhist conquerors would have had to give the island Guanahaní the name Gautama or Bodhisattva, while 'The Prophet' would have been a likely choice for Muslim invaders. After the English pirate John Watlin occupied the now deserted island in 1680 and made it his base, it retained the name 'Watlin's Island' until the start of the twentieth century, as if it had been the pirate's natural vocation to continue the legacy of the discoverer. The pirate's island was only given back its Columbian name in 1926 – not entirely without conflict, as five other Bahaman islands now also claimed to be the historical Guanahaní. The island known today as Rum Cay had been named *Santa Maria de la Concepción* by Columbus, establishing the Holy Family in the Caribbean. For a time, the later Haiti enjoyed the privilege of being dubbed *Hispaniola*, 'Little Spain'. Similarly, thanks to Columbus, dozens of islands and coastal places assumed names from the Christian and dynastic nomenclature of Europe, though few of them had any historical longevity.

Admittedly the continent discovered by Columbus, that of Central and South America, was not named after him, as the rules of the globalization game would normally require, but after one of his rivals in the race for the exploration of the New World. Owing to a problematic naming hypothesis advanced by the German cartographer Marin Waldseemüller in 1507, the feminized (because continents, as vessels of life, must be feminine) first name of the merchant-discoverer Amerigo Vespucci came to be used for the continent, whose eastern coast the Florentine had, according to questionable sources, supposedly explored as far as the mouth of the Amazon in 1500. This naming success reflects the assertiveness of a roughly heart-shaped planispheric world map published by Waldseemüller – it is also (coming shortly after Contarini's 1506 map, produced as a copperplate) the oldest *printed* map made using the woodcut technique.[14] Its establishment – there were supposedly 1,000 copies, of which only one has survived – was assisted by an accompanying text that had to be reprinted three times in the year of its publication alone. The year of Waldseemüller's map also saw the production of his globe, which suggests the same name for the southern half of the New World: *America*. One might ask whether the heart-like shape of the map – even if it is not developed as fully as in the later heart-shaped world maps of Oronce Finé and Giovanni Cimerlino[15] – contributed decisively to the triumph of Waldseemüller's brilliant cosmographic feat; for what could seize the world-envisaging imagination more than the idea of depicting the surface of the terrestrial orb on a great heart? Waldseemüller's later abandonment of his Vespucci hypothesis could no longer impede the triumph of the name he (and Matthias Ringman) had advanced.[16] On this foundation, the lands of the New World would develop into the United States of the Misnamed.

The Paris *Globe Vert* of 1515 seems to have been the first on which the name *America* was also applied to the northern part of the double continent. For a considerable time, however, more than a few rival labels for this part of the *mundus novus* were in circulation. As late as 1595, it appeared on a map by Michael Mercator as *America sive Nova India*; a Venetian map from 1511, on the other hand, calls the Columbian continent *Terra sanctae crucis*; on a Genoese world map from 1543, the entire North American continent remains nameless, while the southern part simply bears the aspecific marking *Mundus Novus*. For centuries, the North-east United States appeared as *Nova Francia* or *Terra francisca*, while the West and Midwest fell to their British name-givers as New Albion. The eastern coast of North America, which later became New England, was in fact temporarily termed *Nova Belgia* – meaning 'New Netherlands' – while Australia was known in the seventeenth century as *Nova Hollandia*.

These confusing traces of early name nationalism indicate the dawn of the age of civil imperialisms on the basis of capitalized nation-states. For an entire era, the prefix 'new' proved to be the most powerful module in the creation of names, matched only by the prefix 'south' during the race for *Terra Australis*, the hypothetical giant continent in the southern hemisphere. With the christening of 'new' cities (New Amsterdam), 'new' countries (New Helvetia), 'south' countries (South Georgia, New South Wales), saints' islands (San Salvador), monarchic archipelagos (the Philippines) and conquistador countries (Bolivia, Rhodesia), Europeans enjoyed the prerogative of semantically cloning their own world and appropriating distant and foreign points through the lexical recurrence of the same.

Owing to the sum of its effects, the role of cartography in the actual progress of globalization cannot be overestimated. Maps and views of the globe not only served as the greatest lures of the first discovery

periods; they were a manner of land register, documents of appropria-
tive acts and archives of locating knowledge that accumulated over
centuries, as well as route maps for seafaring. They also constitute
the memory media of the Age of Discovery, containing countless
names of nautical heroes and finders of foreign parts of the world
– from the Straits of Magellan in southern Patagonia to Hudson Bay
in northern Canada, from Tasmania in the South Pacific to Cape
Chelyuskin in Siberia, from Stanley Falls in the Congo to the Ross
Ice Shelf in the Antarctic. In parallel with the history of artists, which
was taking shape during the same time, the history of discoverers
had created its own hall of fame on the maps. Many of the later
undertakings were already candidates in tournaments for the prize
of an idealized status in charted history. Long before art and art
history drew profit from the concept of the avant-garde, the van-
guards of earth acquisition were moving on all fronts of future cartographical fame. They often set off from European ports as those
who, if successful, would be the first to have reached some point
or other.

Theatrical projects such as the 'conquest' of the North Pole and
South Pole in particular were entirely guided by that mania of immortalization for which going down in the annals of discovery history
was the highest distinction. Alpinism was also a variety of the vanguard hysteria that wanted no eminent point on the earth's surface
to remain unconquered. For a long time, the hunt for the fame promised by the first visits to the poles would remain the purest form of
this learned delirium. Contemporaries of aviation and space travel
can no longer comprehend the popular fascination and scientific
prestige that were still attached to the two polar projects around
1900. The earth's poles not only epitomized that which was distant,
devoid of humans and difficult to reach; they were also the focus of
the dream of an absolute centre or axial zero point, which was barely
anything other than the continuation of the search for God in the
geographical element.

In this context it is appropriate to remind ourselves that the era in
which Sigmund Freud would make a name for himself as the 'discoverer of the unconscious' also saw the climax of the races for the
earth's poles and the grand coalition of Europeans to extinguish the
last white spots on the map of Africa. In its habitus of disclosure and
foundation, the enterprise of psychoanalysis belongs to the age of
empire builders such as Henry Morton Stanley and Cecil Rhodes ('I
would annex the planets if I could'). These were joined not long
afterwards by Freud's age-mate, the young Hanoverian Carl Peters
(briefly a *Privatdozent* in Leipzig), the later founder of German East

Africa, whose philosophical treatise *Willenswelt und Weltwille* (1883) had conceptually realized the imperialization of the irrational ground of life in advance. Freud's ambition can only be explained in relation to the projects of those men. Had the unconscious not been present in vague outlines on the maps of the reflective spirit since the days of the young Schelling? Was it not natural to claim that its dark interior had finally become ripe for the 'sickle of civilization'? If Freud, who was familiar with the works of the Africa-conquerors Stanley and Baker, chose the 'true inner Africa' in the psyche of every person on his path to fame, this choice of research area testified to an excellent imperial instinct.[17]

The Austro-Hungarian Arctic expedition of 1872–4, led by Karl Weyprecht and Julius von Payer, had achieved some *succès d'estime* with the discovery and naming of Franz Joseph Land and Prince Rudolf Island; as a whole, however, their results were only of frosty and provincial significance. Freud's self-assured scientism manifested itself in the fact that he claimed not an island on the icy outskirts, but rather a hot and centrally situated meta-continent for himself. His ingenuity exhibited itself impressively when, thanks to his topological maps, he succeeded in acquiring the unconscious *de facto* as Sigmund Freud Land. That he drew its borders with a ruler was in keeping with his time's ideal of rational territorial planning. He stoically took the white man's burden upon his shoulders when, summarizing his work, he stated: 'Psychoanalysis is an instrument to enable the ego to achieve a progressive conquest of the id.'[18] Even if the sad tropics of the id are meanwhile increasingly being managed by new occupiers, and unanalysable Calibans are even declaring their decolonization, the old Freudian landmarks remain clearly visible in many places. Whether they will be able to command more than touristic interest in the long run, however, is uncertain.

19

The Pure Outside

Like Freud's allusion to the 'dark continent' of the unconscious,[1] the reference to the 'terrors of ice and darkness'[2] encountered by polar explorers is suitable for presenting the spherological meaning of discovery projects in the age of globalization in the correct light. When European merchants and heroes set off to 'take' distant points on the globe, they could only make their decisions in so far as the globalized locational space had already been conceived as a homogeneous, open and passable outside. All European expeditions of land and sea acquisition – which now take on their most general form through ecological environment acquisition – aim for exospheric spaces that, in the eyes of the expedition groups, in no way belong to their own lifeworlds. Here Heidegger's existential-topological statement 'In Dasein there lies an essential tendency towards closeness'[3] no longer applies. The strong characteristic of externality is that it is *not* 'always already' disclosed in the mode of dwelling – rather, the possibility of disclosure is supposed in a projective anticipation, from which it follows that the difference between inhabiting and exploiting will never again become clear. With the advent of discoverers and conquerors, global camping was established as a modus vivendi. Here Merleau-Ponty's subtle theorem 'our body is not primarily *in* space: it is of it' falls short.[4] The remark by the same author that 'science manipulates things and gives up living in them'[5] is equally applicable to piracy or international trade; like the natural sciences, neither of them has a habitative relationship with the world. For the pirate's and the liberal's eye, it is no longer true that they inhabit being 'as a man lives in his house'.[6] In truth, the seafarers and colonizers – to say nothing of the desperados and *degradados* from all the gutters of the Old World – are sooner scattered about outside like displaced bodies in an abandoned space. Only rarely do they find the way, through the transference of domesticity, to what one calls a 'second home'. They no longer live off the warmth of their own hearth, but rather from the frictional heat of their plunge into the maritime action space. Their hardened bodies are, to paraphrase Deleuze and Guattari, 'thermometers of a becoming' towards previously unexperienced states of moral deterritorialization.[7] In the external space, a type of human is rewarded that, thanks to the weakness of its ties to objects, can appear everywhere as internally controlled, speculative, unfaithful and available.[8]

Perhaps this explains the mysterious ease with which those men who encounter one another on the outside as strangers exterminate one another over fleeting matters. The other, viewed as a body in the external space, is no cohabitant of a shared lifeworldly sphere, no fellow carrier of a sensory-moral resonator, 'culture' or shared life, but rather an arbitrary component of welcome or unwelcome *external circumstances*. If the psychodynamic problem of an over-sheltered settled existence is container masochism, then that of the excessively uninsured life lies in exterminism – a para-sadistic phenomenon that had already revealed itself in the disinhibitions of the Christian crusaders from the twelfth century onwards. The disposition for this stems from spatial alienation: in the watery wastes and new lands on the earth's surface, the agents of globalization are never active as dwellers on their own property. Their behaviour is that of unleashed actors who no longer see a reason to respect any house rules. As house-leavers, the conquerors traverse indifferent space, yet without joining the 'path' in a Buddhist sense. When they step out of the shared house of the Old European world interior, they give the impression of projectiles that have discarded all restraints to look around in a general non-sphere and non-closeness, a smooth and indifferent outside world of resources – guided only by their mandates and appetites, and kept in shape with cruelty workouts. The landing successes – in both the narrower and the broader sense – of these unleashed agents of the earth will one day decide whether they will fall prey to their internal centrifugal forces and disappear into nothingness as feral expedition psychotics, or whether, as it were, through 'new object relationships', they will succeed in a restoration of mainland conditions, a renewed encasement in a distant world or in the recovered old one.

On his first voyage to India in 1497, after looting an Arab merchant vessel with over two hundred pilgrims to Mecca on board, including women and children, Vasco da Gama had it burned and sunk for no particular reason – the prelude to a 'world history' of external atrocities. That the European historical awareness never truly integrated these into its image of the Modern Age, except in isolated publications of the black books of colonialism, in no way lessens the excessive violence of these incidents.[9] Globalized liquidation activity breaks away from all pretexts and, as pure extermination, brings about a state beyond war and conquest. The boundlessness of the waters calls up the moral desert in the seafarers – 'I exterminate, therefore I am' is the message conveyed by every *acte gratuit* of the piratical temper. The colonies and the seas beyond the line were the practice sites for the exterminism that would return to Europeans in the twentieth century as the style of total war. If it takes place on the outside, the battling of a foe can no longer be clearly distinguished from the extermination of a thing. Carl Schmitt rightly pointed out the role of the 'friendship lines' agreed upon by the European naval powers, whose purpose was to mark out a civilized space beyond which the outside, as an extralegal space, could formally begin.[10]

20

Theory of the Pirate:
The White Terror

In this context, piracy – next to the slave trade (which one could also describe as the deportation industry), the foremost manifestation of a naïve globalization criminality – takes on a marked historico-philosophical significance. It is the first entrepreneurial form of atheism: where God is dead, or where He is not looking – in the region without a state, on the ship without a priest on board, on the lawless seas outside of the agreed zones of respect, in the space with no witnesses, and in the moral emptiness beyond the line – the unimaginable is indeed possible. The open sea has, at times, been the site of (almost) the greatest atrocities that can be perpetrated among humans.

At the same time, piracy established itself as an economic sector (comparable to the kidnapping industry of the twentieth century), resolutely settled in the security market's gaps between the sixteenth and nineteenth centuries. (Not without an aftermath at the turn of the twenty-first: in the light of recent events, some speak today of the 'return of the pirate', especially in the prey-rich waters of the Strait of Malacca and other zones in which an absence of naval policing gives a colourful new people of attackers free rein; in 2002, 350 hijackings were recorded worldwide, with a strong upward trend.[1] Furthermore, chaotic maritime law provides ideal conditions for terrorist groups; it is no coincidence that Osama bin Laden and his ilk switched to the shipping business, where they maintain(ed) a considerable fleet of old freighters under exotic flags.) The corsair industry was so closely connected to regular business that Goethe could have

his Mephistopheles present a theory of economic globalization that
testifies to more than the barbed tongue of its speaker:

> One asks the What and skips the How,
> No need to know much navigation;
> War, trade and piracy are one
> Inseparable combination.[2]

The lesson of capture capitalism is a lasting one: the moderns conceive of the dangers of libertarian and anarchist disinhibition in terms
of piratical atheism – the conservative phobia of partisans stems from
this. The fear of innovators among the guardians of law and order,
notorious since antiquity, changed during the Modern Age into the
land-dweller's fear of the seagoing entrepreneur; for even if he wears
a top hat and knows how to use a fish knife at the table, the pirate
still lurks behind his exterior. Hence no terran can imagine without
horror a state of the world in which the primacy of the political –
which here means of mainland things – were no longer in force. For
if the pirate goes ashore, what criminal plans is he carrying in his
breast pocket? Where is he hiding his weapons? What enticing arguments does he use to advertise his speculations? What humanitarian
masks does he don to hide his despicable intentions? When robbers
appear in good company, their sophists – the advisers – are never far
away. The citizens have been arranging their fears for two hundred
years: in the best case, the anarcho-maritime figure on land becomes
a Raskolnikov (who does as he pleases, but regrets it), in the less
favourable case a de Sade (who does as he pleases and negates
remorse), and in the worst case a neo-liberal (who does as he pleases
and then, quoting Ayn Rand, proclaims himself a man of the future).

Piracy does, admittedly, influence bourgeois thought in a different
way: from early on, it was idealized in the fantasies of the mainland-
ers as an alternative libertarian world in which anything was possible
– except boredom. Centuries before the artistic bohemian world, the
maritime one provided an inexhaustible supply of simulations for the
dreams of ordinary citizens who wanted to be more than just citizens.
In eighteenth-century engravings, female corsairs enter the stage –
with cutlasses drawn and blouses open, their breasts bursting out – as
if to prove that at sea, the new woman is a raider in her own right.
Up to Brecht's *The Threepenny Opera* (1928) and Pasolini's *Scritti
corsair* (1973–5), one can follow the criminal-romantic longing that
sees the Great Freedom coming from the sea. Friedrich Schiller, in the
sketches for his *Sea Plays*, also toyed with the idea of portraying the
'floating republic of the filibusterers'. The author of *The Robbers* had

to admit that buccaneers represented the more impressive counterculture.

In the figure of Captain Ahab, Herman Melville erected a monument to those who have fallen out of society, to the seafarers without return who spend their 'pitiless old age' on the outside – a monument that soars up to a higher and darker sky than any statue of liberty. Ahab embodies the Luciferian, lost side of European-American seafaring, indeed the whole night side of the project of colonial modernity. In psychological or microspherological terms, the evidence is compelling that the inner and outer double of the possessed seaman do not assume a personified form. The genius of Ahab's existence is not a spirit in the proximity field, let alone a lord on high, but rather a god of below and outside, an animal sovereign that appears from the deep and defies all appropriation – precisely that white whale of which the author noted in his etymological mottos:

> 'This animal is named from roundness or rolling; for in Dan. *hvalt* is arched or vaulted.'
> *Webster's Dictionary*
>   'Whale. *** It is more immediately from the Dut. and Ger. *Wallen*; A.S. *wealwian*, to roll, to wallow.
> *Richardson's Dictionary*[3]

Through its 'rolling' form, the whale appears to both its admirers and its haters as the epitome of a power that turns exclusively within itself in the sea's ominous depths. Moby Dick's grandeur represents the eternal resistance of an unfathomable life to the calculus of hunters. His white simultaneously stands for the non-spheric, homogeneous, unmarked space in which travellers will feel cheated of any feeling of intimacy, arrival or home. It is no coincidence that his colour was reserved by cartographers for *terra incognita*. Melville called white 'a colourless all-colour of atheism from which we shrink',[4] because it reminds us of the Milky Way's white depth, of the 'heartless voids and immensities of the universe';[5] it infuses the observer with the thought of their annihilation in the indifferent outside. Ahab's whale must wear this colour, as it symbolizes an exteriority that is otherwise neither in need nor capable of a manifestation. But if the outside should ever show itself as such, then:

> the palsied universe lies before us a leper; and like wilful travellers in Lapland, who refuse to wear coloured and colouring glasses upon their eyes, so the wretched infidel gazes himself blind at the monumental white shroud that wraps all the prospect around him.[6]

Almost a century before Sartre would let one of the figures in a play state that 'hell is other people', Melville had touched on a deeper foundation: hell is the outside. The disconnected modern point-individuals are scattered in this methodological inferno, this indifference of a space in which no dwelling occurs. It is therefore not, as the Existentialists claimed, only a matter of giving oneself a direction through a freely chosen commitment amid the larger senselessness; after the general exposure of humans on the surfaces of the earth and the systems, it is rather a matter of inhabiting the indifferent outside as if ensouled bubbles could achieve longer-term stability within it. Humans must bet that they will succeed – in the face of the shroud that covers everything external – in taking their relationships with one another in an interior to be created artificially as seriously as if no external facts existed. Couples, communes, choirs, teams, people and churches all try their hand at fragile spatial creations against the primacy of the white hell. Only in such self-producing vessels can the wilted word 'solidarity' be fulfilled in the most radical layer of its meaning: the living-arts of modernity aim to establish the non-indifferent within the indifferent. This creates inexhaustible horizons for projection and invention in the face of a geographically exhausted world.[7]

Perhaps the 'free peoples' of which the nineteenth century spoke – without realizing that it was thereby assisting the emergence of the modernized obsession collectives, the patriots with their demands for sacrifices – will only exist as associations of people who, faced with an actually universalized indifference, join forces anew in a manner vaguely anticipated by congregations and academies, but previously unknown.

21

The Modern Age and the
New Land Syndrome
Americanology 1

The reading room in the modern annex of the Library of Congress features an inscription by Thomas Jefferson that sums up the spirit of the land acquisition age with unsurpassed clarity: 'The earth belongs always to the living generation. They may manage it then, and what proceeds from it, as they please, during their usufruct.'

Although the Washington thesis dates from the end of the eighteenth century, it encapsulates an impulse that affected the expansionist behaviour of Europeans from Columbus's time onwards: the view of the earth as found property and a resource. Old Testament and colonizatory references are as unmistakable in Jefferson's statement as the grand gesture of the advocate of the present: the generation granted usufruct is, of course, none other than that of the New England Americans who broke away from the British Crown and believed they had found the promised land on the North Atlantic coast. For the Yankees (supposedly the Native American pronunciation of *les anglais*) of the eighteenth century, the Judaizing language games of the Pilgrim Fathers, who thought they were repeating the exodus of the Israelites from Egypt across the ocean, had long become rhetorical small change. They did not have to lisp when expressing their belief that a chosen people must be granted a land suited to its status. And as they had now found it, it would have been a betrayal of their mission to abstain from taking resolute possession of it.

The statement about the handing-over of the earth to the present generation of usufructuaries, shimmering with the jargon of natural right, unmistakably conveys the shock of world reforms triggered by the transatlantic discoveries at the end of the fifteenth century and by Magellan's voyage. While the Pacific 'revolution', the realization of the oceanic character of the earth's communicating water areas, remained an abstract and unwelcome, at best utopia-inspiring piece of 'information' for the vast majority of Europeans over centuries, the discovery of the Fourth Continent, the two Americas, was a more than geographical sensation. It was mirrored in countless expressions of a new theological and mercantile appetite. Americanists have offered manifold paraphrases of the salvation-historical interpretations of the double continent's discovery presented by its contemporaries and their successors. For the Biblicists among the occupiers, America was undoubtedly the ace God had kept up His sleeve for a millennium and a half to play it in the time of greatest need, in the religio-political agony of the Occident. By allowing His Catholic servant Columbus to find America just in time, God used the ploy of divine providence to show His Protestant followers the way in the second exodus.

We shall leave aside the historico-theological deliriums that became real historical factors through the emigrants and their strong faith. Anyone interested in the serious North American appendix to *The Divine Comedy* should get their money's worth from *Magnalia Christi Americana* (The Glorious Works of Christ in the New World), penned in 1698 by the Bostonian minister Cotton Mather. Since then, every century has produced further prize pieces of American political theology – extending to the mirages of George W. Bush's divinely ordained election fraud in the year of the Lord 2000. What made the America effect one of the central psychopolitical facts of the Modern Age, beyond its character as a geographical sensation and the theological idealizations thereof, is its irradiation into the awareness of space, soil and chances among the post-Columbian Europeans from whom the Americans would be recruited.

America rose from the Atlantic like an auxiliary universe in which God's experiment with mankind could be started from scratch – a land in which arriving, seeing and taking seemed to become synonymous. While, in the feudalized and territorialized Old Europe, every strip of arable land had had an owner for a thousand years, and every forest path, cobblestone or bridge was subject to age-old rights of way and restrictive privileges in favour of some princely exploiter, America offered countless arrivals the exciting contrasting experience of a virtually lordless land that, in its immeasurability, wanted only to be occupied and cultivated so as to belong to the occupier and cultivator. A world in which the settlers arrive before the land registers – a paradise for new beginners and strong takers. Hence feelings of the world's breadth in the Modern Age were co-conditioned by the basic American experience: the ease with which possession can be taken of land and resources. This produced – along with numerous other social characters – a world-historically unprecedented type of peasant who no longer resided on a lord's property, but rather managed his new, self-owned soil as an armed land-taker in his own right and a farmer under God.[1] Anyone seeking their fortune on the chance-grounds of the overseas commonwealth must therefore be as much of a chance-taker as goes with being a land-taker. Indeed, perhaps what theologians and jurists called natural law is simply the formal explication of the new taker-subjectivity, which has set itself the task of taking what is its own, by land and by sea. Human rights are the legal soul of the life that takes what belongs to it wherever it can. Melville, once again: 'Is it not a saying in every one's mouth, Possession is half of the law: that is, regardless of how the thing came into possession? But often possession is the whole of the law.'[2] Nonetheless, the taker-entrepreneurs on the colonial fronts act, to speak in Kantian terms, under a maxim that is usually more suitable for the definition of crime than that of a noble participation in the exploration of the world: for, by seeking to become owners of goods by pure taking, they elude the impertinent demands of fair exchange. Their consciences are barely ever damaged by this, as history shows, as they invoke the right of the supreme moment: in this instant, justice must lie in the appropriation itself, not in fair trade and mutual acknowledgement. The agents of expansion, in the American West and the rest of the globe, exculpated themselves in their interventional acts through an implicit theory of the moral gap: there are seemingly times in which action must be ahead of legislation, and we are now in such a moment. With this argument they apply for acquittal due to extraordinary circumstances. In the historical gap, people who would be looters in ordinary times are pioneers. Whoever found themselves charged with a crime during juridified, inhibited post-historical years would, in the turbulence of history in action, be considered an adventurer, hero and missionary of civilization. Can anyone overlook the fact that the current crime film industry continues to dream of the gap? One can define it as the special zone in which the human right to take without exchange is still valid.

Who could defend the American soldiers who, with genocidal intent, sent pox-ridden woollen blankets into the camps of their Native American enemies? Who would stand up for the slave traders who sometimes lost a third of their perishable wares on their trans-atlantic human animal transports? Who would take the side of Leopold II of Belgium, who turned his private colony, the Congo, into the 'worst forced labour camp of the Modern Age' (as Peter

Scholl-Latour phrased it) – with ten million massacred? Faced with these events, historians have had to become prosecutors of their own cultures. Their dossiers show how the relationship between justice and history can shift after the fact.[3]

The tribunalization of the past has meanwhile affected the heroic period of terrestrial globalization in its entirety. The file on the Modern Age reads like a giant indictment of imperial incorrectnesses, infringements and crimes, and the only solace offered by a study of its contents is the thought that these deeds and misdeeds have become unrepeatable. Perhaps terrestrial globalization, like world history as a whole, is the crime that can only be committed once.

22

The Five Canopies of Globalization: Aspects of European Space Exportation

To understand the spherological secrets of advanced terrestrial globalization, one must not only attempt to go back *before* the negation of spatial differences through traffic technologies and storms of images in the late twentieth century. What is even more necessary is to recover the criteria to assess the immeasurable work of European humans and their collaborators in all parts of the world on the reinvention and transference of liveable conditions to other locations. The reaching out into the planetary white could never have become the 'success story' for Europeans and their descendants that it was, in all its outgrowths, in geopolitical and technological terms, if the departing risk-takers had not managed to preserve or regenerate minimal endospheric conditions on the way and at the other shores. Thus the true history of terrestrial globalization should first of all be told as a history of shells brought along, and as a crossing of enclosing husks, visible and invisible ones alike.

One can say with good reason that it was the specific European art to export canopies – portable symbolizations of the sky that could also be appropriated outside by the travellers as a 'sky for us'. It was not so much their fatal exterminism that made Europeans leaders in the conquest of the outside for centuries as their ability to preserve a minimal native space in the most remote locations. Islanders imported to Europe usually lost their coordinates fairly soon, whereas Europeans took themselves everywhere by drawing strengths from their ships, their missions and their egotechnics. One could say that the European settlers were the inventors of worldwide camping. Wherever they appeared, they usually proved the better observers: an observer is someone who perceives the other through a window of theory while themselves eluding counter-observation. As they had portable mental windows at their disposal, the managing Europeans were usually ahead of the discovered others by an entire dimension of descriptive, analytical and acting capacity. There are essentially five forms in which the relationship between the attackers and the white space could be spherologically handled:

- nautical mythology
- the Christian religion
- loyalty to the princes of one's mother country
- the scientific documentation of the external space
- linguistic translation

Each of these methods produced its own spatial poetics, and all of these contributed to the epochal task of making the outside liveable for the voyagers and invaders or feigning its integration and domination.

23

The Poetics of the Ship's Hold

The psychodynamic aspects of the ship's-hold experience are most accessible to present-day people, as they have points of reference from dealing with caravan interiors and car cabins. The availability of such 'traffic' means would not have become an indispensable, and usually enjoyable, method of movement for the considerable majority of modern individuals if the interior forms of the vehicles themselves did not adapt elementary structures of sphere formation on a small scale. The ship, like – more moderately proportioned – the car and the caravan, is the mobilized nest or the absolute house.[1] From an existential perspective, the task is a mobilization of the interior – which amounts to squaring the circle of life. Because the ship simultaneously embodies the realization of the longing for being-with-oneself and evasion, it is (especially in its early modern, seaworthy form) the archetype of the resolved contradiction. It balances out the diametrically opposing strivings towards habitation and adventure. It makes symbiotic relationships possible – and yet it can be experienced like a projectile striking the unheard-of. The vehicle is experienced as a belly that holds a litter of newcomers; they will go ashore where they can, and do as they please in front of their context-free front door.

At the same time, the ship is a magical-technospheric self-expansion of the crews – like all modern container-vehicles, it is a homeostatic dream machine that can be steered through the outer element like a manipulable Great Mother. (A psychohistorically convincing history of vehicle superstition has yet to be written.) Thus ships can become mobile homelands for their crews. In recognizing ships as extensions of the country under whose flag they sail, maritime law follows an original spherological intuition: being-on-land here changes in spatio-logical and international law terms into being-on-board; central aspects of the earth's *nomos*, the 'peace' of the native space, are transferred to the floating endosphere.

The decisive function of the ship's hull, admittedly, is to push back, both in physical and in symbolic terms: because it moves through the damp element, whose displaceability aids the fulfilment of the ship's spatial demands, the floating body wins out over the resistance of its carrier. At the social level, this corresponds to the rule that human ensembles which throw themselves outwards only remain coherent if they succeed in stopping their leaks and asserting the precedence of the interior amid the unliveable element. Just as church naves[2] once transferred this act of displacement to the mainland in order to be vehicles for Christian souls on the earthly sea of life, expedition ships in the outer space will have to rely all the more on their displacement space as the spatially self-disposing shelter form they have brought with them.

24

Onboard Clerics:
The Religious Network

From here it is obvious: the fact that the larger expeditions of heroic nautical times could barely ever embark without a priest on board was not simply a religious convention, or a mere concession to the demands of the church not to let groups of seafarers leave without some form of spiritual control. The omnipresence of the religious factor in early seafaring (Columbus's first voyage is the only one whose crew list shows no clergyman – though it does include overseers sent by the Spanish Crown) points rather to a second, overpowering spheropoetic mechanism. If the expeditions of the first ocean travellers were to succeed, the crews had to rely not only on their profession for assurance, but also on the metaphysical routines of their home countries. Because seafaring was a practice that involved extreme situations, experts on the extreme had to be on board whenever possible. The possibility of shipwreck belongs to any ship as distress belongs to the sea, and the holy emergency helpers and their connoisseurs, the priests, could at least offer symbolic protection from the latter. The fact that European seafaring could call itself Christian – and long before the dawn of the oceanic age – shows its orientation towards this indispensable metaphysical insurance system. If the white outside seemed terrifying, it was also because for countless people it meant death, and thus the prospect of being buried in an element devoid of all conciliatory qualities.[1] Without any connection to Old European ideas of burial and the hereafter, the notion of perishing outside was doubly unbearable.

The seafaring clerics would have mistaken their function, however, if they had not looked out on two sides from the start: for the seamen on board who had to be ritually stabilized and motivationally controlled, and also for the new humans outside, who became increasingly interesting as future recipients of the Christian message.

On the board side, the Christian religion offered incentive and refuge – the latter especially on the expeditions of Catholic nations under the ubiquitous figure of the protecting Virgin Mary, the *regina maris* who was also presented after the victory of Lepanto as Santa Maria della Vittoria – the Great Mother of seamen and rescuer-intercessor in mortal danger and distress. *In periculis maris esto nobis protectio.* Rulers, merchant princes, captains, sailors and baptized natives all found refuge beneath her protective cloak – when they crossed beneath Mary's cloak, the rigged fleets only seemed exposed to friendly winds. On the cult pictures in seamen's chapels, the high lady wraps her own in the shell of a world womb as if for the last time – the entire navy under a single garment (a plausible argument in favour of loose clothes for women, and one of the last concessions of the Modern Age to the morphological dream of the living being contained in the living). Here, once again, an enclosing sphere in the sky is elevated to a sealed, personally coloured symbolic shell – even though by this time cosmologists had already begun to make the heavens metaphysically comfortless.

On the side of new land, the meaning of the Christian religion in the Age of Discovery was essentially mission in its second era – consistently in its dual function as a neo-apostolic extension of the church and a religious protection on the flank of colonialism. One cause of the militant colonial church and 'battlefront church' tendencies of overseas missionary practice was the almost unconditional papal approval of the Portuguese and Spanish forays into the New World, as the Curia initially saw 'the providential arm of the great commission in the Iberian states'.[2] In its universalist appetite, Rome granted the conquerors such far-reaching privileges that the Catholic Church soon found itself in the position of a disempowered second next to the *de facto* autocratically colonizing states. Nonetheless, the pope had entered the Modern Age stage – especially in the first era of expansion – not only as its supreme client, but also as the notary of globalization; this was evident early on from his eminent role in confirming the Portuguese discoveries in Africa (with the bulls *Romanus Pontifex* of 1455 and *Inter cetera* of 1456), and then from his mediating function in the dispute between Portuguese and Spanish pretentions over world domination: sanctioning the Treaty of Tordesillas in 1494 had inevitably been a matter for the Holy See.

Post-Columbian Catholicism's claims to majesty came to light most explicitly when the pope, citing the sources of his office, proclaimed himself the true overlord of the circumnavigated world.[3] Under these circumstances, the national monarchies of Europe – the Catholic ones too – had to resist the papal claims to primacy with increasing vehemence. The tone of these national-dynastic rebellions became apparent in 1540, when Francis I ordered the imperial envoy to show him Adam's will and the papal clause therein stating that the French king should be excluded from the division of the world.

As far as the Protestant missions are concerned, these were devoted from the start to national-colonial functions even more obviously than the Catholic ones; missionaries for the Dutch colonial empire were trained in Leiden at a seminary of the United East India Company, as if the church's vocation to proselytize came not from Matthew 28:19 but through a mandate of the North Atlantic free trade associations. Certainly the Christian mission – or, more generally, the exportation of confessions – was the most important agent of a sociospherological continuum principle in the transition from the Old World to the New World because, when encountering the strangers, the motifs of possible generic and cultic commonalities between discoverers and discovered could be foregrounded.

The opening of the Second Vatican Council in 1962 showed under spectacular auspices how successful the Catholic missions in particular believed their globalization efforts over four and a half centuries had been, with bishops from no fewer than 133 countries entering St Peter's Basilica in Rome – an act of assembly that one would have to call unique, had it not been regularly outdone at the opening celebrations of the Olympic Games in the Modern Age. Councils and Olympiads – both exemplary manifestations of European assembly projects – illustrate what universalist umbrellas can achieve. Precisely these, however, as imposing as their expansive gestures may be, bring to light the insurmountable exclusivity of such gatherings. To construct a religious or athletic interior of humanity *in actu*, those who actually come together must be representatives, 'overseers' or 'choices' – the virtual totality can only arise through the synchronized attention of an observing humanity in the media of transference. The totalizing quality of such gatherings is therefore expressed less through those present than through the universalist symbolism of the assembly's architectural container – the typical superlatives of macrospherically committed architecture: the Catholic cathedral and the secular sports arena. In the cathedral, the nave and the dome indicate the assembling power of the Roman Catholic creed, while in the stadium, the neo-fatalistic arena motif exhibits itself as a symbol of the closed world sphere.[4]

Because the churches only exist as uncollected *communio sancto-rum* in their everyday mode of being, however, and have to prove themselves in local gatherings, they are constantly confronted with the task of organizing themselves in less spectacular, always opera-tively accessible and traditionalizable media. In addition, centrifugal forces take effect far more powerfully in Protestant churches, with their more autonomous units. The New England Puritan communi-ties left behind were especially reliant on their ability to achieve stability through their own ritual practice. To understand the condi-tions under which this attachment to brought-along forms took place, it is useful to call to mind the reconstruction of the primitive wooden chapel in which the Pilgrim Fathers and their families gathered for their services after landing in New Plymouth, at Cape Cod in the Massachusetts Bay on 19 November 1620. Nothing could highlight the precedence of the ritual framework over the physical building more clearly than this raw, draughty barn in the middle of a hastily erected, fear-infused palisade village. It is not only in Heidegger's provinces that humans are those who dwell in their language as the House of Being; in the scattered points of the newly disclosed global space too, they set up camp under the tent roofs of the traditions and ritual safeguards they have brought with them.

25

The Book of Vice-Kings

As well as their religious notions, the leaders of the globalization expeditions – the vice-kings – the admirals and their officers also carried their dynastic models in themselves and out into the distant expanse. The internalized images of the royal clients, no less than their real portraits, ensured that the expansion into the outer space, both in critical moments and in hours of triumph, could be experienced as an effective emanation from the personal centre of power. When the carriers of discovery firms return physically or think back sentimentally, they make inner and outer gestures that convey their allegiance to the European origin of power. Their activity can be compared to the behaviour of the Platonic ray of light, which erupted from the centre, turned around after arriving at its point of reflection, and returned to its source of emission. In this sense, all loyal European conquerors and discoverers were on their way as the executive rays of distant sun kings. Even the crudest emissaries of imperialism in the nineteenth century, the 'men on the spot', considered themselves bringers of light in the service of their nations. If the European agents presented themselves as the great bringers, it was also because they carried their dynastic splendour outside with them, while appropriating the treasures of the New World with the demeanour of harvest hands. They move about in the nimbus of their native majesty systems, and most or all of their finds remain tied to the throne rooms and halls of fame at home. What has been termed the exploitation of colonies merely conveys the most intensive form of bond to the colonizers' homeland – most especially the Spanish, who unfolded a complicated bureaucracy of looting. Relics of this can still be viewed today in the Archivo de las Indias in Seville. The subject of looted art is as old as terrestrial globalization: gold treasures of the Aztecs were exhibited in Antwerp at the start of the sixteenth century, and the question of their rightful owners was never asked. Albrecht Dürer looked with his own eyes upon these works of an art from an entirely different place.

Without their inner royal icons, most expedition leaders of early globalization would not have known for whom – except themselves – they should achieve their successes; most of all, however, they would not have learned whose acknowledgement would have augmented, justified and transfigured them. Even the atrocities of the Spanish conquistadors in Central and South America were metastases of loyalty to their native majesties, who could be represented by extraordinary means. The title of vice-king thus has more than simply legal and protocol significance; it is also a category that sees to the very psychopolitical heart of the Conquista. The books of the vice-kings have yet to be written. It is because of them that the European kings were present always and everywhere in the outer expansions of the Old World, despite never visiting their colonies themselves.[1] The conquistadors and princes' pirates collected their spoils under imaginary majestic canopies – and whatever part of it they transferred home was appropriated by the treasurers of their kings like a wild tax. In these happy days of globalization, the riches from across the ocean proved that the wide world followed no other destiny than to owe tribute to the European houses.

In a sense, this is also true of the spiritual king of kings, the pope, who, as the wearer of the three-tiered crown, wanted to expand his throne into a hyper-majesty for the entire globe. For it was his elite troops – the Jesuits, who were pledged to him with their fourth oath as the commander of martial Catholicism – who covered the globe with a net of prayers for the pope and considerations for Rome: an Internet of fervent obedience formed by distant devotees of the centre. This was the model for the worldwide operations of today's telecommunications companies; the long-distance call was prefigured by the long-distance prayer for the pope. The Jesuits were the prototypical news group, communicating via their organization-specific network. The other missionary orders – Franciscans, Dominicans, Theatines, Augustinians, Conceptionists, Clarists of the first and fifth rules, Hieronymites, canonesses, Barefoot Carmelites and many others – were likewise committed through their Rome connection to the project of procuring successes for the spiritual Conquista. It was their ambition to spread a papally supervised commonwealth over all the earth's continents. Only in the twentieth century did the pope have the mass-medially correct idea of travelling to the provinces of his moral empire as the ambassador of his own state. This marked Catholicism's transition into undisguised telematic charismocracy: the Roman path to modernity.

In keeping with the laws of metaphysical communication in large-scale social bodies, however, Catholic telecommunication before the age of actual papal presence could still not dispense entirely with magical-telepathic mechanisms. The corpse of the first great Jesuit missionary in Asia, Francis Xavier, who had opened up India and Japan to the Roman church, found its final resting place in Goa. The saint's right arm was brought back to Europe, 'tired from the baptism of thousands'; it is still preserved today in the order's mother church, Il Gesù in Rome, as the most precious relic of globalization.

26

The Library of Globalization

But what if the participants in the commando operations of early terrestrial globalization were neither captains loyal to the crown nor missionaries who obeyed the pope or Christ? They did not need to feel excluded from the higher chances of shelter or from the idealizations of European expansion. For the worldly minded pioneers of world-disclosure, there were ways and means to step beneath one of the secular canopies of globalization, and even a spirit not religiously committed had good prospects of getting its money's worth in the Last Bullet project. Anyone who did not acquire new lands for a European king or believers for the church could nonetheless sail into European ports as a conqueror and bringer of riches if they knew how to make themselves useful as agents of the European experiential sciences. These open-minded disciplines, which grew around geography and anthropology, constituted themselves emphatically in the incipient era of expansion as *new* sciences; they served an accumulation of knowledge whose methodological modernity and allegiance to the age of European world-taking were plain for all to see.

It is characteristic of these insights that they accumulated like a second capital – albeit a capital that would belong to an enlightened humanity as a whole, and not be withdrawn from public and civil use by princes and their keepers of secrets. Against the background of the new sciences of the outer humans, of usable nature and of the inhabited earth, an alphabetized European could never feel entirely cut off from the flow of their native systems of meaning, even in the most desolate abandonment on distant islands and continents. Every life on the outer front potentially bore an aura of cumulative experience that could be projected into literary documentations. I have already spoken of the immortalization of countless seafarers and explorers on land and sea maps; cartographical fame is only a special example of what one could call the general canopy function of the European experiential sciences during the globalization process. It currently and potentially protects the actors on the outer lines from the danger of sinking into the senseless white and being engulfed by the depressions that can be triggered by collisions with unassimilable newness, otherness, strangeness and bleakness.

The empirical sciences, with their affiliated literary genres of travel account, utopia and exotic novel, tend towards a transformation of all outside conditions into observations, and all observations into announcements that find their way into the great book of new European theory – 'observers', after all, exist only as subjects who will write what they have *seen* or *found*. The constructivist assumption that observation is description of facts with the aid of a central distinction already applied to the early long-distance travellers, in so far as they applied the distinction between taking or not taking with them throughout the world. I am thinking especially of the golden age of explorer-writers, from which names such as Louis Antoine de Bougainville, Jacques-Etienne-Victor Arago, Reinhold and Georg Forster, Johann Gottfried Seume, Charles Darwin, Alexander von Humboldt, Henry Morton Stanley have occasionally risen to the level of world literature – as far as the breadth of their readership was concerned, at least. It is typical of the Modern Age habitus of acquiring, bringing, contributing, collaborating, going forwards and systematizing that the principal research takes place in the form of competitions. Corresponding to the races for goals to be reached, there is a writing competition on the field of scientific honour – which applied particularly to the fundamentally hystericized domain of polar research, whose protagonists mostly appeared as their own rhapsodists and publicizers of their research woes. This entanglement of research and theatre made it recognizable at a popular level that all forms of scientific expedition would also be media matters in future; one can illustrate this in the present with the amply hystericizable enterprises of genetic research, brain research and cancer research. Concerning the heroic days of globalization, one can say that had its heroes not been mirrored in an idealizing medium, their goals would never have become adequately clear or unclear to them.

Initially, however, it was not so much the mass media that observed the expeditions as they set off. Rather, all literate participants in the voyages into the unknown looked towards an imaginary hyper-medium, the only one in which the history of the lonely successes outside could be recorded and brought back: the canopy that could hold all the solitudes of researchers had to be a fantastic integral book – a book of cognitive records in which no one would be forgotten who had ever stood out as a bringer-back of experience and a contributor to the great text of world-disclosure. It was inevitable that, sooner or later, someone would attempt the actual publication of this imaginary hyper-book of European experiential knowledge. It is characteristic of the practical genius of French Enlightenment figures that as early as the mid-eighteenth century, at half-time in terrestrial globalization, so to speak, they summoned the energy to carry out the project of an *Encyclopedia* of valuable knowledge. It lent the previously informal theoretical canopy the edifying shape of the circle which orders and holds all knowledge – a circle that could, furthermore, be straightened into a section of the bookshelf encompassing seventeen volumes of text and sixteen of illustrations. In this work, items of knowledge from the remotest sources could be promoted to their cognitive value-forms. Thus the black of print celebrated its triumph over white in the hyper-book of the sciences.

That collecting and bringing home experiences can also have a subversive, or in some cases at least a tactless side, however, was learned by Frederick II of Prussia in his dealings with the globetrotter and naturalist Georg Forster. At his first audience with the king after acquiring a professorship for natural science in Halle, Forster supposedly said – somewhat more frankly than was customary at the royal court – that he had seen five kings in his life, three of them savage and two tame, 'but none like Your Majesty'. Frederick the Great considered these the words of a 'most uncouth fellow'. But how else should one have told the princes? Once the kings of the Old World could be viewed empirically like exotic chieftains (and once European residences could be observed as mere locations of royalty), it could no longer be kept from the noble lords and their followers that their time was coming to an end.[1]

27

The Translators

While participation in the European experiential sciences was able to develop under the super-canopy of an encyclopedic book phantasm, it was the task of linguists and ethnologists to work away at the linguistic outside in a wealth of individual encounters with different foreign languages. The European explorer-languages found themselves faced with a semiotic multiverse of incredible variety comprising at least five thousand authentic languages (6,700 at a recent UNESCO count) and a virtually inestimable multiplicity of dialects and sub-dialects that always include mythologies, 'religions', ritualisms, arts and gestures. Considering this diversity, which defies any attempt at an overview, the dream of an all-integrating hyper-language must disappear almost automatically. Only two strategies offered themselves to the discoverers and the discovered alike to find their bearings in this neo-Babylonian situation: firstly, the forced establishment of the colonial rulers' languages as general languages of interaction – which at least succeeded in the cases of English, Spanish and French, with varying success in different parts of the world – and secondly, the infusion of the individual languages with the translated words of the new masters. Both paths had to be taken simultaneously, and on both of them, learning languages – and translation along with them – proved the key to the regional spheropoetic processes. Whether one leans towards pessimistic or optimistic theories of translation, bilingualism or plurilingualism performed one of the most important canopy functions during terrestrial globalization. It remains a fact that the language of the European rulers pulled the local languages over to its side, rather than the respective indigenous

languages absorbing the idioms of the colonizers.[1] It testified to the
wise intuition of the politician-historian Winston Churchill that he
wrote the history of the British world power not only as that of an
empire, but also that of a language area: *History of the English-
Speaking Peoples* (4 vols., 1956–8). He evidently foresaw that the
most long-lived aspect of the Commonwealth would be its common-
speak. This arrangement not only satisfied the English need to present
the rift between Great Britain and the United States as a mere question of pronunciation; it also kept open the option of new political
groups and cultural circles entering the club of English-speaking
peoples. As far as the language criterion is concerned, all natural
scientists, pilots, diplomats and businesspersons have indeed been
incorporated into the inescapable Anglophone language network like
artificial new peoples – followed by the brave new world of pop
music. In Anglophony, as in religion and the most basic forms of
entertainment, the medium is the message.

As far as the Christian message is concerned, it could not wait in
its second missionary cycle for demand to arise among the five thousand foreign languages; it had to translate itself into the language of
the others in order to explain its salvific significance to them. Probably
the work of Christian translators in the last five hundred years to
express their faith in other languages, at least in quantitative, and
perhaps also in qualitative terms, constitutes the most extraordinary
cultural achievement in the history of mankind – at least, the self-
translation of modern Christianity into the countless individual cultures is, for the time being, the most powerful testament to the
possibilities and difficulties of an operatively concrete trans-cultural
ecumene. (If anything, it would be comparable to the number of
Homer translations into the plethora of European and non-European
idioms.) At the end of the twentieth century, the New Testament had
been translated into over 1,800 genuine languages – from which connoisseurs of the linguistic atlas can conclude that the Christian
message has gained access to at least one in three language communities on the planet, including more than a few in which the New
Testament was the first book ever published.

This fact, which could be described in church-historical immanence as the continuation of the Pentecost miracle by Gutenbergian
means, at once reveals the insurmountable particularity of even the
most inclusive message: the inaccessibility of 'small' languages places
a limit on the effectively universal spread of the Gospel. Consequently,
the apostolic methods of dissemination, as invasive as they may
have been, were unable to fulfil the dream of erecting a worldwide
message empire, penetrating as far as the capillary level, founded on

Mediterranean transmitters and content providers. This observation could only be retracted if one interpreted the triumphal procession of the natural sciences through the modern nations as a missionary success of Hellenism in its modern phase – perhaps Athens as a sender can reach the places where the missives from Rome and Jerusalem cannot be read.

In any case, Hollywood, the Pacific metropolis of images, outstripped the Mediterranean emission bases for morals and mysteries – Rome and Jerusalem – half a century ago. Its messages were never directed at the smaller cultures, whose markets are too narrow for the products of the new amusing imperialism. If they can be promoted in two dozen dubbed versions, however, they promise adequate profits.

Second Part

The Grand Interior

But just as every point on the earth is the top,
the *present* is the form of all life.

Arthur Schopenhauer, *The World as Will and Representation*

28

Synchronous World

Modern times: half a millennium after the four voyages of Columbus, the circumnavigated, uncovered, depicted, occupied and used earth presents itself as a body wrapped in dense fabrics of traffic movements and telecommunication routines. Virtual shells have replaced the imagined ethereal sky; thanks to radio-electronic systems, the meaning of distances has effectively been negated in the centres of power and consumption. The global players live in a world without gaps. In aeronautical terms, the earth has been reduced to a flying route of fifty hours at most; for the orbits of satellites and the *Mir* station, and recently the International Space Station (ISS), units of ninety minutes became the norm. For radio and light messages, the earth has virtually shrunk to a single point – it rotates, as a temporally compact orb, in an electronic layer that surrounds it like a second atmosphere.

Terrestrial globalization, then, has advanced so far that it would seem bizarre to demand now that it justify itself. Just as the actual occupation of a country had become the final argument of European nation-states for the realization of colonial claims until the nineteenth century, the effective consummation of terrestrial globalization has become the self-supporting argument for the process itself. After a start-up phase of several centuries, the world system is increasingly stabilizing itself as a complex of rotating and oscillating movements that maintain themselves on their own power. In the realm of circulating capital, momentum has overtaken reasons. Execution replaces legitimation, and facts have become *forces majeures*. Anyone speaking of globalization could just as easily refer to 'destiny'.

What the sixteenth century set in motion was perfected by the twentieth: no point on the earth's surface, once money had stopped off there, could escape the fate of becoming a location – and a location is not a blind spot in a field, but rather a place in which one sees that one is seen. The liquefaction 'revolution' rolls on, the tides rise. All cities have meanwhile become ports, as explained above; for where cities have not gone to the sea, the sea comes to them. For the super-commodity of information in particular does not reach its investors via highways – as an incorrect metaphor from the early days of the network discourse suggested – but rather through currents flowing into the more aptly named data oceans. Through its old and new media, 'globalization' constantly conveys the message that it is occurring and advancing, with disregard for any alternatives. Hence its peculiar independence from philosophy and other manifestations of reflective theory; now it talks only to itself, celebrating itself as the dominant subject of its soliloquies. Briefings have replaced critique. At most, the course of the world can read itself as the most comprehensive form of an act of God, realized through human actions – and no will to desist, however widespread, could prevent their continuation. No theoretical or practical engagement with the present can undo the fact that the earth has been circumnavigated and its peoples and cultures forced into mediation. The worldwide 'anti-globalization' movement proves the ineluctable nature of the new status quo through its mere existence: by pointing to dysfunctions in the world system, the critics bear witness to its functioning. It would be equally impossible for opponents of the earth's rotation to escape the fate of participating in the daily circulation of the ground beneath their feet.

That is why terrestrial globalization, like an axiom, is the first and only precondition for a theory of the present age. Even though the scattered peoples of the world have, until recently, existed in their endospheres as if on separate stars, concealed from the outside in their linguistic retreats, immunized through their ignorance of others and enchanted through their own misery and fame – they are forced by the distance-destroying 'revolution' of modernity to admit that from now on, because they are reachable by mobile others, they live on one and the same planet: the planet of the unconcealed.

Because terrestrial globalization is a mere fact that came into effect late on, and under singular circumstances, it cannot be interpreted as the manifestation of an eternal truth or an inescapable necessity. It would be far-fetched to see it as an expression of the biological theorem that all people on earth form a single species. Nor does it support the metaphysical idea that the human race shares in one and the same store of unrevisable truths – even if some believe that, or purport to. And least of all does it mirror a moral law that all people should think of all others in their species as considerately and compassionately as possible. The naïve supposition of a potential openness of all to all is taken *ad absurdum* by the facts of globalization. On the contrary: the inevitable finitude of human interest in other humans becomes ever clearer as global interconnection progresses – it is only the moral accent that changes, tending towards expectations of greater capacity despite an increasing nervous strain. It should come as no surprise if it transpires that the symptoms of misanthropy increase with the progressive interconnection of the world. If fear of humans is a primal response to unwelcome neighbours, an unprecedented misanthropic epidemic would be a foreseeable result of the imposed long-distance vicinity between most people and most others. This should only amaze those who have forgotten that the words 'neighbour' and 'enemy' were traditionally almost synonymous. Viewed in this light, such terms as 'education' or 'cosmopolitanism' take on a different meaning: in future, they will indicate the horizon of misanthropy-inhibiting measures.

What characterized 'all people', without exception, 'by nature' until very recently was their shared inclination to ignore the vast majority of people outside of their own ethnic container. This interignorant constitution of 'mankind' should initially be understood as a guiltless state. As members of a scattered species – whose factual diaspora remained insurmountable even after the 'revolution' of global traffic – humans in their clans, their ethnicities, their districts, their clubs and their interest groups turn naturally and quietly away from those who belong to other units of identity or mixture scenes, and even the club of universalists makes no exceptions to this rule. To put it anthropologically, one could say that of all creatures, *Homo sapiens* has the broadest back; he needs it to turn on those around him. Being-in-the-world has always had elements of an overwhelmingly extended non-consideration-of-whatever-cannot-be-integrated. One of the outstanding mental effects of 'globalization' is the fact that it has made the greatest anthropological improbability – constantly taking into account the distant other, the invisible rival, the stranger to one's container – the norm.

The globalized world is the synchronized world; its form is produced simultaneity, and it finds its convergence in things that are current.[1] Where it is night, countries and people will still lie in the earth's shadow; but the world as such has become shadowless, and will remain bound by a pervasive diurnal imperative for the foreseeable future. There are no more time-outs in the disclosed and depicted global space. In addition, the mindsets of the global market and of burgeoning world-domestic politics besiege the habitual ignorance towards distant and foreign people, pushing together those involved in an arena of real chances for encounter and chronic necessities of contact. The result of globalization, namely the logical synthesis of humanity in a powerful concept of species and its joining in a compact world of traffic, is a product of compelling abstractions and compulsion-creating expeditions.

What was said above concerning the precedence of the outward journey in the history of world traffic now becomes the crux of the matter: 'man' and 'mankind' have only existed since, after centuries of European one-way journeys to others, the anthropological horizon has been explored as a plenum of peoples and cultures – a movement that has recently begun to be balanced out and complicated by growing two-way traffic. This two-way traffic mingles with the gestures of Europeans returning to themselves; the result of the mixture is multiculturalism, its modus operandi the hybridization of symbolic worlds.[2] 'Mankind' – it enters the stage of contemporary thought in a state of progressive self-discovery and interconnection as the vague and splintered para-subject in a universal history of the coincidental,[3] a latecomer whose emergence, if not its character, remains entirely determined by the chance circumstances of its discovery.

29

The Second Ecumene

'Mankind' is no means constituted by the libido of forming a total organization and procuring the necessary media for it. Rather, the anthropological assembly resulted initially from the coercive ties of colonialism and, following its dissolution, through the compulsion of interconnections that take effect via physical movement of goods, credit systems, investments, tourism, cultural exports, scientific exchange, world-policing interventionism and expansion of ecological norms. The impositions of the current Second Ecumene reveal themselves less in the fact that people everywhere are supposed to admit that people from elsewhere are their equals (though the number of those who deny this, openly or covertly, remains considerable), and more in the circumstance that they must endure the increasing pressure to co-operate that forces them together as a self-coercing commune in the face of shared risks and transnational threats. The results of analysing nation-states – which state that they can only be kept in shape through a constant self-stressing communication – increasingly prove true for the as yet inadequately aggregated planetary 'community of states'. Autogenous stress is the foundation for all large-scale mechanisms of consensus and co-operation.[1]

Faced with the growing pressure to encounter between world actors, international politics is transforming itself in a significant fashion: before our eyes, it seems to be leaving the era of great actions in favour of the age of great themes – that is, of generalized risks that solidify into semantic institutions, and thus universals of a new kind. These must be worked out in minute detail in endless meetings. Theme politics and the corresponding cycle of conferences only

progress as a production of autogenous global stress. Their carriers
act for a humanity that increasingly constitutes itself as the integral
of mutually approaching stress communes.

This virtual plenum of an actually interconnected, theme-moti-
vated humanity of traffic that has developed from modern terrestrial
globalization through the colonial empires and their sublation in
global market conditions (and latent neo-colonial alliances) is not the
first manifestation of the anthropological commune that was conceived in the history of human self-discoveries and self-organizations.
Pre-Columbian Europeans too had already conceived a nation of
species unity, articulated in the Greek concept of the *oikumene* or
'inhabited world'. That these colonies of the 'human being' were
essentially restricted to Roman-Hellenistic Mediterranean culture,
and knew no periphery but the Ptolemaic-terran continental trinity
of (residual) Europe, (Western) Asia and (North) Africa, does not
reduce the generosity of this first species-related idea. The point of
the ancient ecumenical concept does not lie in the notion that people
always have to be at home somewhere; it never occurred to the
ancients to teach that the mortals of all peoples were economic
animals (*oikein*, to dwell, inhabit) or deficient, house-dependent
beings who could not live without a roof over their heads and whatever else were considered the basic necessities. In ancient ecumenism,
people were *not* those beings which had rights because they all had
more or less the same physical needs, and recognized themselves in
one another as a result. Rather, in the thought of the early philosophers, humans are ontologically unified as members of a species that
shares a single world secret beyond their respective local symbolisms.
They all gaze into the same light, and all have the same *question*
towering over them. This view of a universal participation in a manifest *and* concealed super-ground of reality constitutes what, to use
Eric Voegelin's terms, one can call the First Ecumene of the West
(there was, as we know, also a Chinese version of the idea of a civilized totality expressed in the concept of *t'ien-hsia*, 'everything under
the sky' – usually translated simply as 'realm').[2] Voegelin incisively
formulates the metaphysical structure of the first idea of a united
mankind in Western antiquity:

> Universal mankind is not a society existing in the world, but a symbol
> that indicates man's consciousness of participating, in his earthly exist-
> ence, in the mystery of a reality that moves towards its transfiguration.
> Universal mankind is an eschatological index.
> [. . .] Without universality, there would be no mankind other than
> the aggregate of members of a biological species; there would be no

more a history of mankind than there is a history of catkind or horse-kind. If mankind is to have history, its members must be able to respond to the movement of divine presence in their souls. But if that is the condition, then the mankind who has history is constituted by the God to whom man responds. A scattering of societies, belonging to the same biological type, is discovered to be the one mankind with one history, by virtue of participation in the same flux of divine presence.[3]

From this perspective, the basis for the unity of a 'mankind' thus projected is to be found neither in the Mediterranean movement of goods nor in the imperialistic synthesis of peoples under Roman rule. Rather, the people of antiquity, in the most thorough reconstruction of their self-interpretations, were a 'problem community'; they were illuminated through participation in similar facts and solidarized through sharing the same riddle structure of existence. What gave the human race its dignity was that it encompassed the beings that were towered over by the same immeasurable 'ground'. It would, admit-tedly, be reserved for the Romans to develop the war machines and means of transportation that would place the inhabited world all around the Mediterranean Sea at their feet; once they had spread out in all directions, however, the conquerors in turn found themselves conquered by the spirits of two conquered peoples. If first of all, as Horace wrote, 'Captured Greece took her savage victor captive', this was because the philosophical theology of the Greeks had revealed the structures of a generally perceptible voice of reason – or rather an exportable technique of evidence – that could potentially *show itself* in pure thought to all people, with no concern for their ethnic allegiances. Voegelin celebrates this 'noetic epiphany' as Greece's contribution to a world-culturally relevant *philosophia perennis*.[4] If the Christian Jerusalem later also won out over Rome, it was through its message of the intimate and public community of God with the souls of the faithful in the *ecclesia*: thanks to this doctrine, the motif of a 'pneumatic theophany' was likewise developed in general, no longer ethnically restricted terms.

Rome thus rose to become the Eternal City less in the name of its rooted success gods – Jupiter, Mars, Venus, Virtus or Victoria – than because it was capable of changing into a Second Jerusalem, and within narrower limits even a Second Athens. Through its powers of assimilation and translation, the city of Caesars and popes was able to raise itself to the city of the First Ecumene. Long before the uni-versities and modern academies, *Roma aeterna*, that metaphysical power point of Old Europe, presented itself as the earthly seat of evidence: after Athens and Jerusalem, it wanted to be the city where that which *is shows itself*. It demanded of its visitors that the journey to Rome become a pilgrimage both to evidence and to mystery.

In the meantime, terrestrial globalization has decentred the city of cities too, turning the metaphysical broadcasting headquarters of the Old European globe into a location among locations. One should not underestimate the fact that the fifty-six men who signed the American Declaration of Independence of 4 July 1776, almost all of them free-masons and amateur metaphysicians, refer to the evidence first, only then declaring the human rights – as if they had intuitively under-stood that attempts to break away from Europe do not succeed unless the truth is conveyed across the Atlantic first: 'We hold these truths to be self-evident, that all men are created equal.' For the anthropo-logical commune of the Global Age, however, a metaphysical ground of unity in the manner of the 'divine presence' which Voegelin claims inhabits every soul is no longer in sight. A different medium of uni-versal coexistence will therefore have to be found.

The Second Ecumene broke open the universals of the first in all directions. It labelled both the Christian and the Greek conceptions of the world, with their supposed logical evidence, provincial – however vehemently they insisted on their universality. Christianity too had to face being told of its particularity, and time will tell whether it will manage to expand its authority through attempts to become a 'world ethos' – a project on which Hans Küng and others are working with the élan of belated Church Fathers.

This much is certain, however: none of the so-called world religions can qualify as the Great Vehicle for all factions of human-ity. In the long term, every one of them will have difficulty keeping its shares on the global market of metaphysical needs, and the pros-pects for synthetic universal religions of practically implanting a unified language or final vocabulary for the anthropological commune are non-existent.[5] Under these circumstances, it seems plausible to lower the requirements for the concept of a ground of unity for the species.

What the Second Ecumene can learn from the First, at least, is that it will not do to invoke biological 'foundations' as a ground of unity for mankind – not even after the emergence of a younger, politically correct genetics that affords all humans a place in a largely homoge-neous gene pool. This Adamitic racism is a delusional system whose structure is similar to all earlier biological collectivisms, even if genetic arguments are now no longer used to discriminate between races, but rather to unify them.

Consequently, the Second Ecumene too will be able to formulate the 'unity of the human race' – to adopt the language of the eighteenth century for one moment – not through a shared *physis*, but only through a shared situation. The situation can only be determined ecologically and immunologically, and it points everywhere to the compulsion to civilize cultures. This means that none of the life forms in local traditions are adequate to the new situation with only their onboard means. The 'unity of humans' in their scattered species is now based on the fact that all of them, in their respective regions and histories, have become synchronized, affected from a distance, shamed, torn open, connected and overtaxed: locations of a vital illusion, addresses of capital, points in the homogeneous space to which one returns and which return to themselves – more seen than seeing, more acquired than acquiring, more reached than reaching. Every person must now, in returning to themselves, make sense of the advantage or disadvantage of being who they are. 'Mankind' after globalization consists mostly of those left behind in their own skins, victims of the locational disadvantage of oneself.

The development of the world has, without any philosophy, shifted people away from the middle in an unexpected fashion. In the course of globalization, they not only experience themselves as antiquated, as some theorists of alienation have lamented, but now actually perceive themselves as located on the outside – beings looking at themselves from without, not knowing whether anyone will be at home when they want to get into their own places.

If the exemplary human in the First Ecumene was the wise man who meditated on his dysfunctional relationship with the absolute, and the saint who could feel closer to God than ordinary sinners through grace, then the exemplary human in the Second Ecumene is the world star who will never understand why they had more success than other people, and the anonymous thinker who opens themselves up to the two key experiences of the age: firstly, to constantly recommencing 'revolutions' as the 'presentations of the infinite in the here and now',[6] and secondly, to the shame which affects every thinking life today more than original sin: never rebelling enough against the ubiquitous degradation of all that lives.

On the last orb, the location of the Second Ecumene, there will be no sphere of all spheres – neither an informatically produced nor a world-state sphere, let alone a religious one (for anyone who would join Habermas and Ratzinger in relying on the unifying power of religion would need to be more resilient to disappointment than the people of today). Even the super-inclusive system of the Internet, as manifold as its potential might be, inevitably produces a complementary super-exclusivity. The orb consisting only of a surface is not a house for all, but rather an epitome of markets on which no one can be 'at home'; no one is meant to settle where money, commodities and fictions are changing hands. The global market is a concept for the realization (and demand) that all suppliers and customers should meet in a general externality. As long as the global market or global markets exist, all speculations on the recovery of a domestically or capital city-centred circumspection in an integral interior of humanity are doomed to failure.

If the Middle Ages already proved incapable of placing the world orb and the orb of God within each other concentrically,[7] modernity would only produce even more folly if it attempted the hubristic project of integrating the multitude of cultural and entrepreneurial locations as sub-spheres within a concentrically built monosphere. Marshall McLuhan seems to have underestimated this when he embraced the vision of the global village for a time, before disappointment had caught up with him: 'The media extensions of man are the hominization of the planet.'[8] Today, such words could not even be repeated in missionary sects. As generous as the media theorists expectations were, the dying-out of imperial-centrist world-form creations also destroyed the basis for electronic Catholicism (the central position of the sender).

The last orb allows further constructs only in the horizontal – which does not rule out individual high-rise buildings. It stimulates neighbourhoods, joint ventures and intercultural transactions under artificial, not overly steep skies; it demands forums, podiums, canopies, patronages, alliances and sponsorships; it favours gatherings of interest groups at tables of different formats in conference rooms of graduated sizes. In future, it will no longer support the idea of a super-monosphere or a power-holding centre of all centres.

30

The Immunological Transformation: On the Way to Thin-Walled 'Societies'

From the noisy monotony of the current sociological and political literature on globalization, a number of patterns can be abstracted that have good chances of becoming journalistic universals of a sort for the coming decades, perhaps even centuries. The first of these almost timeless themes is the claim that a new modus vivendi between the local and the global must be negotiated time and again; the second is that political communities 'after modernity' have entered a new constellation 'beyond the nation-state'.[1] The third is that the gaping divide between rich and poor has brought the globalized world to a state of political and moral tension and the fourth is that the progressive consumption of the biosphere along with the pollution of water, air and soil changes 'humanity' willy-nilly into an ecological community of interests whose reflection and dialogue must bring forth a new, far-sighted culture of reason. It is not hard to perceive a common tendency in all these themes: the blurring of traditional notions of political subjects and social units. Wherever one looks, one notes that the most important trends have slipped from the hands of those responsible for them, and that the problem-solvers of yesterday and the problems of today (let alone the problem-solvers of today and the problems of tomorrow) make a poor match.

We intend to translate these perceptions from the sociological debate into our own context: a political poetics of space or 'macrospherology'.[2] After this shift of perspective, all questions of social and personal identity pose themselves in morphological and immunological terms, which is to say in terms of how something resembling liveable forms of 'dwelling' or being-with-oneself-and-one's-own can be accommodated in historically active macro-worlds. Contemporary nervousness about globalization mirrors the fact that with the nation-state, what was previously the largest possible scale of political dwelling – the living and conference room of democratic (or imagined) peoples, as it were – is now subject to negotiation, and that this national living room already has some very unpleasant draughts – most of all in those places where high unemployment rates converge with routines of lamentation at high standards. Looking back, we can see more clearly the extraordinary achievement of the nation-state, which was to offer the majority of those dwelling there a form of domesticity, a simultaneously imaginary and real immune structure, that could be experienced as a convergence of place and self, or as a regional identity in the most favourable sense of the word. This service was performed most impressively where the welfare state had successfully tamed the power state.

The immunological construction of political-ethnic identity has been set in motion, and it is clear that the connection between place and self is not always as stable as the political folklores of territorialism (from ancient agrarian cultures to the modern welfare state) had demanded and pretended. Weakening or dissolving the link of places and selves can allow us to see the two extreme positions that reveal the structure of the social field in an almost experimental state of disintegration: a self without a place and a place without a self. It is clear that all actually existing societies have always had to seek their modus vivendi somewhere between the poles – ideal-typically at the most favourable distance from each extreme position, and one can easily understand that in future too, every genuine political community will have to give an answer to the double imperative of self-determination and place-determination.

The first extreme of dissolution – the *self without a place* – is probably approached most closely by the diaspora Judaism of the previous two millennia, which has been described not unjustly as a people without a land – a fact that Heinrich Heine put in a nutshell when he stated that the Jews are not at home in a country, but rather in a book: the Torah, which they carried with them like a 'portable fatherland'.[3] This profound and elegant comment illuminates a fact that is frequently passed over: 'nomadizing' or 'deterritorialized' groups construct their symbolic immunity and ethnic coherence not – or only marginally – from a supporting soil; rather, their communications amongst themselves act directly as an 'autogenous vessel'[4] in which the participants are enclosed and stay in shape, while the group moves through external landscapes. A landless people rooted in a scriptural tradition, therefore, cannot fall prey to the misconception that has imposed itself on virtually all settled groups throughout human history: understanding the land itself as the container of the people, and viewing their native soil as the a priori of their life's meaning or their identity. This territorial fallacy endures as one of the effective and problematic heirlooms of the sedentary age, as the basic reflex underlying all seemingly legitimate applications of political force. Indeed what is termed 'national defence' relates directly to it. National defence is based on the obsessive equation of place and self – the axiomatic logical error of territorialized reason (which struck the great majority of Israeli citizens after 1948 as a desirable one to make). This error has increasingly been exposed since an unprecedented wave of transnational mobility began to ensure that peoples and territories everywhere qualify their liaison. The trend towards a multi-local self is characteristic of advanced modernity – like the trend towards a polyethnic or denationalized place.

The Indo-American cultural anthropologist Arjun Appadurai has drawn attention to this state of affairs with his conceptual creation of the 'ethnoscape', allowing us to examine issues like the progressive deterritorialization of ethnic connections, or the formation of 'imaginary communities' outside nation-states and the imaginary sharing of the images of life forms from other cultures among countless individuals.[5] As far as Judaism during its period of exile is concerned, its provocation lay in the fact that it constantly reminded the peoples of the Western hemisphere of the seeming paradox and actual scandal of a factually existing self without a place.

At the other extreme, the phenomenon of the *place without a self* becomes increasingly clear. The earth's uninhabitable regions – the white deserts (polar world), the grey ones (high mountains), the green ones (jungles), the yellow ones (sand deserts) and the blue deserts (oceans) – are paradigmatic of this extreme 'selflessness'; the secondary man-made deserts can be placed alongside them. In the context of our investigation of spheric conditions, the latter are of interest by way of contrast as they constitute places with which people do not usually develop any cultivating relationship, let alone attempt any identification. This applies to all transit spaces, in both the narrower and wider sense of the term, be they facilities intended for traffic such as train stations, docks and airports, roads, squares and shopping centres, or complexes designed for limited stays such as holiday villages and tourist cities, factory premises or night shelters. Such places may have their own atmospheres – but these do not depend on a populace or collective self that would be at home in them. By definition, they do not hold on to those who pass through them. They are the alternately overrun or empty no man's lands; the transit deserts that proliferate in the enucleated centres and hybrid peripheries of contemporary 'societies'.

It does not take much analytical effort to see that in these 'societies', globalizing tendencies work against a prior normality – life in massive, ethnic or national containers (along with their specific phantasms of origin and mission) and the unendangered licence to confuse land with self, decisively infringed upon by globalizing tendencies. On the one hand, such 'societies' loosen their regional ties through large populations acquiring unprecedented mobility. On the other hand, there is an increasing number of transit places that cannot be inhabited by those who frequent them. Thus globalizing and mobilizing 'societies' simultaneously approach both the 'nomadic' pole, a self without a place, and the desert pole, a place without a self – with a shrinking middle ground of regional cultures and grounded contentments.

The formal crisis of modern 'mass societies', which is now seen chiefly as a loss of meaning for the nation-state, thus results from the advanced erosion of ethnic container functions. What was previously understood as 'society' and invoked with it was usually, in fact, nothing other than the content of a thick-walled, territorially grounded, symbol-assisted and generally monolingual container – that is, a collective which found its self-assurance in a certain national hermeticism and flourished in redundancies of its own (that could never be entirely understood by strangers).[6] Because of their self-containing qualities, such historical communities – known as peoples – stayed on the point of intersection between self and place and usually relied on a considerable asymmetry between inside and outside; this usually manifested itself in pre-political cultures as naïve ethnocentrism, and at the political level in the substantive difference between inner (domestic) and outer (foreign) policy. The effects of globalization increasingly evened out this difference and asymmetry; the immunity offered by the national container is perceived as increasingly endangered by those who profit from it. Certainly no one who has tasted the advantages of free transnational movement is likely to desire a return to the militant enclosures of older nation-states in earnest, much less the totalitarian self-hypnoses that often characterized tribal life forms. Yet for numerous people today, the purpose and risk of the trend towards a world of thin-walled and mixed 'societies' are neither clear nor welcome. Globalization, Roland Robertson rightly observes, is a 'basically contested process'.[7] The protest against globalization is *also* globalization itself – it is part of the inevitable and indispensable immune reaction of local organs to infections through the larger format of the world.

The psychopolitical challenge of the Global Age, which Martin Albrow aptly describes as a wilful result stage of the Modern Age, lies in the fact that the weakening of container immunities must not be dealt with simply as decadence and loss of form, that is to say as an ambivalent or cynical abetment of self-destruction. What is at stake for the postmoderns is successful new designs for liveable, immune relationships, and these are precisely what can and will develop anew in 'societies' with permeable walls – albeit, as has always been the case, not among all and not for all.

In this context the epochal trend towards individualistic life forms reveals its immunological significance: today, in advanced 'societies', it is individuals who – perhaps for the first time in the history of hominid coexistence – break away from their group bodies as carriers of immune competencies, groups which had to that point functioned primarily as protection. They seek in great numbers to disconnect their happiness and unhappiness from the being-in-shape of the political commune. We are now experiencing what is probably the irreversible transformation of political security collectives into groups with individualistic immune designs. (This trend would remain in force even if a purported or genuine 'return of war' were to lead to a renewed primacy of the political. Such a returned war would certainly have a therapeutic, defensive and immunitary character; the re-militarized individualistic group could only relapse into collectivist moods episodically.)

This tendency manifests itself most clearly in the pilot nation of the Western world, the USA, where the concept of the pursuit of happiness has nominally been the foundation for the 'social contract' since the Declaration of Independence. The centrifugal effects of making individual happiness the guiding concept have thus far been balanced out by the combined energies of communities and civil societies such that the traditional immunological precedence of the group over its members also seemed embodied in that synthetic people, United States Americans. Meanwhile, the tables have been turned: no country, population or culture on earth practises as much biological, psychotechnic and religioid self-concern in parallel with a growing abstinence from political commitments. In the 1996 presidential election, the USA saw its first voter turnout of under 50 per cent (Clinton's re-election). In the November 1998 elections to the House of Representatives and the Senate in 1998, roughly two out of three voters stayed at home (though experts did not view the 38 per cent turnout as a particularly bad result).[8] It was only through an exceptionally hard-fought election campaign that some 60 per cent of eligible voters were mobilized to cast their votes in the re-election of George W. Bush in November 2004. This testifies to a situation in which the majority feel sure that they can largely abandon solidarity with the fates of their political commune – guided by the highly plausible notion that the individual will, in future, no longer (or only in exceptional cases) find their immunological optimum in the national collective, but at best in the solidary system of their own community, or more precisely the victimological collective, though most clearly in private insurance arrangements.

The axiom of the individualistic immune order gained currency in populations of self-centred individuals like some new vital insight: that, ultimately, no one would do for them what they do not do for themselves. The new immunity techniques (in their institutional centre, private insurances and pension funds, and at their individual periphery, dietetics and biotechnology) presented themselves as existential strategies for 'societies' of individuals in which the long road to flexibilization, the weakening of 'object relationships' and the general authorization of disloyal or reversible inter-human relationships had led to the 'goal', to what Spengler rightly prophesied as the final stage of every culture: the state in which it is impossible to determine whether individuals are diligent or decadent (but diligent in what respect, and decadent in relation to which height?[9]). It is the state in which individuals have lost their ability of exemplary world-formation. The individualized humans behaved as if they had realized that the optimum immunization cannot be attained by absorbing 'the world' in a multi-faceted way, but rather by defining one's contact with it very narrowly. As a result, the last metaphorical difference, namely the distinction between noble and common, lost its meaning. The end of the heroic age of discovery and creation was also the end of great men, those all-encompassing individuals who seemed capable of unifying their respective epochs and collectives in themselves. They were followed by the individualistic cycle in which everyone made themselves their own speciality. The consequences are well known. One of them was that the anthropological phantom of the Modern Age, *l'homme monde* – the microcosmic, the variously receptive and expressive, the complete human – disappeared like a face drawn in sand at the edge of the sea.

31

Believing and Knowing:
In hoc signo (sc. globi) vinces

Martin Albrow's concept of the Global Age accommodates the need of a narrative theory for division into phases amid unfinished sequences. It proposes that the era of globalization – in our terminology, terrestrial globalization – must be considered finished, and is now in an indefinitely long period of added time appended to history proper, an added time that constitutes an era in its own right. As noted above, some authors have described this expired epoch as the 'millennium of Europe',[1] or even the 'world history of Europe' – formulations that, however anachronistic and questionable they may be, have the merit of highlighting the asymmetry between the activities of European agents and those of non-Europeans.

What one calls 'asymmetry' in systemic terms means domination from a political perspective. The term 'colonialism' is a catch-all for the procedures and results of 'European expansion', which are now universally deplored.[2] Though this label discards the methods of the period, it cannot ignore their result: the establishment of the world context. Colonialist practice was based on the conviction of the European 'great nations' – and every one of them felt entitled to be great during its times of attack – that unilateralism was their birthright. But what to do if the time of one-sidedness is over and a period of numerous other sides has begun? The recent efforts towards a symmetrical worldview as articulated in post-colonial studies presuppose not only the endogenous expiry of European central power, but also the transition to a different understanding of strike and counterstrike. The concern for symmetry results in alterity being given precedence. One is now even free to conclude that Europeans were discovered by Caribbean natives in October 1492. For the sorrowful discoverers, it subsequently proved wise to collect data about their visitors; today, these archives are open to analysis.

The consequence of the age of European offensives was (one has to repeat it like a postmodern mantra) the development and consolidation of the world system. This implies the interconnection of the global players on several levels: states, business enterprises, banks and stock exchanges, academic life, the art scene, the world of sport, prostitution, the drug trade, arms dealing, and so on. This repercussion-infested system, as unstable as it may seem, for now constitutes the final working level of countless routines that have enabled consideration for spatially distant, but materially close opponents to become the dominant style of being-in-the-world. In its present definition, then, the concept of 'civilization' amounts to tele-realism.

'Terrestrial globalization is finished' – this means that we now know once and for all that one is never the first to reach any place in the world; and one must also explicitly take into account that one cannot speak on any subject in the world independently of the respective discourse. Wherever one looks, the traces of discoverers and previous voices are present in compact forms. The most convincing argument against the ambition to attempt new things in spite of all lies in the conditions themselves – although innovation (or, more precisely, climbing ever higher up the tower of improbabilities) is demanded pro forma incessantly and on all sides. Constantly used routes show the transformation of earlier expeditions into regular traffic; ingrained disciplines ensure that ideas and hypotheses are embedded in academia. If the age of globalization was defined by explorations and pioneering, the Global Age was defined by travel schedules and increasing traffic density – including density of chatter. Adventuring belongs to globalization, and reservation to globality. The discoverers in the age of globalization boarded departing ships with muskets, machetes and vague maps, while the lecturers of the Global Age board aeroplanes with reservation cards and finished scripts.

One can best explain the continuous and the novel aspects of the globalization era and the Global Age by drawing an analogy with the saturation of urban cultures. Most contemporary metropolises have grown through several centuries of settlement, planning and building; nonetheless, thanks to regional booms, some major cities like Kuala Lumpur, Shanghai or Berlin are currently experiencing architectural fevers whose results will influence the silhouettes of tomorrow. The constitutive phases of urban formation, however, ended some time ago for most traditional metropolises; what follows is a crystallization phase in which buildings are modified through remodellings, extensions and superstructures – the key terms here are interconnection, optimization and aestheticization. Where only very little can be newly erected, one must make more intensive use of what is already standing. The alliance of traffic policy and culture-city marketing becomes characteristic of this phase; the cities of the successful want to be event locations, 'life quality providers' and nodal points in metropolitan corridors, which is why the construction of high-speed roads between capital cities expresses the ambitions of crystallized city culture as strikingly as the building of such indispensable urban collectors as exhibition centres, sports arenas, museums of modern art and branches of international hotel chains.[3]

Just as one meanwhile finds crystallized urban cultures at all focal points in the world, there is also a routine internationality and interculturality developing in the world system, embodied in diplomacies, markets, academic organizations and providers of tour-compatible music. Similarly, one finds medical institutions, police forces, museums and secret services striving for transnational hook-up. Viewed from areas of affluence, the world, generally speaking, gives the impression of a thoroughly colonized space – or, as the word 'colony' is frowned upon in common parlance today: a web of spaces that have imposed a self-determined civil order on themselves, usually the respective nation-state constitution, which has already ceded certain responsibilities to supra-national authorities (UN, IMF, EU), over ethnic substrates. With the establishment of this political-cultural network, the age of globalization has reached its immanent conclusion.

I propose here that the era of terrestrial globalization is the only one that can be termed 'world history' or 'history' without adding any epithets. Its content is the drama of the earth's disclosure as the carrier of local cultures and its compression into an interconnected and foamed world context. If one takes this definition of 'history' seriously, it follows that only the sequence of events between 1492 and 1945 can be characterized thus, while the existence of peoples and cultures before and after this does not display 'historical' qualities – though the exact dates remain open for debate. Naturally all groups, institutions and practices are always subject to the laws of becoming; they go through their periods at the quiet pace of varying repetition, and experience the leaps and catastrophes that interrupt longer series. This waiting and drifting have nothing to do with the

things that happened in 'history', however. Only history gives narrative answers to the ontological questions: how did we arrive at the
conditions of the Global Age? What enabled the disclosure of the
earth as the carrier of the connection between cultures? How were
Europeans able to draw their maps and spread their networks over
the inhabited world? And what part did modern money play, in its
threefold guise as trading capital, industrial capital and financial
capital?

'History' is the myth of the birth of the world system.[4] The only
rightful way to tell it would be as the heroic epic of terrestrial globalization – the novel of successful one-sidedness dictated by the
European actors to their chroniclers. This heroic song goes far beyond
the usual complicity between the heroes and their singers; in the
course of being sung, it unfolds as the untellably long grand narrative
of the self-provocation of 'mankind'. As often as one might vary it,
no version will ever quite reach the level of the event.

This hubristic epic, often attempted but never rendered adequately
in all its details, forms an eminent section of the universal history of
the coincidental, which, despite its contingency, seems infused with
an internal sense of purpose. The globalization account is not only a
history in the strict sense of the word because, as is proper, it has a
beginning, a middle and an end; it is also history in the teleological
sense, as it holds the criterion for its conclusion within itself.

We have symbolically laden scenes to mark its beginning:
Columbus's three caravels left the 'bar of Saltés' near Palos at 8 a.m.
on Friday 3 August 1492,[5] heading for the Canary Islands – with
consequences that will be discussed here. Land was sighted after
sixty-nine days, and on the seventieth, another Friday, the men set
foot in the New World.[6] In the autumn of the same year, Martin
Behaim presented his 'earth apple' to the councillors of Nuremberg;
he brought the terrestrial truth to the Franconian trading town. The
end is marked by equally clear images: during the Nuremberg Rally
of 1937, Hitler had the Behaim Globe brought to his hotel, Deutscher
Hof – firstly to cast an occasional glance at the restoration work on
the heavily blackened piece, which he had financed, and secondly to
draw motivation for his imperial plans from the sight of that venerable object. At the Bretton Woods conference in July 1944, the agreement on the gold exchange standard of the dollar and the pound
sterling established the first binding world currency of the Global
Age; in 1969, American astronauts brought back photographs of the
rising earth from their moon voyage. Between these dates lie millions
of scenes that all reinforce the same point: life punishes those who
do not take the globe seriously.

Towards the end of the Middle Ages, the hypothesis that the earth
is spherical, and can thus be adequately represented by an earth globe
with two-dimensional images of landmasses and seas, did not occupy
more than a handful of theologians, cartographers and merchants
stimulated by long-distance appetites. For the vast majority of
Europeans from the sixteenth century to the American Declaration
of Independence, it was merely a tentative speculation without notable
effects on their own lives, even after the voyages of Columbus, Vasco
da Gama and Magellan had brought about a clear empirical vote in
favour of this onetime assumption. Certainly the maps gradually
became more precise, atlases, globes and planispheres appeared in
princely libraries, and the new media of earth knowledge found their
way into the studies of bourgeois households – and yet the reality
content of the globe-image continued, for the great majority of
Europeans, to be an uncertain and more or less trivial factor. The
roundness of the earth was one of those truths that was only caught
up by its providential recipients centuries after being made public.

For some actors, however, the hypothesis quickly became a faith
strong enough to stake their lives on. In the cases of Columbus,
Magellan and del Cano, faith went in search of intellect. For this faith
to declare itself, it required seaworthy ships and crews who could be
induced by money and good words to accept the madness of the
captains. Thanks to a happy coincidence, the payroll of the 1492
crews has survived; it states that the *piloto* Sancho Ruiz de Gama
received twenty ducats for participating in the journey, the *marinero*
Juan de Moguer four thousand maravedís, and so on.[7] The implicit
creed of the early circumnavigators can only be reconstructed from
the acts and legacies of these men, however. It might have resembled
the following:

*Credo in unam terram rotundam, vitae matrem, fontem divitiarum,
populorum domum, et in marem universalem, fecundam naviga-
bilemque, palatium ventorum, amicam gubernatoris vectorisque, et in
aerem liberam, ubique respirabilem, velivolantium motricem velorum,
libertatum omnium aulam.*

[I believe in one round earth, the mother of life, the source of riches,
the house of peoples, and in the universal sea, fertile and navigable,
the palace of winds, the friend of the helmsmen and the passenger, and
in the free air, breathable everywhere, mover of fast-sailing sails, hall
of all freedoms.]

Columbus, as we know, was driven by the hope of finding enough
gold in the West to finance a crusade to liberate the Holy Sepulchre
from Muslim rule – and in this sense too, the westward route would

open up the eastward one: this Christophorus was not the last to place the Modern Age in the service of the Middle Ages.[8] And yet: after Magellan and del Cano, after Francis Drake and Henry Hudson, allegiance to the globality of the earth became stronger each decade, culminating in a doctrine whose catholicity was a match for any church orthodoxy. Like the Christian faith, belief in the orb on which we live and move and have our being had not only to be recited, but also tested in practice. The statement that the earth was spherical ceased to be an esoteric hypothesis, and began to merge with the central convictions of modern humans. Faith includes the ontological function of 'being serious about an idea'; it means taking the step from imagining to being.

Thus the account of the discovery and interconnection of the earth tells a story that is a history of faith from start to finish. It tells of the faith of the discoverers who did not doubt that they would find new things, of the conquerors who looked at the horizon until their prey appeared, and of the seafarers who clung in all seriousness to the claim that one could travel around the earth and still return home. The impossible became a reality: they found the new things, the prey appeared on the horizons, and the ships returned – those that had not smashed on reefs and come to rest at the bottom of the sea. For the actors in these events, there was ultimately only one possible explanation for this finding, appearing and returning: God had called them to be discoverers, conquerors and homecomers.

In retrospect, the successes of the European globonauts take on a different complexion. We understand today that the belief in the spherical shape of the earth was not a belief in the reality of fantasies. The faith of the *marineros* was rewarded by the goodwill of the real – it gave ontological weight to the hypotheses, maps, images, stories, perceptions and feelings concerning the world, to the point where the object itself gained the support of the believers. From that point, the increasing conviction of the earth's being-round, being-whole and being-navigable determined the taste of the real. Just as there are paranoids who are actually persecuted, there are seafarers who fancy there is a water-covered, round earth and genuinely sail around it.

At this point in our deliberations, the curtain rises for the appearance of a great word: the faith of the geomanic on the eve of the sixteenth century was a faith in the *truth* – initially concealed but then uncovered, once distant but then brought closer. Because the uncovering, approaching and disclosure of the spherical earth and its treasures took centuries, world history existed as action, as a transcript and postscript of the great adventure; because the uncovering and approaching of the earth were relatively finite tasks, the history that tells of them needed – taken with a grain of salt – a beginning, a middle and an end. In fact, the goal-directedness of its course is so suggestive that an enlightened reader would be more likely to suspect some distortion through the retrospective view than a real event. Are we not dealing with one of the usual teleological insinuations, hinting to us that we can draw conclusions about original intentions from coincidental later results?

With the history examined here, the case is different: for half a millennium, the notion of the round earth settled in the consciousnesses of Western people and their media like a self-fulfilling prophecy. It drew a very small, active minority of these into an unprecedented departure – a pragmatic mixture of a conquering expedition, apostolic history and research process. But the idea of the earth's spherical shape did not remain merely a symbolic figure; monogeism was more than a postulation of beautiful physics. The carriers of this true, as yet unproved idea – tough seafarers, patient cartographers, metal-addicted monarchs and noble-minded spice merchants – piled proof upon proof until the last deniers, ignoramuses and indifferents had to yield before the advancing evidence. The story of the Modern Age reads like a long commentary on the statement *In hoc signo vinces*[9] – but now the *signum globi* is meant, not the *signum crucis*. The sign of the orb trumps that of the cross: it is this observation that contains 'history'. As long as the cross and the orb were even, the outcome of 'history' still seemed open. The conclusion of the overtaking manoeuvre, which relegated the cross to second place, closed the field on which the phenomenon of 'history' could proceed as the success story of belief in the orb.

The globe mission was only resolved for the people of today through its all-pervading success. Since no remotely sensible person would dream of questioning the validity of the belief in the round earth, the new sign paled in a similar fashion to the old; it perished through its own redundancy. Possible doubters of monogeism must tolerate being labelled revisionists. The faith of the seafarers changed into knowledge, and that knowledge became trivial and specialized; the earth-believers of the sixteenth century are now postmodern geoscientists – eleven thousand of them gathered in Nice in April 2003 for a Euro-American working conference.[10] On the flight, most of them would only have cast a brief glance from the air at the strange object of their theoretical desire.

In the wake of the new state of knowledge, all pre-Columbian and pre-Copernican notions of the earth's form and location in the cosmos have had to undergo demotion to obsolete 'world pictures'. With his interpretation of the Modern Age as the 'Time of the World Picture', then, Heidegger did not quite hit the mark. He would only have been right *toto genere* if Europeans had never been bold enough to sail around the earth in their ships. Because the earth was circumnavigated, however, and because there has consequently been valid new knowledge of the earth since then – even if all we see of it at home are the pale maps and their echoes in the ranting of imperialists – all statements about the world made by non-circumnavigators, rooted rhapsodists and shamans must be declared 'world pictures' in their visible and invisible landscapes. They are indeed no more than past world-figments, figures with no real knowledge or idea of what to do next, regional poetries from the time before encompassing seafaring. Although the knowledge of the moderns about the world is bound to visual representations to an unknown extent, it does not – as Heidegger failed to recognize – ultimately constitute a picture, but rather the roaring of the oceans in the bodies of seafarers. Anyone who places their ear against an earth globe should hear the breaking of the waves in it.

Schopenhauer noted the following in the introduction to *The World as Will and Representation* concerning the philosophically sound human being after the transcendental-philosophical turn: 'It immediately becomes clear and certain to him that he is not acquainted with either the sun or the earth, but rather only with an eye that sees a sun, with a hand that feels an earth, and that the surrounding world exists only as representation [. . .].'[11] From the perspective of seafarers and all others active in globalization, one would have to add that in future there will not only be an earth for the feeling hand. After Magellan and Mercator, it became clear and certain that we only know the ships that have sailed around the earth, and only the maps and globes in which the truth of these great voyages is represented. Now we are also familiar with the telephones and monitors that provide us with notions of voices and pictures from the other side of the world.

The success of the earth-sphere mission was so overwhelming that it is no longer even perceived as such by its heirs. The Christians of the post-Constantine era, faced with the wondrous spread of their faith from the Sea of Galilee to the Milvian Bridge, had felt compelled to call upon the Holy Spirit, which had decided that the church would triumph over the empire. The people of the postmodern era content themselves with the view that the earth was always round, and the truth had to come out sooner or later. When it comes to stable triviality, not even a Holy Spirit can achieve anything. Maybe help from such powers would be dispensable if we could call to mind with sufficient intensity how the world finally became the terrestrial orb. Such a narrative would prove *en passant* that every single scene could have taken place quite differently, whereas all the episodes together, with any number of changes to their content and sequence, could still not have failed to arrive at a state of realized globality. When the time was ripe, the FACT revealed itself in the lives of the seamen and the logbooks of the pilots.

Some 'anti-globalization activists' in recent times have openly stated their belief that it would have been better if humans had never reached the global stage – or, having informed themselves, had avoided the high seas and remained in their villages and small towns. But what is that if not a belated form of disbelief in the message that the earth constitutes a navigable unity – accompanied by the doubt that people can react productively to the truth about the orb beneath their feet? The unbelievers would evidently have preferred to remain Ptolemaians. They favour the provincial, plant-like mode of being for humans because they believe the price of the truth is too high; who can find sufficient arguments against them? Speaking of the willingness among Europeans to suffer (and make others suffer) for the new to become, Immanuel Wallerstein declared: 'It was to Europe's credit that it was done, since without the thrust of the sixteenth century the modern world would not have been born and, for all its cruelties, it was better that it was born than that it had not been.'[12] If philosophy too were able to make declarations of belief, this would be one of them. If all that exists is essentially good, then its goodness must also extend to what is becoming. Could the world-becoming of the earth be an exception to this?

The logical consequence of these reflections is, as hinted above, to demand that the concept of 'history', in the sense of world history, should in future be limited to a relatively short sequence of events: those between 1492 – the date of Columbus's first voyage – and 1945, or 1974, the year in which the last Portuguese colonies separated from the motherland in the wake of the Carnation Revolution. There are two attractive merits to this reduction: firstly, it can be used to contain the normative excesses of evolutionism, which sought to impose the capitalist path of development in its European variety on all peoples and cultures – in keeping with the dogma 'as in the West, so on earth'. Secondly, this restriction can preserve the productive elements of earlier theorems about the 'end of history' in a minimalist version. The 'end' in this case is a state in which, for the vast majority of earth-dwellers, the geographical image of the earth globe speaks the truth about their situation. The 'end of history' can be expressed in a near-tautology: the history of the 'world' reaches its end when the picture of the world as earth is more or less complete and has been universally disseminated. Once this picture has established itself, it is no longer especially important who drew it first; the decisive point is that most have accepted it as the valid representation of their situation in the terrestrial context.

32

Post-History

With the transition to the Global Age – marked by the confirmation of the irreducible diversity of cultures, albeit one that requires taming for civilizatory purposes, in the framework of the crystallized world system – the added time after the official Modern Age has begun. Since 1945, it has been clear that the history-making potency of the carriers of European expansion has expired. The Old World has exhausted its first strike capability in the disclosure of the planet and burned up its surplus energies in two major wars, of which the second was the almost unavoidable consequence of the far more avoidable first. Since then, the agents of the resulting constellation have had to write scripts with a non-European emphasis for their interactions – scripts that perhaps still work on the background assumption that the forming of the world system took place in the known fashion, but otherwise have more important concerns to address.[1] Looking to Europe's past has no significance for the projection of the world's future as a whole. The European present, by contrast, has become a model in a different way, as it holds an almost fully matured concept of post-imperial politics – a concept that is also beginning to seduce Americans who have grown weary of America.[2] As an example of a gentle world power, it could soon be encouraging others to follow suit, especially in Asia and South America. As far as the utility of history for life is concerned, it consisted after 1945 primarily in gathering together the files for possible damage surveys. Moralized history names addresses for the victims' return to the scene of the crime – where they hope the perpetrators will also have returned, without taking into account that this only happens in fairy tales. It forms a global Gauck Office that provides access to the files documenting the harassment of humans by humans.[3]

Otherwise, 'history' is precisely what is commonly known as water under the bridge; the decolonization after 1945 and the military stalemate of the Cold War give an idea of just how quickly it flows. In 1947, India and Pakistan broke away from the association of the British empire; after 1953, the French withdrew from Indochina; the majority of African states achieved independence in the course of the 1950s and 1960s; in 1974, as mentioned above, the leftovers of the Portuguese empire evaporated; and in 1990, with the collapse of the Soviet Union, the last Old European missionary power left the stage and its disintegration released the world's last tribute states into capitalism or chaos. Regarding the national communism of the Chinese, one can note that it does not hold a world project – but remains significant because it proves the separability of capitalism and democracy on a grand scale – a fact that makes law-and-order politicians all over the world dream. It could, therefore, become the paradigm for a basic line of the twenty-first century that is already becoming visible: the turn of the world system towards authoritarian capitalism.

It would be naïve to think that the view of things proposed here could gain currency among historians and the general public without further ado. The resistance of the profession will ensure that the illusion of still living 'in history' remains virulent for a long time. One can easily evade the realization of the world system's post-historical character in the Global Age by continuing, as is customary in the trade, to refer to every sequence of events at both the macro- and micro-level as history. Thanks to this terminological rigidity, any matter can be 'taken historically' – in the great night of history, one grey cat more or less is not so important. In this way, none of the things that make a difference between heaven and earth elude the tireless historians. Wherever something occurs, they adjust it to fit the mould of historical material, convinced as they are of the utility of their activities for the common good.

They write the history of menstruation in the Middle Ages; they write the history of projectiles from the Ice Age hunting spear to intercontinental missiles; they write the history of aerosol art and gangsta rap; the history of the ten largest private fortunes in the world; the history of pirate copies since China opened up; and they also write the history of body-oriented psychotherapy in the Sauerland. They write the history of plastic materials, the history of contributions by Afro-Caribbean intellectuals to the critique of Eurocentrism, the history of fatty degeneration among pets in the USA before 9/11, the history of Nobel Prizes and the history of artificial sweeteners. They stop neither at the history of disabled sports nor at the history of seating furniture in Africa and the history of inflations. The members of the profession behave as if they had been treated with the trance-inducing axiom that there is only one science: the science of history. Those with a 'senior point of view' write the history of historiography, declaring their conviction that history has not ended yet – notwithstanding theses to the contrary penned by insolent philosophers.

But it would be hasty, at the very least, to take the mass appearance of historians as evidence of the continuation of 'history'. One of the strongest signs pointing to the post-historical modality of contemporary streams of events can be found precisely in the activities of an internationally scattered guild of historians, whose approach to finding subject matter constantly opens up new fields. Their existence testifies to the crystallization of every kind of past into the plasma for a history of everything. Whether something happened a few weeks or a hundred thousand years ago is of secondary importance for the universal past-worker.

Yet alongside neutralized history, which, like an academic Midas, turns everything it touches into monographs, morally oriented discussion of the past and the future in nations and institutions is thriving as much as it always has. In historical groups and institutes, this form of historical awareness constitutes an effective mythodynamic function that acts as a psychological tool in the struggle of collectives for survival. Thanks to mediological enlightenment, it is increasingly being understood how much the success collectives on the world stage, be they nations, peoples, cultures or businesses, are controlled by autoplastic communications – with self-building histories occupying an especially prominent position. There is no longer any need to prove that the continued survival of mythodynamics in long-term groups tells us nothing whatsoever about the progress of 'history' as such.

Against this background, it becomes clear that the European historicism which Nietzsche fought out of an anachronistic, heroic mentality was no more than the twilight of the era of terrestrial globalization. We know today that this twilight lasted for over a century, and entailed the destruction of Old Europe in its last battles for 'world power'. During that time, the historians in the precise sense of the word were those authors whose writings described the historical complex as such, or local aspects thereof: the five-hundred-year drama of the world system's formation, including the endgame-like 'age of extremes'. This drama also features the two major attempts at a one-sided breakthrough to post-historical civilization: the USA and the Soviet Union.[4] It is hardly surprising in this context that most classical historians are limited to a clearly nationally oriented perspective. The grand narratives of the modern nations and their role in the world were, on the whole, not merely presented as auto-suggestive histories of education and freedom among collective subjects; often enough, they directly supported the imperial pretentions of the narrating nations. Only historians of art, philosophy and economics had freer access to extra- and supra-national views; it was among them that the spirit of academic pacifism had the best chances of shaking off the leash of the noble lie in the service of one's own power collective.

An important fact should be pointed out to critics of Eurocentrism in this context: there has never been a shared plan for European world-taking, so *in actu*, there has never been a centralized inspirational narrative detailing the actions of a conquering collective either. Aside from the earth globe and cartographical works, the colonial powers did not have any higher coordinating authority – leaving aside certain powerless universal gestures from the Holy See. With this lack of coordination, there was only a loose number of national projections on the grand scale – a world history of Spain, a world history of England, a world history of France, a world history of Portugal, and perhaps also a world history of the Netherlands. As far as the world history of the Germans is concerned, the historian's courtesy encourages silence for the time being. The splintering of political expansions was repeated at the level of the Christian missionary powers. Far from following any ecclesiological master plan, the Jesuits, the Franciscans, the Dominicans, the Moravian Church and other agents of faith all worked on their respective neo-apostolic empires.[5] Initially, all these histories describing the spread of salvation across the inhabited earth were still written entirely in the heat of actions and their reflexes in the national and ecclesiastical memory. Need it be emphasized that the time has now come to file all of these away in a larger archive? Because there has never been a single actor known as 'Europe', only the competing national imperialisms of colonizing countries and the networks of rival missionary orders, the common criticism of Eurocentrism mostly come to nothing. The agent targeted by this criticism is a post-colonial fiction: Europe only exists as a subject of self-criticism and an object of outside criticism *post festum*. The EU became possible once all member nations had entered their post-imperial situations.

33

The Crystal Palace

Among those nineteenth-century authors who observed the advanced games of aggressive world-disclosure with critical reserve from the 'retarded' Eastern European periphery, it is Fyodor Dostoyevsky who proved the most prescient. In his tale *Notes from Underground*, published in 1864 – which was not only the founding certificate of modern *ressentiment* psychology, but also the first expression of an anti-globalization stance, assuming such backdating is legitimate – there is a formulation that encapsulates the world-becoming of the world at the incipient end of the globalization age with unsurpassed metaphorical power: I am thinking of the reference to Western civilization as a 'crystal palace'. On his visit to London in 1862, Dostoyevsky had visited the site built for the International Exhibition in South Kensington (which was meant to surpass the Crystal Palace of 1851 in size) and instinctively grasped the immeasurable symbolic and programmatic dimensions of the hubristic construction. As the exhibition building bore no name of its own, it seems likely that Dostoyevsky transferred the name 'Crystal Palace' to it.[1]

The gigantic original, designed by the garden building expert Joseph Paxton, had been erected in London's Hyde Park in the autumn of 1850 as a prefabricated construction, and opened on 1 May 1851 in the presence of the young Queen Victoria (before being rebuilt on an even larger scale in the suburb of Sydenham Hill in 1854); until its destruction in an enormous blaze in 1936, it was considered a technological world wonder – a triumph of serial production with military precision.[2] From that point on, a new aesthetics of immersion began its triumphal march through modernity. The psychedelic capitalism of today was already a *fait accompli* in the almost immaterialized, artificially climatized building. In the course of the first world exhibition it hosted some 17,000 exhibitors, of whom 7,200 came from Great Britain and its thirty-two colonies alone. With its construction, the principle of the interior overstepped a critical boundary: from then on, it meant neither the middle- or upper-class home nor its projection onto the sphere of urban shopping arcades; rather, it began to endow the outside world as a whole with a magical immanence transfigured by luxury and cosmopolitanism. Once it had been converted into a large hothouse and an imperial culture museum, it revealed the timely tendency to make both nature and culture indoor affairs. And, although the Crystal Palace was not originally intended for musical performances, it became the site of remarkable concerts, anticipating the era of stadium pop with classical programmes presented to huge audiences.[3]

Not long afterwards, Dostoyevsky associated the sceptical impressions from his London visit with the intense aversions he felt when reading Chernyshevsky's 1863 novel *What Is to Be Done?*, developing the most powerful vision of civilization critique in the nineteenth century from this combination of ideas. In his resolutely pro-Western book, which enjoyed considerable fame at the time, he had announced, with consequences that extended all the way to Lenin, the birth of the New Human Being, who, having found the technological solution to the social question, would live with its kind in a communal palace of glass and metal – the archetype of living communities in the East and the West. Chernyshevsky's culture palace had been designed as a climatized luxury shell in which there would be an eternal spring of consensus. Here the sun of good intentions would shine day and night, and the peaceful coexistence of all with all could be taken for granted. Boundless sentimentality would characterize the internal climate, and an overstretched humanitarian domestic morality would result in a spontaneous empathy of all with the fates of all. For Dostoyevsky, the image of the whole of 'society' moving into the palace of civilization symbolized the will of the Western branch of humanity to conclude the initiative it had started – to make the world happy and achieve mutual understanding between peoples – in a post-historically relaxed state. After the writer had become acquainted with existence in a 'house of the dead' through his deportation to Siberia, the prospect of a closed house of life now revealed itself to him: biopolitics begins as enclosure-building.

This is where the motif of the 'end of history' began its triumph. The visionaries of the nineteenth century, like the communists of the twentieth, already understood that after the expiry of combatant history, social life could only take place in an expanded interior, a domestically organized and artificially climatized inner space. Whatever one considers real history to be, it should – like its spearheads, namely seafaring and wars of expansion – remain an epitome of open-air enterprises. If historical struggles are to lead to eternal peace, however, social life in its entirety would have to be integrated into a protective shell. No more historic events could take place under such conditions – at most, domestic accidents. Accordingly, there would no longer be politics or voters, only mood competitions between parties and the fluctuations among their consumers. Who can deny that in its primary aspects, the Western world – especially the European Union, after its relative completion in May 2004 and the signing of its constitution in October of the same year – embodies precisely such a great interior today?

This gigantic hothouse of relaxation is devoted to a merry and hectic cult of Baal for which the twentieth century suggested the term 'consumerism'. The capitalist Baal that Dostoyevsky saw in the shocking sight of the world exhibition palace and the amusement-seeking London masses takes shape as much in the enclosure itself as in the hedonistic tumult within it. Here a new doctrine of Last Things is formulated as a dogmatics of consumption. The construction of the crystal palace can only be followed by the 'crystallization' of circumstances as a whole – with this fateful term, Arnold Gehlen follows on directly from Dostoyevsky. Crystallization means the intention to generalize boredom normatively and prevent the re-irruption of 'history' into the post-historical world; furthering and protecting benevolent ossification would be the goal of all future state power. Naturally the boredom guaranteed by the constitution will cloak itself in the project form: its psychosocial signature tune is the atmosphere of departure, its basic key optimism. Everything in the post-historical world must actually be geared towards the future, as it offers the only promise that can be made unconditionally to an association of consumers: that comfort and convenience will never stop flowing and growing. Thus the concept of human rights is inseparable from the great departure to comfort, in that the freedoms those rights entail prepare the self-fulfilment of the consumer. They are, consistently enough, only on everyone's lips where there is an intention to set up the institutional, legal and psychodynamic sub-structure of consumerism.

Dostoyevsky was quite convinced, however, that eternal peace in the crystal palace would mentally compromise its inhabitants. In humans, the Christian psychologist tells us, relaxation inevitably leads to the release of evil. In the climate of universal comfort, what was once original sin comes to light as trivial freedoms to do evil. In addition, once evil is deprived of its historical pretexts and utilitarian facades, it can only crystallize into its quintessential form in the state of post-historical boredom (*skuka*): purged of all excuses, it now becomes apparent – perhaps surprisingly for the naïve – that evil possesses the quality of a mere mood. It manifests itself as a fathomless positing, a wilful taste for making oneself and others suffer, a roaming destruction with no specific reason. Modern evil is unemployed negativity – an unmistakable product of the post-historical situation. Its popular edition is the sado-masochism of the middle-class household, where harmless people tie each other to the bedpost for the sake of new experiences, and its luxury version is aesthetic snobbery, which asserts the primacy of coincidental preference. On the youth markets, where the *prêt-à-revolter* is distributed, integrated evil appears as cool. Worthy or unworthy – both depend on a roll of the dice. In boredom, one thing is valued and the other discarded for no particular reason. Whether one joins Kant and calls this evil radical is, in real terms, of no consequence. As its root cannot extend any deeper than the mood, there is nothing to be gained by calling it 'radical' – this raises an ontological thunderstorm to declare that no one knows where evil ultimately comes from.

Do we still need to point out that Heidegger's great phenomenology of boredom from 1929/30 can only be understood as an escape from the crystal palace established throughout Europe (albeit heavily damaged by the effects of war), whose inner moral and cognitive climate – the inevitable absence of any valid conviction and the superfluity of all personal decisions – is grasped more clearly in those deliberations than anywhere else? With his description of inauthentic existence in the notorious sections on the 'They' (probably inspired by Kierkegaard's invectives against 'the audience' in *A Literary Review*) in *Being and Time* (1927), Heidegger prepared his investigation into the basic disposition of bored Dasein. This is where the phenomenological revolt against the hardships of residing in the technological shell took form. What he later calls 'enframing' [*Ge-stell*] is presented in detail for the first time here – especially in terms of inauthentic, self-deprived existence. Where everyone is the other and no one themselves, humans are cheated of their ecstasy, their loneliness, their own decisions, and their own direct connection to the absolute outside, namely death. Mass culture, humanism and biologism are the cheerful masks that, according to the insights of philosophers, conceal the profound boredom of an existence devoid of challenge. The task of philosophy would then be to shatter the glass roof over one's own head and directly make the individual the monstrous once again.

Anyone who remembers the phenomenon of punk, which haunted youth cultures in the 1970s and 1980s, has a second example to illustrate the connection between the omnipresent fluidum of boredom and generalized aggression. In a sense, Heidegger was the punk philosopher of the 1920s, an angry young intellectual who shook at the imprisoning bars of institutional philosophy – not only those, however, but also the bars of urban comfort and the welfare state's systems of existential expropriation. To appreciate his philosophical motifs – that is to say, the core of temporal logic in his reflections – one must recognize them as an attempt wilfully to re-dramatize the post-historical world of boredom, even at the price of making catastrophe the teacher of life. In this sense, Heidegger could have said of the 'national revolution' to which he temporarily showed allegiance that an age of re-historization had begun in that time and place, and that he not only was there, but had also thought it in advance and heroically deduced its meaning. As the dramaturge of a being that was meant to take place anew, Heidegger articulated the aim of escaping post-historical shallowness from the position of the centre of reflection that was Germany, allowing history to return as if at the last moment. By this logic, one should note, 'history' is medially suffered rather than made. As the only people capable of suffering from the open and monstrous, the Germans should have their turn on a grand scale once more and call upon the world to witness their passion. According to the philosopher, they would have been entitled to prove that amid the comfortable and the arbitrary, there is still an 'evidence' that can command historical actions – an evidence that presents itself more readily to the obedient ear than the sceptical eye. For no one can see outside, but there are some who hear the call from without. Had the Germans achieved what Heidegger's fabulation expected of them, they would have made it clear to friends and foes alike that they were the ones for whom the light of necessity was shining as if for the last time.[4]

The historico-philosophical might of Dostoyevsky's crystal palace metaphor can best be judged by placing it next to Walter Benjamin's interpretation of the Parisian arcades. The comparison is a natural one, for in both cases, an architectural form was declared the key to understanding the capitalist condition of the world. Viewed synchronously, it immediately becomes clear why Benjamin falls behind Dostoyevsky – even though the latter contented himself with a rather laconic poetic vision, while the former immersed himself in studying his subject for many years. Benjamin's investigations of being-in-the-world as dazzlement by the capitalist Maya were doomed to implausibility through their choice of object, especially as they took the risk, from the outset, of explaining using an anachronistic phenomenon to explain a current one: they remained fixated on an architecturally, economically, urbanistically and aesthetically obsolete type of building, which was then meant to carry the full burden of a hermeneutics of capital. The well-known statement that he had wanted to write a 'prehistory of the nineteenth century' using the arcades reveals Benjamin's unclear pretensions in searching for the timeless within the outdated. Benjamin wanted to see the ciphers of alienation in all expressions of the modern monetary context, as if not only the good Lord was in the details, as Spinozists and Warburgians believe,[5] but also the Adversary. The ideology of the detail fed off the supposition that exchange value, the *genius malignus* of the modern world which, supposedly, is otherwise invisible, takes form in the ornaments of commodity and reveals itself in the arabesques of arcade architecture. Following such a superstition of details, Benjamin's investigations became stuck in subterranean library studies, forced into a dead end by a constrained ingenuity. The more material they accumulated, the more they buried the enterprise's fruitful idea of exposing the interior-and-context-creating power of the capitalist modus vivendi. Benjamin's interpretation of the arcades was inspired by the realistic, albeit trivial Marxist observation that the shiny surfaces of the commodity world conceal a less pleasant, sometimes bleak working world; this insight was distorted by the suggestion that the capitalist world context as such was hell – populated by damned souls who regrettably learned no political lessons from their damnation. With dark allusions, he implied that the pretty world under glass was a metamorphosis of Dante's inferno. Against this background, it was impossible to gain an idea of how the arcades could be converted democratically, and, more importantly still, to clarify whether it would be conceivable, or at least desirable, for the 'masses' to break out of the matrix or 'field' of capitalism. Viewed as a whole, Benjamin's studies document the vengeful joy of the melancholic who compiles an archive of evidence to show that the world has gone wrong.

If one were to attempt a continuation of Benjamin's important suggestions for the later twentieth and early twenty-first centuries, they would require not only a number of indispensable methodological rectifications, but also a fundamental re-orientation. They would have to be adapted to the architectural models of today – above all the shopping malls (which, from the opening of Southdale near

Minneapolis, the first complex of this kind, in October 1954 spread through the USA and the rest of the world like an epidemic), exhibition centres, major hotels, sports arenas and indoor amusement parks. Such studies could then bear titles closer to *The Crystal Palaces Project* or *The Hothouses Project*, or ultimately even *The Space Stations Project*.[6] The arcades undeniably embodied a suggestive spatial idea in the age of incipient consumerism – they carried out in a public interior that merging of the salon and the universe which Benjamin found so stimulating. In the researcher's eyes, they were the 'temples of commodity capital', streets 'of lascivious commerce only',[7] a projection of the Oriental bazaar into the bourgeois world symbolizing the metamorphosis of all things by the light of buyability – the scene of a *féerie* that enchants customers into rulers of the world for the duration of their visit. The Crystal Palace, however, the one in London that housed the Great Exhibition and later a leisure park (devoted to 'education of the people'), and even more so the one in Dostoyevsky's text, which was intended to make 'society' as a whole an exhibit in itself, already pointed far beyond the architecture of the arcades. Benjamin made frequent reference to the building, but saw little more in it than a magnified arcade (just as he saw only 'cities of arcades' in Fourier's plans for utopian communities) – here his admirable physiognomic vision let him down. He disregarded the basic rule of media analysis, namely that the format is the message. For while the elitist arcades, which never reached a large scale, served the 'cosification'[8] and urbane *mise-en-scène* of the world of commodities in a sheltered promenade, the gigantic Crystal Palace – the valid prophetic building form of the nineteenth century (which was immediately copied all over the world) – already anticipated an integral, experience-oriented, popular capitalism in which no less than the comprehensive absorption of the outside world in a fully calculated interior was at stake. The arcades formed a canopied intermezzo between streets or squares; the crystal palace, on the other hand, invoked the idea of an enclosure so spacious that one might never have to leave it. (A possibility Dostoyevsky went through with the thought experiment of a 'fenced-in palace' in *The House of the Dead*.) Its growing integrativity, admittedly, did not serve the elevation of capitalism to a religion that universalized guilt and debt, as Benjamin surmised in an eccentric early fragment.[9] On the contrary, it led to the replacement of the psychosemantic shield offered by the historical religions with activistic systems of provisions for existence. This larger and more abstract interior cannot be brought to light with Benjamin's methods of digging for treasure in libraries.[10]

Having accepted the crystal palace metaphor as an emblem for the final ambitions of modernity, one can restate the oft-noted and oft-denied symmetry between the capitalist and socialist programmes: the socialist-communist project was simply the second building site of the palace project. After its closure, it seemed likely that communism was a stage on the way to consumerism. The streams of desire can unfold far more powerfully in the capitalist interpretation of consumerism; gradually, even those who had bought bonds in socialism on the stock exchange of illusions – bonds of which a few will be preserved, like yellowed one million Reichsmark notes from 1923 – had to admit this. As for capitalism, we can only now say that it always meant more than the relations of production; its shaping power had always gone much further than can be encapsulated in the thought figure of the 'global market'. It implies the project of placing the entire working life, wish life and expressive life of the people it affected within the immanence of spending power.

34

The Dense World and Secondary Disinhibition: Terrorism as the Romanticism of the Pure Attack

The hallmark of established globality is the state of forced neighbourhood with countless fortuitously coexisting individuals. This state of affairs can best be examined using the topological term 'density'. A statement about density describes the degree of coexistence pressure between particles and agents. Anyone using this word holds a tool that not only keeps its distance from the common mythologies of alienation (as if all agents had originally formed a single family and later, after some disaster, grown distant from one another); it also helps to overcome the romanticism of closeness with which modern moral philosophers have sought to generalize unduly the openness, be it voluntary or forced, of the subject for the other.[1]

Increased density implies an increasing likelihood of encounters between centres of action, whether in the sense of transactions or of collisions and near-collisions. Where dense states dominate, the basic conditions for commodity and information traffic change in a manner that demands far-reaching moral adjustments: one-sided dictates and sustained non-communications now become equally implausible. At the same time, high density guarantees the chronic resistance of the milieu to unilateral extension – a resistance that, in cognitive terms, can be viewed as a bracing climate for learning processes. Sufficiently strong actors make each other friendly, astute and co-operative – and trivialize one another too, of course.[2] They do so because they successfully stand in each other's way, and have learned to offset their respective interests. By co-operating only when there are prospects of shared profit, they reinforce the plausibility of the postulate that the rules of reciprocity should make as much sense to the others as to themselves. This applies as much to interacting states as to private actors.

Through chronic stays in dense milieus, inhibition becomes second nature to us. If it is sufficiently morally and physically rehearsed, a merely one-sided seizure of the initiative will seem a utopia that no longer corresponds to real conditions. Freedom to act, as it was once understood, now seems like a fairy-tale motif from the time when attacking still helped. If one still finds isolated cases of one-sided expansion here and there, this indicates that certain actors still think they are living in pre-dense circumstances which are conducive to disinhibition. Generally, however, one can say that all patches of 'virgin soil', wherever they might have been, have found their settlers. In process-theoretical terms, high density means that the success phase of unilateral practices is over – though one cannot rule out an occasional strong aftershock. The actors have been driven out of the historical Eden in which salvation was promised to the one-sided.

What makes telecommunication a concept of some ontological gravity is that it refers to the practical execution of densification. Today's style of telecommunication results in a world whose updating involves ten million e-mails per minute and electronic financial transactions totalling one billion dollars daily. This overly common term, then, cannot be adequately understood as long as it fails to emphasize very explicitly the production of the reciprocal world context built on co-operation, that is to say mutual inhibition – including all long-distance business relations, long-distance aids, long-distance constraints and long-distance conflicts. Only this strong concept of telecommunication as the capitalist form of *actio in distans* is suitable to describe the tonicity and mode of existence in the expanded glass palace. Telecommunication gives operative support to the old dream of the moralists, namely a world where the inhibitions are a match for the disinhibitions.

Hope, then – may Ernst Bloch forgive us – is not a principle, but rather an effect. Two things give us hope from one case to the next (and are perhaps suitable for process-theoretical generalization): firstly, the fact that people occasionally have new ideas that effect changes in life in the transition from the model to its application, both at the micro-level and on a large scale; these sometimes include inventions with few side effects and a high epidemic potential. Secondly, the observation that under sufficiently dense conditions, a practicable remainder is usually sifted out from the flood of ideas which some are willing to realize, and presents the better option for many, though perhaps not for all. Density-based reason has the effect of a sequence of filters ensuring the elimination of one-sided offensives and immediately harmful innovations – such as those violent crimes which can only be committed once or in short series. In this way, for example, accident-prone new technologies can already be eliminated while in development, or, if they are indispensable, optimized far enough for the operating risk to be tolerable.

One can call density's mode of effect communicative, but only in so far as one can term mutual restrictions of manoeuvring room communications. Once the fog has lifted, what remains of the phenomenon known in poor visibility as communicative competency is reciprocal inhibition. The much-vaunted consensus of the reasonable is the outside of the ability to prevent one another from taking one-sided actions. Likewise, the concept of acknowledgement, which is granted slightly too high a profile in moral philosophy, refers more to the power of an agent to earn recognition as a potential or actual preventer of someone else's initiative. It is Jürgen Habermas's achievement to have recognized the 'inclusion of the other' as a procedure for expanding the field in which mutually inhibiting mechanisms are valid – even if, clinging to the idealist tradition, he dialogically misinterprets this process: the 'inclusion of the other' is not the expansion of the sphere of action towards commonality but rather, on the contrary, the trace left by the tendency to disable action as such – and its replacement with role-playing in collective projects. The more others are 'included', the more the possibilities of taking action oneself are liquidated. The mass unemployment of 'perpetrators' is the sign of the time. It is important, however, to read this as a good sign: one must praise the build-up of capacities for mutual inhibition as the most effective civilizatory mechanism – albeit without forgetting that when the unwelcome and unbearable aspects of unilateral action are eliminated, the good ones are often filtered out along with them.

From this perspective, we can explain why the globalization of crime is instructive for the post-historical situation: the criminal usages inside the crystal palace and along its periphery indicate how and where active disinhibition – once idealized as 'praxis' – can constantly achieve new local advantages over inhibiting forces. Organized crime is based on a professionalized improvement of disinhibition that keeps finding new ideas between the gaps of awkward everyday circumstances. Spontaneous crime, however, expresses no more than a momentary loss of self-control among confused individuals, who in legal jargon are doggedly termed 'perpetrators'. Sustained crime is mostly a nose for the gap, in the market as well as the law, combined with unperturbed vigour. This vigour fulfils the requirements of perpetration, both in a legal and in a philosophically significant sense. Successfully organized criminals are not victims of their nerves; on the contrary, they are key witnesses to freedom of action, despite the universal context of inhibition.

These findings apply especially to what has recently become known as 'global terrorism', of which there have been brilliant partial analyses, but as yet no satisfactory explanation. One can best do justice to its strong manifestations on a theoretical level, in particular the inconceivably simple act of 9/11, if one reads it as an indication of how the disinhibition motif was appropriated by active losers from the non-Western camp against the post-historical background. This does not mean that evil came all the way to Manhattan, as the moralistic newspaper supplements, never at a loss for quick slogans, announced. It rather shows how a new wave of actors is discovering the joys of one-sidedness for itself. They do not, like previous loser movements after 1789, follow the pattern of a 'revolution'; instead, they directly imitate the original momentum of European expansions since 1492: the elimination of sluggishness with the act of striking out, the euphoria-inducing asymmetry of the pure attack, the irreversible headstart gained by those who are on the scene first and make their mark before the others. The antecedence of offensive violence can thus establish itself anew – though this time from the side that was previously the more disadvantaged. But as it is too late to revise the distribution of objects and territories on the globe, even for perpetrators of Islamist terror, they seize large terrains in the wide-open space of world news. There they raise their fiery coat of arms, just as the Portuguese once erected their banners of stone after landing on the coasts of Africa and India.

If one realized why circumstances play into the hands of the terrorists, one could also gain a more precise impression of one's own situation: the bombers have understood, better than many production companies, that the lords of the cables cannot manufacture all content in the studio, and remain dependent on an outside supply of events. By now they have learned from experience that they themselves offer the most sought-after events, as they have a virtual monopoly as content providers in the real-life violence sector. The infospace in the Great Installation is, for the time being, as open as amorphous Africa was to the most brutal European interventions in the nineteenth century. This means that attack always sells, and the more ruthlessly it is carried out, the higher the medial reward. With evil amusement, the attackers see why: the nervous systems of the crystal palace's inhabitants can be effortlessly occupied by any number of invaders, as palace boredom makes the residents wait for news from the outside.

The underworked paranoid programmes of the affluent citizens demand that the slightest signals proving the existence of an external enemy be captured and amplified. In the hystericized infosphere, such magnifications are disseminated as a picture of the situation to the terror consumers, who absorb the indirect feeling of being under threat into their metabolism as a stimulant.

Among the terrorists, the sum of these effectively theoretical insights leads to a coherent practice: when they position their tele-genic explosions in the right places, they intuitively exploit the hyper-communicative constitution of the Western infosphere. They influence the entire system through minimal invasions by – if the phrase is permissible – stimulating its acupressure points.[3] They can rely on the fact that the only anti-terror measure with guaranteed success, namely absolute silence about new attacks in the media (or the intro-duction of an information quarantine to create a distance between the attack and its sensation-echo), is reliably prevented by their insist-ence on the duty to report. 'Our' nervous conductions therefore pass on the local terror impulses almost automatically to the adult terror consumers in the crystal palace. The compulsion to report indefinitely maintains the status of terrorism as the art of making oneself talked-about. Because of this, the directors of terror, like all conquerors before them, can equate success with truth. Bizarre or not, the result of this transaction reveals itself in the fact that one is truly talking about them – with a constancy that virtually places terror alongside the weather, the secrets of women and the latest movements on the stock market. Though a phantom that rarely materializes, it enjoys an ontological renown that is normally reserved for existentials. Compared to this, the fact that the authors of major attacks are viewed as heroes in large parts of the world not controlled by the West is only a partial aspect of terror's success.

Terrorism has proved itself as a strategy for one-sided expansion on the post-historical continent known as 'attention': it pervades the brains of the 'masses' without encountering any notable resistance, and secures a considerable segment for itself on the global market of thematic agitations. It is thus closely related to the modern action and media arts, as Boris Groys has shown in sufficiently cold-blooded analyses; perhaps it merely takes the traditions of romantically trans-gressive art to their heightened conclusion.[4] Such art had aimed early on to force its significance and conspicuousness through aggressive expansions of artistic procedures. The development of such tech-niques in the course of the twentieth century made it clear that the use of shocks does not prove the greatness of a work, but is rather a simple marketing mechanism. Karlheinz Stockhausen's rightly world-famous outburst of envy towards the authors of the New York drama says more about the truth of that day than the entire industry of September literature.[5]

From this perspective, we can understand why neo-liberalism and terrorism belong together like the recto and verso of the same page. On both sides one reads the same clearly articulated text:

> For the determined, history is not over. One-sidedness pays as much as it ever did for those who trust in the attack. The chosen can still view the world as a lordless object, and where there is a will to strike out, the witnesses for the pure attack have their prey at their mercy. The freedom to push forwards is the nature of truth.

One should admit that this is a siren song – and there are not enough masts to tie up all who hear it. Such music of disinhibition to action is welcome for tonicized individuals who wish to invest their excess powers, whether to entrepreneurial or avenging ends.

It is only on the surface, then, that a play is being performed on the world stage which is known in the coalition of the well-meaning as the 'attack of the fundamentalists'; at a deeper level, the fundamentalism of attack ensures unrest. Although it belongs to a bygone age, its leftovers are virulent in the post-unilateral world. What drives the most resolute attackers, be they assassins, speculators, criminals, entrepreneurs, artists or chosen ones, is the longing to transform themselves into a beam of pure initiative – and this in a global situation that musters everything it can to contain offensives and discourage initiatives. Consequently Islamic fundamentalism, which is currently perceived as the pinnacle of senseless sovereign aggression, is only interesting as a mental arrangement to ensure the precarious transition from theory to practice – or from *ressentiment* to practice, or from appetite to practice – among a group of action candidates under the most improbable circumstances: we recall that the cognitive function of the 'foundation' has never been any other than to remove the inhibition of the agent whom it spurs on to action. With good reason, today's anti-fundamentalists in the realm of theory flatly deny their clients the right to expect directives of any kind from them, which is of course a protective claim – for those theorists, one should note, who understood after the twentieth century's flood of perpetrators how quickly authors of general statements can find themselves in the zone of complicity.

One does, at least, ask oneself in retrospect why it took so long for the practical significance of giving reasons for deeds to become visible. The effective reason for having a reason is the need for a motive by which a would-be perpetrator is willing to be led. Are these energies not always already in search of an excuse that will give them free rein? Since Descartes, we have known what demanding perpetrators expect of their disinhibitory reasons: anyone wishing to shock their environment through actions in a time of generalized uncertainty will scarcely settle for less than a *fundamentum inconcussum*. The wall that all who would perform the improbable must pass through only becomes penetrable through a strong means of disinhibition – and as the world of today, in the eyes of the ambitious and the insulted, consists purely of walls that discourage activity, the strongest wall-breakers are just good enough for the perpetrators of the last days. As Niklas Luhmann noted, radicalism is the modern way of presenting the implausible as the only plausible option.

Therefore, the only notable thing about current acts of terror against the major structures is that they prove the existence of a post-historical radicalism – which is equivalent to discovering a species of black swans. It will take a great deal of disappointment work before neo-liberals and Islamist terrorists – both of them martyrs of post-history – understand that the joys of the actively asymmetrical life belong ontologically to the *ancien régime*; it remains to be seen whether these swans too will then become white again.

Both types of actor are untimely in every sense of the word. The one side still wants to set off like gold-hungry seafarers in 1492, and the other dreams of riding out like monotheistically inflamed desert tribes in the seventh century. Both, however, must adapt to the situation of the time by pretending that they see modern networks as their great chance, not as the epitome of obstructive circumstances. With their belated philosophies of action, they offer the two main views of a romanticism of the offensive at the dawn of the twenty-first century. This impatient reverie confuses the gap with the open field. Its actors seek to retrieve strong asymmetry in acting out missions, projects and other gestures of a self-rewarding first-strike character in a time that has already given precedence to nicety, symmetry, inhibition, reciprocity and co-operation in East and West alike – but not in the gaps, which, due to the system's nature, are very numerous and very narrow.

From an action-theoretical perspective, then, 'historical existence' could be defined as sharing in a space of action in which acting out inner excesses and making world history occasionally come to the same thing. The seaman Columbus, whom sources portray as a braggart and borderline autist, defined what a historical hero of the old school can achieve. After 'history', however, the only ones who still attempt to make 'history' are those who are unable and unwilling to accept its expiry. This produces autisms without resolutions on the world stage – but with a loud echo in the otherwise uniform droning of the media. 9/11 is the clearest indication to date of complete post-historicity, even though many, in shock, wanted to see it as a histori-cal sign – even as the starting signal for the 'recommencement of history'.[6] It brought an unnecessary date in the world that points to nothing except the day on which it occurred – and the iconoclastic plan that spawned it. The September criminals stood for a one-sided violence with nothing resembling a project up its sleeve, aside from vague references to repeat performances – references insistently mis-understood as a threat by poor strategists. A genuine threat would take on the form of an 'armed suasion', as the strategy theorists say; the September deed, however, suggested nothing; it was a mere dem-onstration of the ability to carry out a single attack on the crystal palace, a 'measure' that spent itself in its execution. The 'Holy War' for the theocratic state is not a project, but rather a virile gesture to defend the honour of the offensive. Who can say if it means any more than an armed inferiority complex? The great assassination showed no striving for the good end by regrettably necessary evil means, as taught in revolutionary meta-ethics since the nineteenth century; it was the pure reclamation of the attack in the middle of a time defined entirely by the primacy of inhibitions and feedbacks. The perpetrators and defendants of 9/11 could at least, like many iconoclasts before them, experience the destruction of a supposed idol as a gratification.

One can tell from 9/11 that on its dramatic side, the content of post-history will continue to be determined by the interactions of the deluded. This is not merely an observation like any other; the impos-sibility, noted by Hegel, of learning anything from history is now augmented by the impossibility of learning from episodes of post-history. Only the providers of security technology can draw their conclusions from post-historical activisms – the remaining observers are at the mercy of the ebb and flow of medial excitation, including the hectic rush of internationalized police forces who use the height-ened public stress to legitimize their expansion. The clients in the great glasshouse experience chains of incidents without statements and gestures without referents; those are addressed at the special focal points. But the news and its material, the actual acts of violence and dramas 'on site', are now only ripples on the surface of the regular operations in the dense space.

The pinpricks of terrorists certainly do not warrant a regression of Western political culture to the 'Hobbesian moment': the question of whether the contemporary Western state can sufficiently protect the lives of its citizens is answered so clearly by the facts that it would be foolish to claim one should still pose it in earnest. Portraying terrorism as a 'mortal danger' for the entire free world is a rhetorical figure with which home secretaries and alarm-brokers go out on a limb. The responsibility for the mental absorption of terror has long since been passed on to 'society' – just as terrorist irritation is passed on to its recipients purely by their media, not via mobilization orders from the state. Today's state is a terror consumer like all the others, and although it is meant to be responsible for fighting it, this does not change the fact that it is just as passive and inaccessible as 'society'. It can therefore neither be directly attacked nor react directly. The talk of the 'war on terror' only distracts from the realization that the attack lives entirely off the secondary medial process. What we call terrorism belongs to the structural change of the public sphere in the age of total mediatization. Anyone who truly wanted to fight it would have to sever its root in the fascination with death among the terrorist actors and their audience – which would contravene the laws of globalized entertainment.

Furthermore, the state's right to exist no longer derives from its Hobbesian functions, but rather from its services as a redistributor of chances in life and accesses to comfort. It proves its aptitude as the imaginary communal therapist of its citizens, as well as a guarantor of material and imaginary pampering for the many.[7] Even its military functions are now indebted to the therapeutic style; the current wars for 'security' draw their impetus largely from puritanically interpreted immunological motifs.

Illiberal reactions on a larger scale are therefore never a match for terror, firstly because they knowingly conceal the immeasurable superiority of the attacked over the attackers, and secondly because they afford a symbolic meaning to isolated attacks that is out of proportion to their material content. Thus numerous commentators inflate the nebulous entity of al-Qaeda, that conglomerate of hatred, unemployment and Koran verses, into a totalitarianism of its own style; some even see in it an Islamofascism capable – in whatever unknown, fantastic way – of threatening the 'free world' as a whole and damping its systemically indispensable consumption-happy atmosphere. Some Western authors even go so far as to stylize the anti-American romanticism of jihad spreading among disoriented young Muslims into the cause of a Fourth World War.[8] The reasons for these distortions and inflations will not be examined more closely here; naturally, the interests of the respective commentators are always involved too. (A more thorough elucidation of this practice would have to include a section on rhetorical control systems dealing with hystericization as a postmodern method of consensus.) This much is certain: the neo-realists feel in their element once more, finally encountering a situation in which they can present themselves as leaders of the undecided – their eyes fixed on the figure of the strong enemy, that old and new benchmark of the real, even if the opponent's strength is mostly the product of interested exaggerations. For the consultants, the 'war' is the source of their own significance. On the pretext of security, the spokesmen for the new militancy reinforce authoritarian tendencies whose impetus comes from quite different sources. The carefully maintained climate of fear in the medial space guarantees that the considerable majority of pampered Western security consumers submit to the comedy of the inevitable. A foretaste of where this leads is enjoyed by all those travellers at airports who, since 9/11, have sacrificed nail scissors in hand luggage to reduce the risk of flying.

35

Twilight of the Perpetrators and the Ethics of Responsibility: The Cybernetic Erinyes

If the ethics of action was inseparable from unfolding 'history', the unstoppable rise of the ethics of responsibility in the twentieth century bore witness to the post-historical situation in the crystal palace. Part of this situation is a barely removable user illusion which makes individuals believe that they are responsible not only for their own direct behaviour, but also for the side effects of local acts, however distant they might be. The mode of being in the great interior favours telecausal and telepathic ways of thinking in which local actions are associated with long-distance effects. In this manner, the concept of responsibility flatters all those who want to believe that despite the unmistakable negligibility of individuals in most matters, one's own actions are of central importance at all times and in all places. At the same time, it helps countless people frustrated by the course of things to demand that those not responsible be made responsible.

Nonetheless, it would be an unjustified concession to psychologism if one viewed the omnipresent appeals to responsibility and the stream of those volunteering to accept it as mere symptoms of megalomania and the manic rejection of complexity. In truth, responsibility, as its more profound thinkers have shown, is less a moral than an ontological, or even more a relation-theoretical concept: it seeks to anchor the responsive relatedness to the real other (as well as third parties and the multitude of others) in the structure of subjectivity itself. It is concerned as much with how the 'you' inhibits the reach of the 'I' as with the inhibition of action as such through a retrospective and prospective feedback of consequences, however far away from the scene of the crime they might manifest themselves. Responsibility points to the expulsion of actors from the paradise of a time before success asked you how you had achieved it.

The ethics of responsibility[1] that developed from overheated theological motifs during the last hundred years, then, serves not only the self-aggrandizement or self-constraint of potential actors, but more still the exemption of actual actors from the unintended consequences and side effects of their actions. In its most current form, it advises actors to incur only as much guilt as can be carried within the framework of functional routines. The postmodernized version of the categorical imperative reads thus: 'Carry out only those actions which, taking into consideration all sound motives for omission in your personal view and that of your functional area, must not remain unperformed.' Behind the mask of the principle of caution, now universally embraced, a pragmatism with a wild past is coming into its own. One can say that it has passed through the complete cycle of modern attitude shifts from hysteria to cool.

Let us look back for a moment to the spirit of action as it presented itself to the mass audience before responsibility-theoretically wearing itself out: for the young Goethe, author of *Faust*, part I, initial being could still simply be claimed for 'the deed' – together with the vice-beginning known as strength, without which deeds would remain mere announcements. The 'Faustian' placing of the deed at the beginning mirrors the basic Modern Age realization that a logos without energy is as unsuitable a 'world ground' [*Weltgrund*] as an energy without spirit; the true, real starting element can only be found in an intermediate quality that encompasses both strength and knowledge (or its newer guise, information). The problem of how the deed finds its executor thus no longer arises for the moderns, as they assume that they always already find themselves as an 'informed energy'; it is only unclear how this energy is disinhibited from a hesitant status to the completion of the deed. One answer to this has been known since the Faust chapbook from the late sixteenth century: an advisory contract with the devil gives the scholar free access to the most effective means of disinhibition in his time.

Goethe was able to follow on from this state of affairs: as is well known, his Faust, whom we first encounter at the moment of the transition from theory to magic, is initially only searching for slogans and means of one-sided self-expansion. He finds support in the tempter spirit, the vice-God, who assists him in disinhibition *lege artis* – and not only assists him, but accompanies him as an observer like an alter ego.[2] The fire of metaphysical asymmetry burns visibly in Faust, placing the animated perpetrator on one side and the raw materials and empty spaces on the other. This lays down the direction of all expansions: 'deeds' are the expressive actions that confirm the subject's claim to a 'world of its own'. World-positing through 'the deed' would henceforth call itself the 'work' in the intransitive or 'life' in the transitive sense, and these combine to form the 'life work'. The other – whether neuter, male or female – offers the experiential, poetic and building material for this. 'Art' was the medium of unilateralism for the individuals.

With the aesthetic expansionism of the bourgeois age, the dream of creating works, of originating and positing worlds of one's own, entered its popular phase – and in this situation, there was no reason not to cast an occasional glance at the sixteenth century to help pluck up the courage to reach out into the nineteenth. Certainly no one on the real stages of Goethe's time who sought success as an inventor, entrepreneur or fictional monster had to confide in the devil any more. Any recent, popular history of culture was sufficient to get in the mood for striking out – and the history of great men saw to the rest. Faith in the natural law of the one-sided offensive had reached a level of dissemination that invited the crudest of vulgarizations. Since the nineteenth century, reports of success in war, seafaring, science and art could be read by ambitious people as direct invitations to imitation. Whoever could did what was necessary to enter their name in the record book of discovery, conquest, art and crime.

In reality, the twilight of the perpetrators had already begun by Goethe's later years. The injured world had begun to make acting subjects liable to recourse; even in the most banal of all seduction stories, the 'Gretchen' affair, the expressive professor, confronted with the fatal outcome of his whim, did not get off without remorse. Goethe's more attentive readers could not fail to notice that *Faust* was not a German heroic play on the tragically great thinker-perpetrator, but rather a drama of resignation. It described in unmistakable terms how the hero is reminded of the limitations we so like to call 'human'. It dealt with a universally pondered self-denial that enabled the wisdom form of modernity, namely self-withdrawal amid expanded ability, to gain its initial outlines. This renunciation joins the pre-hubris of the naïve mind with the post-hubris of the subject with experience of itself and the world; the second humility, having travelled around the world, returns to the first. Nothing remains of the offensive centre but the now objectless effort-making, which can only strive, but no longer succeed. Hence *Faust*, part II, offered the tale of an actor who pushed his expansions ahead in all directions of ambition, only to recognize at the end of his excursions and euphorias that he needed redemption through the unavailable other after all.

The twilight of unilateralism's idols, the epiphany of the monstrous as responsibility in the resonant context of the world: Faust's postmodernity.[3]

All this can be expressed in clear process-logical terms: while 'history' gained momentum with the flaring up of one-sidedness, which speaks to those around it in the dialect of first strikes, expeditions and incursions, post-history had to devote itself entirely to the discovery and toleration of feedbacks. Every beginning has a magic to it, certainly, but what to do when the hour of side effects has come? Now a second phase of world-taking, as self-withdrawal, begins – dominated by the neo-Erinyes of our time. After the ancients renamed Alecto ('the implacable'), Megaera ('the grudging') and Tisiphone ('the vengeful') as the urban Eumenides ('the well-meaning'), it is now time to give them new names once again, in the spirit of the world system. In future they will be called Feedback, Multi-laterality and Responsibility. These are the discreet mistresses of post-historical density, always pulling strings from the nearby A to the remotest B, dragging effects back to their causes by their hair, immersed in accounting, paling over cost analyses, lost in multifactorial lists, sunk into the fathomless interplay of karma and statistics, assessing the damage done and forecasting further losses in case things go on as they have started.

Corroborated by the new state of things, the postmoderns believe in that which has no beginning: almost anywhere, they can now presuppose the existence of intricately tangled situations in which it is all but impossible to trace back who started what, with whom and with what intention. Most of them sense somehow that the isolation of one originator, assuming one could get hold of them, would only create an even knottier conflict. This does not rule out reminding proven villains of the limits now and again; nor is there any reason not to give an obstinate repeat offender in the arts a prize to honour their life's work. There no longer seems to be any real use for the position of the author, however, that great one-sided figure who molests the world with works, as everything is already fully integrated into the post-unilateral forms of action and thought, where resonance is experienced as a deeper phenomenon than authorship; one indication of this is that the more quick-witted protagonists in creative fields today present themselves either as mere artisans or as switchpoints in the intertext. Originality, like monocausality, is a concept for people from yesteryear; it deserves our smiles as richly as the pure truth which the honest of yesterday still want to speak today.

In this situation, the inhibiting factors seem equiprimordial with the 'originary' impulse, or, more precisely put, they precede it just as the commentary surpasses the text and the stage production tears the play to pieces – and rightly so, as every author must pay for the wilfulness of writing their work one-sidedly and without permission. It is truer than ever, furthermore, that postmodernity retroactively forbids 'history' for reasons that, as we now see, transcend insurance concerns about historical action.

As long as 'history' was able to unfold under its early conditions, it asserted the primacy of the attack wherever it could. This initially required no more than the notorious jingoist trinity – the ships, the men, the money too – as well as offensive arms, writing tools and embedded historians. What follows is a natural consequence of the premises: in relaxed situations, the vectors of action go out into the open, the energies flow into the positing space expressively and without much feedback, the world still has the quality of white paper waiting for the quill's attack, the deeds do not return to their doer – and if they do occasionally catch up with them, the closed loop is either celebrated as a jubilee or meditated upon as a tragedy. The tragic feedback and collection of the deeds in the garland of memory, however, only characterize the exceptional situations. In normal cases, however much the bourgeois use of tragedy assists the inhibition of perpetrators, the causes disappear in space like arrows without return – a constellation that is valued by avant-garde artists, innovative criminals and first climbers of unconquered summits.

In post-historically dense situations, by contrast, every impulse is intercepted by its responses, not infrequently before it has properly developed. Everything that pushes forwards, that wants to go far and to build, is mirrored long before the spade first enters the soil in protests, objections, counterproposals and farewells; anything that attempts to be a measure is overtaken by the countermeasure. Most suggestions of reform could be implemented with a twentieth of the energy that is expended for their reformulation, watering-down and postponement. Hammering a nail into a surface requires the agreement of a committee which, before it approaches the actual nail question, selects a chairperson, deputy, treasurer, secretary, gender equality officer, and external member to represent the concerns of the regional Ethics Council for Technology Assessment and Environmental Protection. Today's governments are groups of people who specialize in pretending that one can energetically advance matters in one's country within the general horizon of inhibition. Similarly, artists are usually only concerned with upholding the semblance of innovation.

Unauthorized originality leads to a note in one's personal file. The people one considers criminals are *de facto* usually those caught in the act of committing their final wilful deed. Need it be emphasized that these conditions, even if they seem bizarre at first, are almost entirely beneficial?

In the light of such circumstances, therapy groups can be considered the real training grounds for post-history. There everyone can learn to say how they feel when someone else does and says this or that, preferably before their counterpart has made any proper utterance. Here one can learn lessons for life in the hyper-fed-back world. The great inconsideration must go abroad if it hopes to find any place with the conditions it requires in order to enjoy the ecstasies of one-sidedness. Perhaps its flight will take it all the way to Brazil, where the counterpart of the state is not society, but rather the forest. But even 'the forest' will soon no longer be a reference to the response-free space; before long, it will represent a problem with so many repercussions on the whole that it too will fail as a sheltering zone for the refugees of side effects.

36

The Capitalist World Interior: Rainer Maria Rilke Almost Meets Adam Smith

Regarding world-formation through capital-mediated processes, we can note that the present state of affairs has confirmed Dostoyevsky's anticipations about the moods of being in glass palaces. Whatever happens today within the domain of spending power takes place in the framework of a generalized 'indoor' reality. Wherever one happens to be, one now has to imagine the glass roof above the scene. Even exceptional events cannot escape this fact; the Twin Towers collapsed within the glass palace, and the Berlin Love Parades were palace amusements in a spacious Jeu de Paume, meaningfully guarded by a gilded angel that anachronistically reports a German victory in the West – the date must be so far back that even the ever-vigilant forces of political correctness forgot to demand the demolition of the triumphal column.

The capitalist world palace – the ultra-late Marxists Negri and Hardt recently re-measured it under the name 'empire', albeit leaving its outer boundary deliberately unmarked, presumably to invoke more effectively the chimera of an organic alliance between the outer and inner opposition – is not a coherent architectural structure; it does not resemble a residential building, but rather a comfort installation with the character of a hothouse, or a rhizome of pretentious enclaves and cushioned capsules that form a single artificial continent. Its complexity develops almost exclusively in the horizontal, as it constitutes a structure with neither height nor depth – hence the old metaphors of foundation and superstructure no longer apply. Nor can one speak any more of an 'underground' beneath this flat Babel; we have arrived at a world without moles.[1] It would also be a misinterpretation, as already shown, to demand that the palace

contain 'mankind' in its full numbers. The great comfort structure
will certainly continue to integrate numerous new citizens over a long
period by promoting the inhabitants of the semi-periphery to full
members, but it will also reject former dwellers and threaten many
of the spatially included with social exclusion, that is to say banishment from the preferred interior locations of the comfort context.
Semi-periphery is present wherever 'societies' still contain a broad
sector of conventionally agrarian-economic and artisanal conditions
– most dramatically in China, where the epochal gulf between the
agro-imperial regime (which still encompasses almost 900 million
people) and the modus vivendi of industrial nations (which already
includes over 400 million) grows deeper by the day.[2] The situation is
similar in semi-modern countries such as India and Turkey, where
relatively affluent urban regions of a Western-consumerist orientation
coexist with rural majorities comprising late medieval poverty populations. (One of several reasons why it would be an incalculable
adventure for the European Union to admit the semi-peripheral
country of Turkey to the crystal palace in Brussels.)

Though designed as an indoor universe, the great hothouse does
not require a solid shell – in this sense, even the original Crystal
Palace is a partially obsolete symbol. Only in exceptional cases do its
boundaries manifest themselves in hard material, as with the border
fence between Mexico and the USA or the 'security fence' between
Israel and the West Bank. The comfort installation builds its most
effective walls in the form of discriminations – walls of access to
monetary fortunes that separate the haves and the have-nots, walls
that are erected through the extremely asymmetrical distribution of
chances in life and occupational options. On the inside, the commune
of spending power possessors enact their daydream of comprehensive
immunity with a consistently high and increasing comfort level, while
on the outside, the more or less forgotten minorities attempt to
survive amid their traditions, illusions and improvisations. One can
reasonably say that the concept of apartheid, after its abolition in
South Africa, was generalized to apply to the whole of capitalism by
breaking away from its racist formulation and changing into an
economic-cultural state that is difficult to grasp. In this state, it has
largely managed to avoid scandalization.[3] The modus operandi of
universal apartheid involves making poverty invisible in zones of
affluence on the one hand, and the segregation of the affluent in the
no-hope zones on the other.

The fact that, by the most generous calculations, the crystal palace
contains almost a third of the species *Homo sapiens* at the start of
the twenty-first century, though probably only a quarter or even less

in reality, is partly explained by the systemic impossibility of materially organizing the integration of all members of the human race into a homogeneous welfare system under the current technological, energy-political and ecological conditions. The semantic and charge-free construction of humanity as a collective of carriers of human rights cannot, for insurmountable structural reasons, be converted into the operative and expensive construction of humanity as a collective of possessors of spending power and comfort chances. Herein lies the malaise of globalized 'critique', which exports all over the world the standards for assessing misery, but not the means to overcome it. Against this background, the Internet – like television before it – can be characterized as a tragic instrument: as a medium of easy and global-democratic communications, it supports the illusory conclusion that material and exclusive goods must be equally open to universalization.

Naturally the global capitalist interior, commonly termed 'the West' or 'the Westernized sphere', also possesses architectural structures developed with varying degrees of artistry: it rises above the earth as a web of comfort corridors that, at strategically and culturally vital junctions, are expanded into dense oases for work and consumption – normally in the form of the open metropolis and uniform suburbia, but increasingly often as rural residences, holiday enclaves, e-villages and gated communities. For half a century, an unprecedented form of mass mobility has been gushing over these corridors and junctions. In the Great Installation, dwelling and travelling have entered a symbiotic relationship – as reflected in the discourses on the return of nomadism and the currentness of the Jewish legacy.[4] Numerous holiday hosts, singers and masseurs offer their services as travelling companions in the liquefied life. If tourism today constitutes the pinnacle of the capitalist way of life – and the most profitable business sector worldwide, aside from the oil industry that makes everything else possible – this is because the largest part of all travel movements can take place in the calmed space. To go away, one no longer needs to go outside. Aeroplane crashes and shipwrecks, wherever they might occur, are practically always incidents within the installation, and are accordingly reported as local news for users of the global media. Journeys outside the Great Installation, on the other hand, are rightfully considered risk tourism, which increasingly often makes travellers from Western countries – as police and diplomatic records show – *de facto* accomplices of a kidnapping industry dressed up as civilization critique.

Demographically, as stated above, the capitalist interior encompasses barely a third of the earth's present population of seven billion, and geographically hardly a tenth of the total mainland area. The marine world does not need to be taken into account, as all the world's cruise ships and inhabitable yachts together only cover one millionth of the total water surface. Only the new *Queen Mary 2*, one of Cunard's newest luxury ocean liners, which set off on its maiden voyage to New York in January 2004, with 2,600 passengers on board, perhaps deserves a special mention: as a floating crystal palace, it proves that postmodernized capitalism does not lack any talent for showmanship. This challenging large vessel is the only convincing *Gesamtkunstwerk* of the early twenty-first century – even surpassing Stockhausen's seven-day opera cycle *Licht*, completed in 2002 – in that it encapsulates the current state of affairs with integral symbolic power.

Anyone who says 'globalization', then, is speaking of a dynamized and comfort-animated artificial continent in the ocean of poverty, even if the dominant affirmative rhetoric likes to pretend that the world system is all-inclusive by its nature. The opposite is true, for conclusive ecological and systemic reasons. Exclusivity is inherent in the crystal palace project as such. Any self-pampering endosphere built on stabilized luxury and chronic overabundance is an artificial construct that challenges probability. Its continued existence assumes a durable and, at first, more or less ignorable outside – not least the earth's atmosphere, which is used by almost all actors as a global disposal site. Nonetheless, it is certain that the reaction of the externalized dimensions can only be deferred, not permanently disabled. Accordingly, the phrase 'globalized world' applies exclusively to the dynamic installation that serves as a 'lifeworld' shell for the faction of humanity with spending power. Inside it, ever new heights of stabilized improbability are scaled, as if the competition between consumption-intensive minorities and entropy could continue endlessly.

It is thus no coincidence that the debate on globalization is conducted almost entirely in the form of soliloquies by the zones of affluence; the majority of other regions in the world barely know the word, generally speaking, and certainly not the matter to which it refers – except in its detrimental side effects. The vast proportions of the installation do, at least, inspire a certain cosmopolitan romanticism, whose most characteristic media include the in-flight magazines of the major airlines, to say nothing of other products of the international men's press. Cosmopolitanism, it can be said, is the provincialism of the pampered. The globetrotting mentality has also been described as 'parochialism on its travels'. It lends the capitalist world interior its flair for openness towards anything that money can buy.

'World interior' [*Weltinnenraum*] is a term that Rilke coined in the late summer of 1914, in the context of a life-philosophically and Neoplatonically tinged poetic reflection on space and participation. It is not for nothing that the poem 'Es winkt zu Fühlung aus fast allen Dingen' [Almost All Things Beckon Us to Feeling] is one of the most well-known of his œuvre, containing the following lines:

> Through all beings extends the *one* space:
> world interior space. Silently the birds fly
> through us. O, I who want to grow,
> I look out and the tree grows *in* me.
>
> I care, and the house stands in me.

As this is not the place for a poem interpretation, I shall content myself with pointing out that the compound *Weltinnenraum* was evidently perfect to describe a mode of world-experience typical of primary narcissism. Where this form of atmosphere becomes explicit, the actual environment and its imaginary continuation are poured out from the experiences of warmth and suppositions of meaning in an agile, high-spirited and de-differentiated psyche. It has the proto-magical ability to transform anything it touches into ensouled cohabitants of its universe. In this mode of experience the horizon is encountered not as a boundary and transition to the outside, but rather a frame to hold the inner world. The emanation of the soul can grow into an oceanic feeling of coherence, a feeling that could plausibly be interpreted as a repetition of the foetal sensation in an external scene. (The phrase 'oceanic feeling' was brought into circulation roughly a decade after Rilke's 'world interior'.[5]) Let us note that the poet gave the preposition 'in' the unusual function of affirming the ego as an integral vessel or universal place – in direct contrast to Heidegger's analysis of being-in from *Being and Time* (1927), where the 'in' is used to express the position of ek-sistence, the state of being held out into the open. The opposition could be indicated by the terms 'enstasy' and 'ecstasy'.

In Bachelard's *Poetics of Space*, Rilke's basic stance is associated with the experience of 'intimate immensity'. Where these sensations can be had, the surrounding space loses its foreign quality and is transformed as a whole into the 'house of the soul'. A space which is thus made soulful can legitimately be called a 'friend of being'.[6] For the topophilic temperament, spaces of this quality epitomize containers of a life that feels equally at home in its de-restricted environment or in a cosmic skin.

'Word interior of capital', on the other hand, should be understood as a socio-topological term that is here applied to the interior-creating violence of contemporary traffic and communication media: it traces the horizon of all money-dependent chances of access to places, people, commodities and data – chances based without exception on the fact that the decisive form of subjectivity within the Great Installation is determined by disposal over spending power. Where spending power takes on a shape of its own, interiors and operational radii *sui generis* come into being: the access arcades where spending-power flâneurs of all stripes go to stroll. The early architectural intuition of having markets in halls inevitably led in the early Global Age to the idea of the world-shaped hall, on the model of the Crystal Palace; the reaching-out into the hall-shapedness of the world context as a whole is the logical consequence of this.

Under the technical firmament, Adam Smith and Rainer Maria Rilke meet. The poet of the Great Interior encounters the thinker of the global market – whether by coincidence or by secret arrangement is undecided. As I do not wish to rely unduly on the term 'encounter', it will suffice to hint at a near-encounter. We shall begin with an apocryphal after-dinner speech by Adam Smith in honour of the British prime minister Lord North, the ominous 'Glasgow toast' (also known as the 'pin speech'), which would have been given shortly after Smith's appointment as commissioner of customs in 1778; nonetheless, the text reproduced here is nowhere to be found in the *Glasgow Edition* of Smith's works and letters. It is followed by a lost letter by Rilke to an unknown noblewoman whose style and content indicate that it was written in the spring of 1922; needless to say, this too is absent from editions published thus far.

I shall leave it to the reader's theoretical imagination to extend the impulse lines of both documents far enough that they intersect at a virtual point in the semantic space of maturing Old European self-observation. With the help of the password 'no capitalism without animism', this point should be accessible from most workplaces with up-to-date equipment.

Document I, *Adam Smith*:

Esteemed gentlemen, I address you, my noble patrons, Chancellor, and all of you, friends of the sciences and the fine arts, on this festive evening at the request of our host to present to those gathered here a lecture on the true causes of the wealth of nations. Ah, most honourable Lord, how could I fail to notice that I would today fall victim to your sense of humour? Could I truly be so blinded by vanity that I did not comprehend the elegant trap you set for me in giving me the task of conveying in a few minutes what has cost me decades of arduous studies? But whence, gentlemen, should I summon the courage to attempt the evasion of an ambush devised by the noblest of friendships? What are friends for if one does not permit them, on occasion, to laugh at our expense? Thus I shall take heart and provide you a fragmentary answer by subjecting myself to the exercise of turning a long art into a table anecdote. As you will understand, gentlemen, I do so more for your amusement than for your instruction, and less out of my own boldness than out of respect for the laws of hospitality.

What, gentlemen, am I holding here in my hand? Strain your eyes and take your time, for what I am showing you to explain the alpha and omega of the science of the wealth of nations is truly a pin, an object that could scarcely be more profane, domestic or humble. And yet I claim that this slim something holds the sum of economic wisdom in our time if one only looks at it correctly. Should you now suppose, perchance, that someone is seeking to amuse themselves at your expense? By no means! I will elucidate for you how this dark aphorism is to be understood. Imagine a little-developed country, with no division of labour and no lively bartering, where everyone provides entirely for themselves: in such a country, there is no need to accumulate any capital or reserves. Each man satisfies his own needs as they happen to present themselves. If he is hungry, he goes to the forest to hunt. If his robe is worn out, he clothes himself in the fur of the next big game animal he slays. If his hut is beginning to crumble, he improves it as best he can with twigs and grass from his vicinity. Need I still explain that one would search in vain for pins in such a country, to say nothing of ten thousand other useful objects? There will be no needles here – firstly, because no one would know how to use them, and secondly, because it would not occur to any of the citizens to produce such an item, except in a flight of fancy that would result in neither regular production nor trade. Things would be entirely different in a country where the large majority of people had forsworn the old ways of self-subsistence. Truly, gentlemen, there are already countries whose inhabitants have set sail almost without exception on the open sea of labour division, if you will permit me to use this thoroughly British metaphor. Is it not a tremendous adventure if the businessmen and merchants of a nation decide to manufacture only such products as see the light of day purely for the purpose of being exchanged for other values? A madness, indeed, but a reasonable madness and a daring wisdom! Countless numbers have already embraced it, for a reason that can easily be appreciated: in this one case, there is far more sense in risk than in sluggish caution. Understand me well, gentlemen: in this order of things, every single producer of goods must be prepared to make his fortune and misfortune entirely dependent on the needs of others, who, for their part, base their own fate on the needs of strangers. Though this be madness, yet there is method in it.

See this pin, gentlemen! We can be quite sure that its producer did not create it for his own use or solitary pleasure. Without knowing any more about the man's circumstances, I will gladly wager that his needle fed him well, and perhaps even made him an affluent citizen. And why? Because the decision to place one's own well-being on the point of a needle inevitably led to an unheard-of increase in the art of producing such needles. An untrained worker could, even if he were serious and diligent, barely produce a single usable one in a day, or a small few at best. Now that needle production constitutes an independent industry, however, the specialization of the workers has brought about a rise in production bordering on a miracle. Not only the quantity, but also the perfection of the products deserve admiration. The one worker pulls the wire, the other stretches it, a third cuts it, a fourth sharpens it, a fifth files the upper end so that the head can be attached and so on, until at the very end one worker applies his zeal solely to packaging the finished product. The manufacture of a pin involves some eighteen different steps. I myself recently visited a factory in which ten workers were able to produce 48,000 needles every day, meaning that each of them proportionally made almost 5,000 – whereas a single worker, as I have said, would barely have managed one in the same time. It is in this ingenious division of labour and its equally ingenious new composition, gentlemen, that you should henceforth seek the final causes of the wealth of nations; in this and nothing else.

Admittedly, this vastly increased production and improvement of goods for exchange is not all that is required. For the specialized manufacture of goods requires a society of astute citizens who have developed their needs in all directions. Imagine, gentlemen, a nation with ten or twenty needle factories, each of them no less productive than my previous example: this would also require a population of needle-buyers, a population that, alongside a thousand other extraordinary demands, would also voice its need to be amply equipped with these prickly objects. The necessary numbers will not be small, as you can easily reckon, for each factory produces 48,000 needles on each of more than 300 working days every year, yielding roughly 15 million altogether. If this performance is matched with the same regularity in ten or twenty similar factories, the total production can be multiplied by this factor. A civilized people, an economist would conclude, is therefore a group of humans sufficiently cultivated to consume 150 or 300 million needles every year. Do you understand now? Do you see the consequences? What a flood of other riches we must at once see passing before our eyes, for, gentlemen, where needles are required in such great numbers, mountains of cloth will also be needed, entire halls of fine silk, the most spacious offices, filled with the textile treasures of the world, and gigantic storehouses full of garments, sheets, blankets and curtains in all varieties. It is clear to any observer, after all, that all this must be fastened together, which calls for needles, threads and tens of thousands of hands to fasten and cut whatever they grasp. We immediately see a mental image of countless elegant ladies attired in magnificent robes, turning this way and that in front of their mirrors. We do not only imagine the rich women, however, for the shop girls and maidservants also play their part in these coquettish movements. And consider the ships in the ports and the wagons on the country roads that move such treasures about the world! In short, our domestic needle industry could only achieve its highest performance once all these needs had awakened and grown to exquisite heights. Finally, other countries will also have to take note of our needle factories – indeed, they must envy us for them. Numerous merchants from all over the world visit the British Isles to divert our surplus into their regions. Who would continue to be surprised, then, that the unassuming needle is becoming a source of the greatest wealth for more than a few, and a sufficiently secure source of income for many?

Now, gentlemen, the time has come to utter the full truth about the modern system of needs! The production of such excellent and numerous needles, whether in this nation or another, could never have come to pass without the maturation of a plan in the heart of the first businessman: to stake his entire future on the manufacture of this mundane item. What acumen that manufacturer showed in realizing that a major new market was promising to open up! What courage, to take up a loan with a banker on a mere intuition so that he could pay for tools and machines! What persistence, to look for suitable buildings and seek out diligent workers who would devote their days to the factory, carrying out their procedures under the instruction of the owner and his subordinates! What skill, to choose the dealers, carters and agents without whose services the needles would never go out into the world, into other workshops and into the houses of their uses! What stoic strength, to compete year after year with producers of similar goods without losing heart – indeed, while reflecting constantly on ways to improve the product! To avoid any misunderstandings: I do not intend to praise only the diligent man whose active faith in the needle can offer the whole world such a useful item, provided it is willing to pay the natural price for it. More still, I wish to glorify the secret underlying the connection between all goods available for exchange on the markets. Gentlemen, my heart's greatest desire is that I might succeed in igniting the spark of wonder in you at the daily mystery of our age: join me in marvelling at the circumstance, so simple and yet almost incomprehensible, that millions of needles make their way from the iron mines to the huts, from the huts to the factories, from the factories to the offices and trading houses, and from the trading houses to the workshops and households where they prove their use, as trivial as it may seem, in manifold ways! In a fit of lyricism, one is inclined to become superstitious and indulge in the quixotic fancy of a higher world that shared in our own, and contained a race of needle spirits that accompanied the terrestrial needles in their metamorphosis like lucky daemons. But let us shake off the temptation of poetic images and look coolly at the order of things developing on the markets of this world! Does it become less magical when viewed with scientific eyes? Certainly not, gentlemen! The more soberly we regard the facts, the higher our admiration will rise when we see that not only the needles, but tens of thousands of diverse products trace their orbits with the most amazing punctuality, as if guided to their destinations by an invisible hand.

Esteemed attendees, I fear you must pardon me this bold image I used a moment ago – indeed, you will have to exercise further lenience when I go even further and say that this invisible hand not only guides the separate forms of goods, but in fact guarantees the larger connections between the objects produced solely for exchange in the strangest and most secure fashion. 'For heaven's sake,' you will exclaim, gentlemen, 'has the speaker gone mad? Is he in his right mind to speak of an invisible hand that, coming from who knows where, dares to interfere in the markets to preserve order?' You certainly have good reason to voice this objection, gentlemen, and yet I am bound by duty to reply that the most thorough examination of the markets has brought me to the assumption, indeed the firm conviction, that there must be a higher force of balance at work in them. Perhaps an analogy will make it easier for you to understand my deep belief. Think of the impertinent suitors who once forced Penelope to weave her bridal dress,[7] certain that her husband Odysseus would never return! What anger and distrust these men must have felt upon realizing that a hidden hand undid every night what had been woven during the day. We are much better off today, gentlemen, as we have the prerogative of observing how an invisible hand fabricates the very same piece of work by day and by night, a cloth that is many thousands of times greater, more intricate, and richer in threads and patterns than the bridal dress of Ithaca – and many times more useful, for, as you know, that dress was never to be worn, for Odysseus ultimately returned home. How much more amazed we should be than that crowd of brazen guests competing for the favour of a matron! Whereas her own hand undid what she herself had woven, the world market, following rules that are still opaque for us, mends behind our backs what we dissolved when we entrusted our fate to the division of labour and to trade. Penelope, the cunning weaver, had the advantage over us because she could observe her own actions in both directions. It was she herself who wove and untied. We, however, only know about one side of our dealings. We provide the separate threads and must leave it to the market, the great weaver, and its magic hand to decide whether it will tie them together or cut them off. Gentlemen, I urgently advise you to cling for all time to the belief that the market will always know more about the fabric as a whole than we, with our vision limited to individual threads, can ever hope to grasp!

You will now ask, gentlemen, what bearing all this has on the art of guiding a great body politic, and I do not intend to deny you at least the outline of an answer. In a well-ruled state where the wastefulness of the unproductive is kept in check, there will inevitably be a general state of affluence that will be tangible even in the lowest classes of society. It must result if the rulers know better than to refrain from impeding the great loom and the invisible hand operating it. A rich state is the sum of its flowering cities; but the city is a constant fair in which its environs congregate to ply trade and study innovations. Happy are those nations which are already constant fairs today! Happy the world that will one day be a single great fair, filled with the noise of dealers and buyers! In that world, the philosophers will receive a hint from the needle-manufacturers that guides their thoughts in new directions. They will one day admit that the great treasure known since the ancients as human freedom is nothing other than the reflection of moving things on the markets, whose price, if I may say so, has brought them freedom. For objects, freedom means the possibility of changing owners, while freedom for humans means that they ransom themselves from the service of feudal lords and become owners of themselves.

Gentlemen, I have now done my duty. I beg you, devote a quiet hour to the paradox with which I closed my speech. It is indeed an unfathomable paradox that the freedom which is so precious to us is contingent on submitting to the needs of strangers. For today, let us banish the ghosts of the profundity that seeks to overstep the boundaries of good sense. We shall leave it to our German colleagues to descend to the darkest depths of existence and return to the light of day with fool's gold! Let us raise our glasses to our host, the noble chancellor of England! I know well enough how meagre the aperçu which I had the awkward pleasure of presenting to you. I am well aware that with my words, I am no less indebted to science than to your patience. Be lenient with my hasty speech. Grant me the extenuating circumstances that can apply to a speaker in my situation. But if, as a Scot among English gentlemen, I should have been miserly with my words, I shall certainly not spare any of my gratitude for the honour you have bestowed upon me with your attentiveness, the beautiful daughter of conviviality and manful seriousness.

Document II, *Rainer Maria Rilke*:

Most esteemed Countess, you magnificently lofty spirit, how I suddenly sense so powerfully your presence, now that I have made the decision to ease my soul and leave a secret in a place that can hold it without constraining it. For, this morning, your image came to my memory as if drawn up on threads from dark light by angels. In this hour you are as close to me as a house in which, as a youth, I spent many days. I feel as if I had been allowed to walk once more through this familiar casing of life, until I am shown the exact place where the secret I have brought with me can be deposited, to remain there and live as befits it. Well may you smile, noble lady, at this presumption that makes me an intruder upon you, albeit one who comes bearing a gift on this occasion. Make use of your inalienable privilege of being above poets' secrets and the flailing intimations that follow in their wake. Yet remain well-disposed to me in the magnanimous way that is your birthright, and whose existence has magnified the air I breathe since life showed me the favour of revealing you to me.

You will recall well how, some few months ago, I sent you a festive letter – one could almost call it an epistle – a letter completed while I was yet in the heights of Muzot, in which I gave you news of the Elegies' completion. I do not doubt that you still remember the significance of the event. How mistaken I would be if our pulses did not beat together that day! Perhaps the echo of that message I sent out reverberates once more in your memory? But of course, you remember my call to my friends, stunned by gratitude: that the number was complete, the noble ten, the holy decade, whose vessel I was during years of waiting, ripening and silence.

And now, most esteemed, noble lady, I must summon the audacity to confide in you what I have called my secret. I write down the following confession with a thin, exhausted hand, with a hand that withdraws in shame, even when it gives. That I finally utter it, so that it might thereafter rest in your smile: the Elegies were not ten in number, but eleven. O heavens, now it is written!

I searched my heart in vain to find explanations for this awkward superfluity. When the verses came to me, I wrote down in a storm, like one beside himself, all that I fancied was being dictated to me by earnest angels. Yet once those feverish weeks were past, I gazed upon the work with less burning eyes, but however often I counted off the divine series, there always leapt out one more than the providential ten.

Noble lady, forgive me if this disclosure strikes at your innermost core. I can scarcely bear the thought that this shared secret might give you a heavy heart! I assure you, it is impossible that you should be caused to suffer by what you learn from me! Consoled by this thought, I now present you, and you alone, a copy of the surplus poem, the eleventh. I know no other soul in this world to which I could so confidently entrust these orphaned verses. For what are souls, what are friends, if they are not also sanctuaries for lost poems! Show these lines to no one, or only to the rare few who come close to your heart. Should it so happen that a lonely and unique spirit encounters you, one who hungers for that inner reality whose late witnesses we will have been, you will understand in an instant what is to be done, without betraying your conscience or the poem that is now your silent guest.

Think of me some violet evenings when you wander the cliffs and the pull of heaven lightens your feet, and be full of the sensation that someone is close to you more quietly than ever, namely

your

RMM.

To stand forever beneath self-built roofs is
　　　to be the prisoner of a freedom that it past.
The starry sky, oh, we have
　　　　　　sent it home to a
distant God who already rues having loved us.
In his stead we built arches of pride and
　　　　　　　caution.
Where braces were once spanned between the stars,
there now stand the frameworks of bold iron art.
Glass without secrets represent the high blue,
Hand-made walls prop up the horizon,
as if the universe would end
where the works of men reach their limits.
Now, even for humans, there are only bars,
and no world behind millions of bars.
Once, albeit outside, in the old open
　　　　　　that grew around us over millennia,
where no engineer had more power than a
　　　　　　small animal which
feels the dominance of the open whenever it
　　　　follows the nearby tracks,
outside, I say, and back then it was the pure
　　　　　　truth when the verse
spoke to me: through all beings extends the one space.
I found all things there sworn to
　　　　　　be together,
all that is swayed imperceptibly in its place in
　　　　　　the same breath.
And like a wind that has left the house of summer
to bring the richer autumn,
existence for one another went through the
bodies of separated things.
The space, the one, ruled as the glorious
assembler, the most communicative god, who handed out souls
　　　　　　　　　　to everyone,
as gifts are scattered among the crowd at
　　　　　　princely weddings,
so that the poorest can take home their share.
Breathing like twins, the farmwoman's shoes stood
　　　　　in front of the darkened room,
the hammer was still warm from valuable work
　　　　　　when it
lay in the workshop at night, no different from the sickle,
　　　　　　which glowed quietly
with usefulness, long after the harvest, until winter.
On every working morning, soul flowed from the
　　　　　handles of the tools into

the hands of those who shared their dwelling with such quiet
                                                household
effects, as weathered men share their beds
with the unspeakable scent of their compliant
                                        women.
But now a fate has driven us out of the
                        ensouled.
Everything bought, I called out, threatens the machine.
We live in a machine,
and inner things have become the same as the outside,
as if the soul were but an exhaust fume irksomely
                                pouring from a loud engine.
Things curl up in themselves, buyable and cold,
like sick girls who have forgotten what love,
                                flowers
and seasons are.
Where once lived souls, insolence has moved in.
The ominous animals
hang, cooled-off meat, disappointed in the display cases.
These high living things, the earlier accomplices of our
                    existence, have ceased to look at us,
so that we now lack the witnesses that could
        have sworn in silent wakefulness that we, like
                        them, are alive, listening so far,
so far inside.
All that lies scattered in the brightness of the hall now bears
                                a single price,
                    each object enclosed in its soullessness.
Each thing cries out to us how young and important
                    it is, as wanton as cheapness feigning expense.
Oh, the thing today no longer finds its
                        owner.
For to be buyable means: having forgotten how to belong
                                to the living,
and buying means lightly inviting things
                        home,
like guests for a single occasion whom one greets,
                                uses,
and never regards again.

. If buying, selling, renting, letting, borrowing and lending are operations that affect all aspects of life in the Great Installation, it is inevitable that the accessibility of things through monetary mediation will
produce a corresponding world feeling. First of all, one experiences
an immeasurable increase in accessible objects, and last of all, the
convergence of the world interior and the spending power space –

with consequences for the status of the devices surrounding us on a daily basis. As soon as many previously non-purchasable things are pulled over to the buyable side, and some unavailabilities suddenly appear available and reversible, one feels forced towards the culture-critical exaggeration that all conventional values are subject to revaluation and devaluation. One should make it clear, however, that expanded commodity traffic does not automatically imply universal corruption: anyone who uses money to gain access to commodities, information and people substitutes irrevocable operations for lasting belonging.

This loosening must be comprehended and rehearsed. That 'things' from the world of belonging do not remain untransformed in their transition to the world of options is a fact mirrored in countless nervous reflections. One understands why it constituted one of the most disconcerting human experiences during the technological and monetary metamorphosis of the world: numerous observers of the period (including Baudelaire, whom Benjamin invoked as his chief witness) stated that things were cooling off and revealing a fake, wanton side. As if driven by their own malice, they suddenly seemed to be deliberately infiltrating humanity instead of remaining with a single organic owner. From that point on, treachery was in the air – as if things had committed some breach of fidelity by becoming commodities.

Walter Benjamin's Marx- and Baudelaire-inspired suggestion of interpreting prostitution not simply as a professional exploitation of the sexual illusion, but as a general mode of being among people and things in the money-driven world, responded sensitively to these connections – and twisted them in a manner that was itself not without illusions. By portraying money as a means of acquiring objects of desire as being in the wrong, he supported the anarchic suggestion that the best things should essentially be for free; he did not take into account that access through belonging – on which the utopian principle of zero charge is modelled – is by far the most expensive form of all. Benjaminism provides the historico-philosophical version of a fantasy among melancholy men: that, in the messianic age, whores and other deceptive surfaces might return to the mode of being of pure utility value.

If we sum up what we know about the great transition into the universe of money, it transpires how far all decisive dimensions of existence are modified by monetary mediation: we have access to places first and foremost as buyers of transport titles; we have access to data first and foremost as users of media; we have access to material goods first and foremost as owners of means of payment; and we reach people predominantly to the extent that we can afford admittance to the sites of possible encounter with them. These seem to be trivial observations; but the memory – by now a scarce one – of times in which money was not yet an all-pervasive factor proves that they are not. In pre-monetarily defined conditions, virtually all access to people and things depended on belonging to a group and its environment of things; before modernity, belonging was the price of the world. To have a world, one formerly had to let oneself be devoured by one's place. No access to people or things without possession through one's own culture (as it was later called in neutralizing fashion).

After the shift towards monetarily determined conditions, access came about far more readily through acts of self-purchase and by following offers or open addresses. Today one expects the successful to be capable of putting their allegiances in the background. The subject of 'belonging' is primarily brought up when individuals and groups feel excluded from financial advantages, and therefore seek recourse to an advantage of identity that can be had for free – being German, being Basque, being Serbian, or similar plumes that can be worn at no cost. Belonging, *Zugehörigkeit, appartenance* – words like these have good chances of becoming the losers' catchwords of the twenty-first century. Needless to say, it is not least this that makes them some of the most interesting terms of the future.

The psychosocial hallmark of successful groups in the world interior of capital lies in the adjustment from allegiances to options. This reform in the ontological status of things and people finds its cognitive expression in constructivism. One must constantly show one's awareness that whatever is presented as *found* is inevitably *made*. For any given thing or semblance of nature, brief instruction is sufficient to reveal its 'construction', 'invention' and 'politics'. This dismantling of the 'natural' has inescapable consequences for human self-relationships – which is why fixed identities do not receive a favourable prognosis in the constructivist climate. Only losers still require fixed natures. This does not, however, mean that we can stop saying where we come from and how we situate ourselves within a larger framework.[8]

One can now understand why the way of life that weakens allegiances and reinforces options leads to a psychopolitical rearrangement of clientele in the comfort spheres of the Western and Westernized world – extending to the post-monotheistic remodelling of religious sentiment. Let it be noted: the Christianity of today is part-time monotheism, and the same applies to Judaism and Islam

– even though these stagnating religions, which are forced to fall back on self-regulation and the cultivation of traditions, also have pronounced fundamentalist elements whose spokesmen, usually professional believers, like to pretend that God still has a use for the whole human being. In truth, money has long since proved itself as an operatively successful alternative to God. This affects the overall context of things today more than a Creator of Heaven and Earth ever could.

The most important metamorphosis of the modern psyche concerns the approval of egotism, which had been subject to an unshakeable ban during the entire age of lack and its holistic compensations. It was Nietzsche, the prophet of world-breaking, who gave the decisive response to this with his neo-Cynical doctrine of the revaluation of all values. The revaluation applies primarily to the self-referentiality of human nature, the 'curvature into oneself' which had to be condemned as a betrayal of the Lord, the collective and the order of things during the era of agro-imperial morality and metaphysics. Since the citizens of modern, prosperous states began to understand themselves as voters and free money-users rather than minions, the duty to participate in the 'whole' of altruism for the sake of the Lord and divine norms has shifted towards an openness to commodities and public issues – with the inevitable side effect that a tendency to take oneself seriously as customers, opinion-owners and carriers of personal qualities has spread among the 'subjects'. This was registered first by the moral-critical authors from the eighteenth century onwards who discovered *amour-propre* and *vanity fair* as topics for endless commentary. The rich phenomenology of egotism in all social strata prepared for its moral neutralization. The analytical content of this literature led into Nietzsche's *Gay Science*, while its human-shaping surpluses contributed to demands for the *Übermensch*, whose modern equivalent is the cosmopolitan consumer.

In addition, what spirals out of control in the capitalist world interior is the inclination towards an end use devoid of ulterior motives; in the first uproar a hundred years ago, this had been termed 'nihilism'. The name expresses the observation that consumption and disrespect are adjacent phenomena. And indeed, the consumerist metamorphosis of the 'subject' did create an awareness of the right to destroy the objects of consumption. The model for the revaluation of all values is the organic metabolism. In so far as all that is the case is defined by its absorption through the consumer, waste becomes the universal 'result of life in all classes' – in the words of Rameau's nephew, the forefather of neo-Cynicism. In this framework, revaluation always amounts to devaluation.

The same trend releases vague pantheistic and polytheistic forms of experience, as the global system favours persons without overly fixed qualities – and how could it be otherwise, when the task of the individual in the capital universe is to become involved in ever more numerous commodity offers, ever more diverse role play, ever more invasive advertising and ever more arbitrary art environments. The life of the market erodes convictions, monisms and forms of rugged primalness, replacing them with the awareness that possible choices and side exits are available at all times. The consequence is that the persons become paler and the objects more colourful; but it is the colourless who are called upon to choose between the colourfulnesses. To be sovereign is to decide the colour of the season. The discourse on the 'flexibilized human being' laments these facts, while that on the 'new age' and 'net age' beamingly acknowledges them. Tomorrow's ideal possessor of spending power would be the anti-Bartleby: the person whose training with long lists of options had taught them to respond to most suggestions with a 'Why not?'[9] They would be the habilitated consumer. They could, to adapt the words of another of Melville's figures quoted above, declare: 'The global market was my Yale College and my Harvard.'

37

Mutations in the Pampering Space

Woe to the avant-gardes who are followed by the masses.

The key terms 'boredom', 'hothouse existence' and 'psychopolitical rearrangement' of the part of humanity possessing spending power require additional explanations. They must begin from the observation that among the populations of the comfort sphere, a far-reaching shift is currently taking place from conventional thinking in terms of need and lack to a largely unaccustomed thinking in options.[1] The significance of this transition goes far beyond what can be expressed by a phrase such as 'change of mentality'. These collectives have experienced such a deep caesura that one could be tempted to articulate their meaning with recourse to an exuberant philosophical concept: the realm of necessity, it would seem, has given way to the realm of freedom, however numerous the partisans of necessity who doggedly resist the altered conditions from an underground of old and new conservatism. These include romantic and religious temperaments who react with outrage to the discovery that banality and freedom are converging – which is not how the goal of human endeavour had been envisaged. Indeed, after the shift, weak reasons such as mere moods and personal taste must take over the role of strong reasons, previously embodied by commanding need and its translation into figures of the fundamental, the dominant, the glorious and the inescapable. In a world defined by means of relief, the old imperatives are losing their justifications. Where there was necessity, there can now be mood.

The theoretical reconstruction of the great turn is made easier by the fact that the idolatry of labour which dominated throughout modernity – economically, physically and psychologically – was sufficiently eroded by the postmodernization of consciousness to give a clearer view of living conditions in our poly-dimensionally relieved 'society'. Now we can calmly retrace the outlines of existential sensibilities in the post-necessary space, without fear of any significant distortion of the picture through the propaganda of the parties representing need and seriousness. This situation is unmistakably characterized by a historically singular wave of pampering that includes the great majority of populations from zones of affluence in its increases.

Reference to pampering does not, of course, imply any concessions to conservative pedagogy, which clings stubbornly to the view that humans always depend on being led by a firm hand. Pampering, as a term from historical anthropology, denotes the psychophysical and semantic reflexes of the relieving process that was inherent in the civilizatory process from the start, but could only become fully visible in the age of a radical de-scarcification of goods. In the light of these assumptions (which further develop some of Louis Bolk's and Arnold Gehlen's insights), it can be made clear that the experiment of the modern economic and welfare state constituted a leap in the pampering history of *Homo sapiens* – a leap that opened up an enormously expanded space of existential opportunities for all those who participated in it. For the sake of caution, it should be noted that the anthropologically oriented theory of pampering does not aim for a reversal of relieving effects enabled by civilization; it seeks to optimize the ability for cultural navigation among the subjects of pampering in their hazardous and largely uncomprehended milieu by offering conceptual orientations for existence in heavily relief-defined situations.

The psychosemantic consequences of the stay in the comfort ether of the great hothouse are concisely expressed in the term 'boredom' as expounded by Dostoyevsky and Heidegger. Its nebulous omnipresence shows the mood reflex of an existence that finds constant peace, constant sustenance and constant entertainment in its milieu – though an opposing constant agitation provides a certain balance with themes of stress and competition that tonicize the collective. Even if traditional milieus of socio-critical radicalism cultivate Gothic disaster theories which focus the view immovably on past and present scenes of violence and lack, the pampering tendency is undoubtedly ahead of re-burdening efforts. The effective powers of pampering form an immersion space that calibrates its inhabitants with the atmospheric dictates of a fundamentally advanced existential assurance.

In this space of generalized relief the discovery of stress phenomena was inevitable, as the formulation of a general concept of stress only became possible once the complementary concept of relief had been established in theory and practice. Against the background of the relieving tendency, stress took on the degree of conspicuousness that is indispensable for both the development of a new level of sensitization and the growth of an explicit theory. Because stress constitutes the disappointment of an expectation of relief, its explication belongs to the workload of a theoretical engagement with living conditions in the crystal palace. Diffuse boredom on the one hand and aspecific stress on the other are the atmospheric universals of hothouse existence. Just as boredom means relief as such, relief *sans phrase*, so too stress means irritation as such, irritation *sans phrase*. These two fundamentals of existence in the crystal palace create a chronically ambivalent atmosphere in which the alarm and the all-clear are in constant alternation. Irritations are perceived as stressory figures against a foundation of relief; they all have the form of re-burdenings that counteract a tendency towards relief. Means of relief, in turn, all take the form of stress-reducing measures. Once this is accepted, it is not difficult to show how, after the establishment of the relief system, stress too enters the age of its artificial production.

An architectural image can assist in grasping the new conditions: the interior of the postmodern crystal palace contains an elevator that transports residents to the five expansively constructed floors of relief. Naturally, one should not assume that all passengers are able to alight on whatever floor they like and make use of its specific offers. As significant numbers of beneficiaries are currently present on each level, however, knowledge of the pampering that is possible elsewhere affects all other palace-dwellers. In time, most palace-dwellers walk through all the floors, though they do not all have the same experiences. The first floor is for those who have succeeded in partially or completely fulfilling the dream of income without performance; the second is frequented by an audience of relaxed citizens who profit from political security without themselves having any readiness to fight; the third is where those meet who participate in general provisions of immunity without having their own history of suffering; on the fourth, consumers of a knowledge whose acquisition requires no experience spread themselves out; and on the fifth one finds those who, through direct publication of their own person, have succeeded in becoming famous without presenting any achievement or publishing any work.

We enter the first level of the pampering space when we examine a value aspect of money that is virtually absent from conventional theories of money. I shall call it the 'pampering value', thus referring to two related, albeit clearly distinct phenomena. Both are overlooked if one cannot break with the prejudice that money is a fundamentally scarce commodity and its lack is synonymous with material need. The first aspect of the pampering value of money manifests itself as the fact that the world of objects, in so far as they can be purchased, has become accessible and available to a historically unprecedented degree. By its nature, spending power facilitates access to all commodity-shaped things, and thus has the quasi-magical merit of opening the gate to the world with a gentle movement. The contemporary semantic content of the action we call 'buying' can only be adequately articulated if one takes into account the pampering value of the fundamentally facilitated access to objects. This facilitation, furthermore, comes from the modern transport system, where the universal agent of relief and pampering – petroleum – celebrates one of its most important successes. Thanks to greatly cheapened transport services, the ubiquity of commodities in the vicinity of buyers is ensured almost everywhere. Thus buying also means performing magic by monetary means; and performing magic in turn means – as shown elsewhere[2] – achieving a surplus of effect in relation to cause. The response to this is the amazement of the audience at inexplicable, sudden effects. The amazement does not arise when such surpluses are to be expected and are produced at a constant rate – and the regularity of these effects is the secret of labour division and its market-based synthesis. The great majority of the crystal palace's residents profit from the magical context of the monetary sphere, which, through the immeasurable heightening of possible self-sustenance performance, equips each individual agent with an unprecedented wealth of options, summed up in the formula *shopping and fucking* – as long as they meet the requirement for residence in the space of affluence, namely the possession of spending power.

The pampering value of money manifests itself even more openly as soon as one examines the most fascinating view of modern money ownership: this is evident in great fortunes entirely based on chance acquisition. With a fortune of this kind, it is logical that its accumulation will not be in any measurable proportion to the efforts undertaken to amass it. Consequently, money is perceived here as the ultimate means of relief. To older ears, the word 'millionaire' still expresses something of the formerly widespread amazement that a single person can own more than an individual can 'really' ever earn – unless they draw on the numinous money source whose outflows have, since the start of the Modern Age, been termed 'fortunes'. The greatest pampering value thus comes from undeserved possession of money in which the connection between personal performance and wealth seems completely severed. In such cases, there is no longer a path from what someone does to what someone has: the owning subject, whether as an heir, treasure-finder, fortunate stock exchange speculator or manager who awards himself gratuities of an undisguised looting character, profits from an absolutely disproportionate relief: one simply has it, and does not know how it happened.

It cannot be by chance that the inception of the capitalist economy in Western Europe coincided with the triumphal march of the modern economic fairy tale – the myth of the self-filling purse – through the imaginations of those people who were having their first experiences of the generalized use of money. In the central scene of *Fortunatus*, the chapbook that was published anonymously in Augsburg in 1509 and appeared in numerous editions over the centuries, Lady Luck gives the eponymous hero a purse that will contain forty gold pieces in the relevant currency whenever it is opened – a gift that leads to the endless stalking of its owner Fortunatus and his son until the latter finally withdraws to a monastery, having gained wisdom in the realization that possessions of this kind hold no blessings. This fable of value creation marks the beginning of a long series of fantasies dealing with nothing other than the vertical irruption of relief into effortful life; constantly moving with the fashions, technologies and zeitgeists, they continue into the present, where, thanks to their mass media reinforcement, they have climbed to excessive heights. With each new generation, they proclaim – under different auspices – the good news of the affluence that suddenly appears. A favourable marriage, a large inheritance, a miraculous business deal, an irresistible trick, a valuable piece of inside information, an unexpected bestseller, a successful patent, exaggeratedly high compensation, a gambling jackpot – in these forms and others, any given individual can encounter the great money-making event that catapults them out of their burdened existence and into a more relaxed climate.

The modern welfare state is based on the effect of replicating Fortunatus's purse on a grand scale as a treasury, though the conditions under which one can dip into it must be far more formal than in the fairy tale, where it was enough for the beneficiary to have lost his way in the right forest at the right time. The conditions under which the purse fills itself were likewise developed more soberly in the modern national economy – the fifth book of Adam Smith's *Inquiry into the Nature and Causes of the Wealth of Nations* (1776) can still be considered a central source of state finance theory. This much is certain: the treasury can only carry out its primary functions of financing state tasks and ensuring the redistribution of income if it is connected to a successfully installed system of profits. The present condition of the great comfort hothouse indicates that there is a firm, albeit increasingly nervous bond between capital economy and public funds – with a public spending ratio of over 50 per cent of the national product, one does not have to look far to find the main winner of the game known as capitalism. Once this bond has become stable, the fairy-tale motif of the undeserved fortune can trickle into the most lowly of households and be consolidated as a formally approved claim. Whoever is in need must be given a hand by a legal Fortuna; whoever is not in need is free to dream of higher Fortunas. What Ernst Bloch called the principle of hope has been operationalized by the modern social state to the extent that the principle of relief ensured the elimination of emergencies throughout the system.

The establishment of the 'social safety net' provided the first level of the pampering space with a solid foundation. Consequently, the great majority of the population develops forms of partly atmospheric, partly material participation in any given manifestations of the motif of income without performance. It is against this background that the second universally effective pampering dimension can be discussed. One can still assume that the welfare system is based on procedures for eliminating economic emergency (specifically acute poverty and mortal danger through accidents). If the tendency to reject emergency is extended to foreign policy, the result is a shift of state activity from war preparation to conflict management. The psychopolitical consequence is the 'pacifying' transformation of mentalities in the comfort zone, with the explicit pacifism that became valid as a confession in the nineteenth century constituting a virtually obsolete intensification thereof.

The most visible trace of the change in mentality is the rapid disintegration of historical masculinity. The reason is clear enough: during the last fifty years, the social design of the 'man' became subject to overall relief from war. Specifically, it was liberated from the categorical prohibition on cowardice that applied in traditional cultures. As a result, the 'new man' established himself as a sociopsychological success figure in post-polemogenic culture – with the sole exception of the zone influenced by a military romanticism that continues to enjoy political support and mass media celebration in the imperial front nation on duty, the USA. The new man is the civilly relaxed man, that is to say the consumer in the *genus masculinum*. Where unease in relaxation appears,[3] it is compensated for with symbolic gestures that provide suggestions for the production of designer masculinity. Thanks to such offers, those interested can buy back some of the more robust hallmarks of virility. In the light of this, it is easy to see how far the recently revived friction between pacifists and bellicists is a journalistic phenomenon. It receives further impetus through the politicization of neo-masculinist attitudes – for example, in the context of fighting terrorism and the deployment of Western intervention troops abroad. In truth, warmongering editorialists and young conservative essayists could not transform back into warriors even if they wanted to – warrior existences in the manner of older traditions are now only possible outside the great comfort zone. The authors of neo-realist battle discourses can at least remind us that even for the populations of the space of affluence, security cannot be had entirely for free. Warnings of such tendencies must be voiced whenever there is occasion to consider that the courage to be neutral does not solve all security questions.

In terms of the universal significance of its offers, the second level of the great relief system is every bit the equal of the first – not least because the far-reaching metamorphoses in gender relationships in the twentieth century, including feminism and homoeroticism, would have been unthinkable without the erosion of historical masculinity. This is ultimately responsible if that hallmark of pampering, the unthinking expectation of security without struggle, has infused almost every individual existence today, regardless of gender. The fact that these tendencies currently define the European state of relief from military obligations should be mentioned very explicitly, not least in public discourse, otherwise people will predictably fall prey to the hysteria that will spread once the memory of certain not fully evadable contributions made for the sake of one's own security suddenly re-enters the consciousness of the over-relieved.

On the third floor of the relief system, high security expectations are generalized and expanded to include disturbances and risks in private life such as accidents, illnesses, involvement in natural disasters and the like. This extension of individual security expectations reveals the pampering purpose of the insurance system, whose Modern Age-constituting significance we have already pointed out: insurances can be described as pragmatic immune systems whose function is to institutionalize measures against vaguely expectable, unwelcome burdens. Where hazardous practices generalize, there must be risk compensation procedures – that is why this field (leaving aside the deeply ironic life insurances) is dominated by automobile insurances. These systems must be understood in terms of their relief character, as they protect the insured from the imposition of preparing themselves individually to avoid or cope with unwelcome disturbances. Where the insurance and solidarity systems are as expansive as they are in the European wing of the crystal palace, one can expect a strong surge of frivolity, as thoroughly insured populations inevitably participate in the shift from individual caution to systemic caution – despite the cyclically recurring appeals from reform politicians of all stripes to the spirit of self-provision. The consequence of systemic caution is that individuals profit from expanded margins of immunity. Thus stabilized, anonymous care releases private carefreeness – a classic pampering effect. It should hardly be necessary to demonstrate how much this disposition is connected to the stepping-up of the capitalist markets from the consumption of goods to a consumerism of experiences and risks. In a complementary development, the services for processing accidents and instances of self-harm have ballooned into a multitude of variants unknown in any earlier social formation. They constitute a luxury sector in which one can study the main hallmark of wealth management in the great hothouse – the subjugation of the necessary by the superfluous – more clearly than anywhere else. The sociology of accidents and statistics for illness offers, for the time being, the best introduction to a theory of the present age. The concept of the 'luxury of morbidity', which serves this purpose, has been explained elsewhere.[4]

On the fourth level of the relief system, we address the pampering purpose of the new media. It must be shown how it sets the cognitive economy of relieved populations in motion. Just as the Gutenberg effect set off a strong wave of access facilitations in its time vis-à-vis written knowledge, the popularization of electronic media is currently tied to an unprecedented surge in the availabilization of any given content. It is no coincidence that the concept of information established itself at the same time as the new media. It was not until the age of media abstraction that the homogenization of knowledge, in the sense of uniformly shaped information, could reach technical perfection – via the transcendental-philosophical equalization of all content of consciousness, leading to 'representations' [*Vorstellungen*]. Just as post-Cartesian philosophy presupposed that the printed book and the subject were of the same age, contemporary thought makes the same assumption about information and users of electronic media.

The irruption of the new media into the comfort sphere is of eminent relevance to pampering – not only because they ensure that the so-called worldwide network also becomes practicable for individual users in simple technical routines, but more still because the use of digital media builds a fundamentally new relationship between the content and its users. The tendency is probably best described as externalization, provided one keeps the term free of moral value judgements. Externalization means that a lighter form of subjectivity, let us say the postmodern 'user self', is beginning to replace the more ponderous form of subjectivity, the 'educated self' of the Modern Age.

The technological turn relieves individuals of the impositions of the integral personality formation that exemplified existence in the universe of a knowledge that was read and transmitted through one's own life. The concept of education, which should by no means be taken merely for a German quirk, a luxury variety of apolitical inwardness, referred throughout the European Modern Age to the expectation that each individual should embody the living book of their own life history and reading history; it urged its addressees to hold together the sum of what, not without a certain pathos, they called their experience. However much the book itself constitutes a means of de-contextualization, it remains a model of collectedness as realized in the convergence of being a reader and being an individual. Such collectedness gave the educated individual of the bourgeois period existential weight, provided they distinguished themselves as the living depot of their experiential history.

It is precisely this gravitas of the education-oriented person that the wave of relief triggered by the new media opposes. Their pampering purpose becomes evident to the extent that reader subjectivity dissolves into user subjectivity. The user is the agent who no longer needs to become an educatedly formed subject, as they can ransom themselves from the burden of gathering experiences. The word 'ransom' refers to the relieving effect which homogeneous forms of content – items of information – grant their user as soon as they no longer need to be acquired through time-consuming training, but can simply be 'retrieved' after a brief introduction to the corresponding techniques. The user does not stop collecting – as they must do justice, in their way, to the cumulative quality of successive cognitive events – but what they collect are not experiences, in the sense of personally integrated, narratively and conceptually ordered complexes of knowledge; they are addresses where knowledge aggregates formed to varying extents can be found, should one wish to access them for whatever reason.

The decisive relieving effect in the cognitive realm, then, concerns what one could call the infrastructure costs of education. Whereas the 'whole human being' once had to set off to gain access to scattered, esoteric and expensive sources of education, it is now

increasingly adequate to acquire efficient access techniques in order
to bring the desired content to one's exact location. Easy fetching
develops into a universally available anti-extraversion procedure that
shoots down the principle of experience.[5] While the subject of historical experience was necessarily a searching, indeed a living collecting
point for experience, the current search engines and storage methods
now give it a sign that it can rest from its time-honoured labours.
The present gesture which expresses the transition into the post-
experiential age most perfectly is that of downloading. It exemplifies
liberation from the imposition of gathering experience. Accompanying
it, a post-personal, post-literary, post-academic cognition regime casts
its shadow ahead.

On the fifth floor of the great comfort system, we become aware of
the pampering value of the medially constructed great public sphere,
manifested in the inception of a new category of celebrities. With
these, the question of why they are known or famous has become
practically unanswerable. The traditional meritocracy, as we know,
was based on the willingness of historical 'societies' to reward those
members for outstanding achievements by taking them up into the
small circle of fame. By granting its achievers a celebrity premium, it
indirectly applauded its own willingness to achieve. Recently, with
the establishment of self-referential media worlds in the interior of
the crystal palace, a relieving effect has also become evident with the
phenomenon of celebrity, severing the earlier connection between
achievement and prestige. Ever more people in the comfort system
have registered, whether atmospherically or pragmatically, the fact
that being-in-the-media is an effective equivalent to the usual being-
known-because-of-achievements, which could lead them to believe
– and not without reason – that they are better off avoiding the detour
of work and achievement and heading directly for the studios. The
media act on this attraction of easy prominence, providing an increasing number of platforms on which non-achievers come into view. This
opens up an incalculable market for methods of achievement evasion
that can, however, usually be professionalized before long as secondary achievements. At the centre of the trend stands the figure of the
presenter, who scales the heights of celebrity by introducing celebrities. The moment of truth about the medial pampering spiral comes
when presenters present one another before a large audience; in such
moments, they prove that the stock exchange of fame has also reached
the level of derivative trading. The postmodern art system has reacted
with its own means to the tendency towards relief from the imposition of creating a work, developing strategies to breed workless

artistic fame. This approach is further popularized in mass culture until one arrives at a purely tautological form of celebrity. At their radiant events, all those meet who are known for being known for nothing in particular. Needless to say, a postmodern Fortuna no longer offers her protégé a purse full of gold, but rather the question of whether he would rather be an achiever or become groundlessly famous over night.

In view of the great pampering hothouse as a whole, one is inclined to wonder whether the boredom diagnoses of Dostoyevsky and Heidegger were not simply philosophically and psychologically coded prognoses of decadence. Nietzsche's synonymous vision of the last human being, in this light, would also be nothing other than the anticipation of the consumer who is unspeakably bored and brilliantly entertained at the same time. It consequently addressed the relieved and bored individual who, being equipped with the conveniences of the great capitalist interior, had sufficient resources to praise the attained condition as fulfilment. The concept of decadence would lose its conventional meaning if applied to the new pampering phenomena, however, as those currently pampered are simultaneously participants in ongoing fitness increases. The apparent decadence would then consist in the diligence of the relieved. Its leading figure would be the athlete who cultivates an absurd level of fitness during their period of high performance, usually sacrificing all other aspects of their 'human potential': to be considered the most diligent, they resort without hesitation to doping agents, as everyone else does the same, making doping inevitable in the interests of a level playing field. In such a situation, there is no need to 'wait for the barbarians', as was once the case in declining aristocratic cultures. When the new beneficiaries of relief take over control from their more civilized predecessors, they are identical to the encroaching barbarians. Conventional cultural criticism leads nowhere when confronted with such a situation. It is no great feat to observe that the inhabitants of the crystal palace are growing older, while symptoms of infantilization spread; it is unclear for the time being, however, how such tendencies are to be viewed. There will always be clever apologists for the last human beings who offer proof that they are not only not barbaric, but actually extremely civilized – albeit in a different register.

A far more urgent question is how, in the climate of irrefutable demands for a constant increase of relief, the periodically recurring imperative of re-burdening can be processed without political regressions. In reflections of this kind, one should take Mussolini's dictum that Fascism is a horror of the comfortable life as a reference value. This statement, never taken entirely seriously, is clear enough to elucidate the self-endangerment of the advanced comfort system through protest phenomena that romanticize burdening. The twentieth century amply demonstrated the crass acts to which a taste for the return to harsh realities can lead. If there is a specific risk among the beneficiaries of high relief levels, it can be identified as an inclination towards a second cruelty. This was examined in the discourses that diagnosed an inconceivable 'regression to barbarism' after 1918, and all the more so after 1945. Many like to overlook the fact that these were desired regressions. The chronic unease in culture is accompanied by an acutely erupting aversion to civilized restraint. Anyone wishing to protect themselves from uncontrolled re-burdening movements, from neo-heroism, neo-frugality and a politics of new harshness,[6] should soon begin thinking about how to develop democracy-compatible concepts of burdening.

38

Revaluation of all Values: The Principle of Abundance

On the other hand, anyone enquiring as to the general premises of relief in the age of its technical intensification would receive the best answers from the French early socialists, specifically Saint-Simon and his school, in whose publications – their journal was not named *Le Globe* for nothing – one can find the first elements of an explicit politics of pampering from a genre-theoretical perspective. It is from Saint-Simonism that the formula of the era of relief, still valid to this day in theory and practice, originates; it states that with the rise of major industries in the eighteenth century, the time had come to end the 'exploitation of man by man', replacing it with the methodical exploitation of the earth by humans. In the present context we can acknowledge the epochal content of this formulation: through its use, the human race, represented by its avant-garde (the classes of the *industriels*), is identified as the beneficiary of a comprehensive relief movement – or, in the terminology of the time, as the subject of an emancipation. Its goal was expressed in the secular-evangelical reference to the resurrection of the flesh during one's lifetime.

Such a thing was only conceivable on the condition that the typical distribution of weight in agro-imperial class societies, namely the relief and release of the ruling few through the exploitation of the serving many, could be revised thanks to the relief of all classes through a new universal servant: the earth of resources, taken over using large-scale technology. What the Saint-Simonist keyword 'exploitation' means in process-logical terms could only be articulated once the philosophical anthropology of the twentieth century, especially in the wake of Arnold Gehlen's efforts, had developed a sufficiently abstract concept of relief.[1] Since this concept became available to the cultural sciences, it has been possible to formulate general statements about the evolutionary direction of high-tech social complexes that are substantially more practical in systemic and psychological terms than the palpably naïve nineteenth-century theses on emancipation and progress. If one ties both the phenomenon and the concept of relief back to Saint-Simon's exploitation, it becomes evident that the effect in question cannot be achieved for the many without a shift of exploitation to a new 'down below'.

Against this background, it can be argued that all narratives about the changes in the human condition are narratives about the changing exploitation of energy sources – or descriptions of metabolic regimes.[2] This claim is not only one dimension more general than the Marx–Engels dogma that all history is the history of class struggles; it is also far closer to the empirical findings. Its generality extends further because it encompasses both natural and human energies ('labour power'); it is closer to the facts because it rejects the bad historicism of the doctrine that all states of human culture are connected in a single evolutionary sequence of conflicts; and, in addition, it does not distort the existing data despite its high level of abstraction. Such a distortion can be found in the polemogenic didacticism of *The Communist Manifesto*, which passed over the reality of class compromises in order to generalize the comparably rare phenomenon of open class struggles – at the risk of ascribing exemplary significance to the slave and peasant revolts of earlier history, along with their desperate, undirected and often vandalous tendencies, for the redistribution struggles of wage earners.

The narrative of the exploitation of energy sources reaches its current hot spot as soon as it approaches the event complex known in both older and newer social history as the 'Industrial Revolution' – a misnomer, we now know, as this too was by no means a 'radical change' in which above and below change places; rather, it made explicit the manufacture of products using mechanical substitutes for human movements. The key to the transition from human labour to machine labour (and to new human–machine co-operations) lies in the coupling of power systems with executive systems. Such couplings had usually remained latent in the age of physical labour, in that the worker themselves, as a biological energy converter, embodied the unity of the power system and the executive system. Once a far-reaching leap of innovation had taken place in mechanical power systems, however, they could advance to the stage of explicit working-out.

Thus begins the epic of motors: with their construction, a new generation of heroic agents stepped onto the stage of civilization, a generation whose appearance radically changed the energetic rules of play in conventional cultures. Since the advent of motors, even physical and philosophical principles such as force, energy, expression, action and freedom have taken on radically new meanings. Although their forces are normally tamed ones, bourgeois mythology has never completely lost sight of their unbound, potentially disastrous side, underlining this with throwbacks to the pre-Olympian race of violent Titanic deities. Hence the profound fascination with exploding machines, indeed with explosions in general.

Since the neo-titans appeared in the midst of modern lifeworlds, nations have changed into immigration countries for machinery. A motor is, in a sense, a headless energy subject brought into existence out of interest in the use of its power. It only possesses those attributes of the perpetrator, however, that still cling to the impulses without being burdened with elaborations or reflections. As a beheaded subject, the motor does not move from theory to practice, but rather from standstill to operation. In motors, the shift that has to be effected through disinhibition in human subjects who are meant to take action is triggered by the starting mechanism. Motors are perfect slaves, for there are no complications through human rights concerns if one makes them work day and night. They do not listen to abolitionist preachers who have a dream: the dream of a not-too-distant day when motors and their owners have the same rights, and the children of humans and machines play with one another.

To integrate motors systematically as cultural agents, one requires fuels of a very different nature from the foodstuffs with which human and animal bearers of muscular work were kept alive in the agro-imperial world. Thus the most dramatic sections in the epic of motors are the cantos on energy. One can go so far as to ask whether the formulation of the abstract, homogeneous energy principle – energy *sans phrase* – by modern physics is not merely the scientific reflex of the principle of motorization, whereby the aspecific coupling of nutrition and organism was replaced by the precise relation between fuel and machinery. The evacuation of power from the organism begins a passage in the grand narrative of the procedures and stages of energy source exploitation that meets all the requirements for dictating a permanent final chapter.

The grand narrative of relief among the moderns begins, as we know, with the account of the massive invasion by the first generation of mechanical slaves, which were naturalized from the eighteenth century onwards under the name 'steam engines' in the burgeoning industrial landscapes of North-western Europe. Mythological associations were particularly obvious in the case of these new agents, as their operating principle – the expansion pressure of the trapped water vapour – immediately recalls the Titans of Greek theogony, who were condemned to subterranean bondage. As water vapour initially comes from the combustion of coal (it was only with the thermonuclear power plants of the twentieth century that a completely new agent was introduced), this fossil fuel had to become the heroic energy-bearer of the nascent Industrial Age. It is one of the numerous 'dialectics' of modernity that coal, that powerful pampering agent, usually had to be extracted through the inferno-like labours of underground mining. Thus the miners of the coal-hungry nineteenth and early twentieth centuries could be presented as living proof of the Marxist thesis that the wage labour contract was nothing but the legal mask of a new slavery. This Promethean coal was joined from the later nineteenth century on by rock oils and natural gases as further fossil carriers of energy – likewise relieving and pampering agents of the highest order. Their extraction required overcoming obstacles to development of a different kind from those encountered in underground mining. Occasionally, the process of acquiring them displayed an effect that one is inclined to call an accommodation by nature, as if it wished to make a contribution of its own to ending the agriculturally defined age of scarcity and its reflection in ontologies of lack and miserablisms.

The primal scene of this accommodation of human demand by natural resources took place in 1859 in Pennsylvania, when the first oil well was uncovered near Titusville, and with it the first great oil field of the New World, in a very shallow layer barely more than twenty metres below ground. Since then the image of the eruptive oil well, known among experts as a 'gusher', has been one of the archetypes not only of the American Dream, but of the modern way of life as such, which was opened up by easily accessible energies. The petroleum bath is the baptism of the contemporary human being – and Hollywood would not be the central issuing facility of our valid myths had it not shown one of the great heroes of the twentieth century, James Dean, bathing in his own oil well as the star of *Giant* (1955). The continuously growing influx of energy from so far unexhausted fossil stores not only enabled constant 'growth' – positive feedbacks between work, science, technology and consumption over more than a quarter of a century – together with the implications I have described as the psychosemantic modification of populations through prolonged relieving and pampering effects; it also included such venerable categories of Old European ontology as being, reality and freedom in an abrupt change of meaning.

Thus the concept of the real has now come to include the activist connotation that things could always be different (of which only artists, as guardians of the sense of possibility, have so far had any intimation), in contrast to the view held by tradition, where references to reality were always infused with the pathos of not possibly being any other way. As a result, the concept demanded submission to the power of finitude, harshness and lack. For an entire age, for example, a phrase like 'crop failure' was loaded with the admonitory severity of the classical doctrine of the real. In its way, it reminds us that the ruler of this world can only be death – supported by the Four Horsemen of the Apocalypse, his seasoned entourage. In a world situation like that of today, characterized by the fundamental experience of surplus energy, the ancient and medieval dogma of resignation has lost its validity; now there are new degrees of freedom whose effects extend to the level of existential moods. Small wonder, then, that Catholic theology, which essentially thinks in premodern and miserablist terms, has completely forfeited its connection to the facts of the present – even more than the Calvinist and Lutheran doctrines, which at least take a semi-modern approach. Accordingly, the concept of freedom also had to break away from its conventional meanings over the last hundred years. It makes new dimensions of meaning sound on its current overtone rows, especially the definition of freedom as the right to unlimited mobility and festive squandering of energy.[3] Thus two former lord's prerogatives, namely gratuitous freedom of movement and whimsical spending, are democratically generalized at the expense of a subservient nature – only, of course, where the climatic conditions of the great hothouse are already in force. Because modernity as a whole constitutes a figure on a background of the primary colour abundance, its denizens are challenged by the feeling of constant dissolutions of boundaries. They can and must acknowledge that their lives fall into a time without normality. They pay for their thrownness into the world of excess with the feeling that the horizon is drifting.

The sensitive zone in the reprogramming of existential moods in modernity thus concerns the experience of de-scarcification encountered early on by the inhabitants of the crystal palace – and which they barely ever acknowledge sufficiently. The sense of reality among people in the agro-imperial age was attuned to the scarcity of goods and resources, being based on the experience that their labour, embodied in arduous farming, was just enough to place precarious islands of human artificiality in nature. This was already addressed in the ancient theories of ages, which bear resigned witness to the fact that even the great empires crumble, and the most arrogant towers are levelled by inexorable nature within a few generations. Agrarian conservatism expressed its ecological-moral conclusions in a categorical ban on wastefulness. Because the product of labour could not usually be increased, only augmented by looting at best, people in the ancient world were aware at all times that produced value was a limited, relatively constant factor that had to be protected at all costs. Under these conditions, the squanderer must have been considered insane. The narcissistic profligacies of noble lords could thus only be taken as acts of hubris – and their later reinterpretation as 'culture' could not yet be predicted.

These views were invalidated when, with the breakthrough to the fossil-fuelled style of culture a little more than two centuries ago, a sinister liberalism appeared on the scene and resolutely began to overturn all the criteria. While wastefulness had traditionally been the ultimate sin against subsistence, as it jeopardized the constantly scarce supply of survival means, the age of fossil energy saw a thoroughgoing change in the meaning of wastefulness: we can now calmly term it the first civic duty. Not that supplies of goods and energies have grown into the infinite overnight; but the fact that the limits of the possible are constantly pushed further away gives the 'meaning of being' a fundamentally altered complexion. Now only Stoics still count the stocks; for the ordinary Epicureans in the great comfort hothouse, the 'stocks' are the very things that one can assume are infinitely duplicable. Within a few generations, the collective willingness to consume more was able to ascend to the level of a system premise: mass frivolity is the psychosemantic agent of consumerism. Its blossoming indicates how recklessness is now in the position of the fundamental. The ban on wastefulness has been replaced by the ban on frugality, expressed in the perpetual appeals to encourage domestic demand. Modern civilization is based less on 'humanity's exit from its self-inflicted unproductiveness'[4] than on the constant influx of an undeserved wealth of energy into the space of entrepreneurship and experience.

In a genealogy of the wastefulness motif, it would have to be noted how deeply the verdict of tradition on the luxurious, leisurely and superfluous was rooted in theological value judgements. In the official monotheistic view, everything superfluous could only be displeasing to God and nature – as if they were also counting the stocks.[5] It is notable that even the proto-liberal Adam Smith, as willing as he is to sing the praises of the luxury-stimulated markets, clings to a markedly negative concept of wastefulness – which is why his treatise on *The Wealth of Nations* is pervaded by the refrain that wastefulness is a submission to the 'passion for present enjoyment'.[6] It belongs to the habitus of 'unproductive hands' – priests, aristocrats and soldiers – who, on account of a long-entrenched arrogance, follow the belief that they are called upon to waste the riches generated by the productive majority.

Marx likewise remains bound by the wastefulness concept of the agro-imperial age when, following in Smith's footsteps, he adheres to the distinction between the working and wasting classes, albeit with the nuance that now the owners of capital, far ahead of the feudal 'parasites', occupy the role of malign squanderers. At least he agrees with Smith in conceding that the new economic methods have brought a surplus product into the world that goes beyond the narrow surplus ranges of agrarian times. The author of *Capital* stylizes his bourgeois as a vulgarized aristocrat whose greed and baseness know no bounds. This portrait of the capitalist as a pensioner pays no regard to the fact that the capital system also introduced the new phenomenon of the 'working rich', who balance out 'present enjoyment' through the creation of value. Nor does it take into account that in the modern welfare and redistribution state, unproductiveness switches from the tip of society to the base – leading to the virtually unprecedented phenomenon of the parasitic poor. While it could normally be assumed in the agro-imperial world that the impoverished were exploited productive people, the paupers of the crystal palace – bearing the title of the unemployed – live more or less outside the sphere of value creation (and supporting them is less a matter of the 'justice' one naturally demands than one of national and human solidarity).[7] Their functionaries, however, cannot refrain from asserting that they are exploited individuals who are lawfully entitled to compensation because of their hardships.

So, even if liberals and Marxists alike undertook far-reaching attempts in the nineteenth century to interpret the phenomenon of industrial society, the event of fossil energetics was not even perceived in either system, let alone conceptually penetrated. By making dogmatically inflated labour value the most important of all explanations for wealth, the dominant ideologies of the nineteenth and early twentieth centuries remained chronically incapable of understanding that industrially extracted and utilized coal was not a 'raw material' like any other, but rather the first great agent of relief. It was thanks to this universal 'natural worker' (for which alchemists searched in vain for centuries) that the principle of abundance found its way into the hothouse of civilization.

Nonetheless, even if the pressure of new evidence convinces one to understand fossil energy carriers and the three generations of motors spawned by them – steam engines, combustion engines and electromotors – as the primary agents of relief in modernity, even if one goes so far as to welcome in them the *genius benignus* of a civilization beyond lack and muscular slavery, one cannot do away with the finding that the inevitable shift of exploitation in the fossil energy age has created a new proletariat whose suffering enables the relieved conditions in the palace of affluence. The main emphasis of the current exploitation has moved to livestock, for which the industrialization of farming brought about the age of massive production and use. On this subject, statistics are more informative than sentimental arguments: according to the German government's 2003 Animal Welfare Report, almost 400 million chickens were slaughtered in 2002, along with 31 million turkeys and nearly 14 million ducks; of large mammals, 44.3 million pigs, 4.3 million cows and 2.1 million sheep and goats met their final use. Analogous figures can be assumed in most market societies, not forgetting that the national statistics must be augmented by an enormous amount of imports. Animal proteins constitute the largest legal drug market. The monstrous scale of the figures exceeds any affective judgement – nor do analogies to the martial holocausts of the National Socialists, the Bolshevists and the Maoists fully reflect the unfathomable routines in the production and use of animal carcasses (I shall refrain from addressing the moral and metaphysical implications of comparing large-scale cases of human and animal exterminism). If one considers that intensive livestock farming rests on the agrochemically enabled, explosive growth of animal feed production, it becomes evident that the flooding of the markets with the meat of these animal bio-converters is a consequence of the oil floods unleashed in the twentieth century. 'Ultimately we live on coal and petroleum – now that these have been transformed into edible products through industrial farming.'[8] Under these conditions, one can predict a growing unease among the populations of the great hothouse in the coming century through an internationalized animal rights movement, already almost fully developed, that will emphasize the unbreakable connection between human rights and animal suffering.[9] This movement could transpire as the vanguard of a development that assigns a new meaning to non-urban ways of life.

Thus, if one is to name the axis around which the revaluation of all values in our developed comfort civilization revolves, the only possible answer is the principle of abundance. Current abundance, which always demands to be experienced within the horizon of intensifications and dissolutions of boundaries, will undoubtedly remain the decisive hallmark of future conditions, even if the fossil energy cycle comes to an end a hundred years from now, or slightly thereafter. In broad terms, it is already clear which energy sources will enable a post-fossil era: primarily a spectrum of solar technologies and regenerative fuels. At the start of the twenty-first century, however, the details of the shape it will take are still undecided. We can only be sure that the new system – some simply call it the coming 'global solar economy' – will have to move beyond the compulsions and pathologies of current fossil resource policy.[10]

The solar system inevitably posits a revaluation of the revaluation of all values – and, as the turn towards current solar energy is putting an end to the frenzied consumption of earlier solar energy, one could speak of a partial return to the 'old values'; for all old values were derived from the imperative of managing the energy that was renewed annually. Hence their deep connection to the categories of stability, necessity and lack. At the dawn of the second revaluation, we see the outlines of global civilizatory weather conditions that will quite probably display post-liberal qualities – they will install a hybrid synthesis of technological avant-gardism and eco-conservative moderation. (In terms of political colour symbolism: black-green.)[11] The conditions for the ebullient expressionism of wastefulness in current mass culture will increasingly disappear.

In so far as the expectations created by the principle of abundance in the industrial era remain in force, technological research will have to devote itself first and foremost to finding sources for an alternative wastefulness. Future experiences of abundance will inevitably see a shift of emphasis towards immaterial streams, as ecosystemic factors preclude a constant 'growth' in the material domain. There will presumably be a dramatic reduction of material flow – and thus a revitalization of regional economies. Under such conditions, the time will come for the as yet premature talk of a 'global information or knowledge society' to prove its validity. The decisive abundances will then be perceived primarily in the almost immaterial realm of data streams. They alone will authentically possess the quality of globality.

At this point we can only vaguely predict how post-fossility will remould the present concepts of entrepreneurship and freedom of expression. It seems probable that from the vantage point of future 'soft' solar technologies, the romanticism of explosion – or, more generally speaking, the psychological, aesthetic and political derivatives of the sudden release of energy – will be judged in retrospect as the expressive world of a mass-culturally globalized energy fascism. This is a reflex of the helpless vitalism that springs from the poverty of perspectives in the fossil energy-based world system. Against this background, one understands why the culture scene in the crystal palace betrays a profound disorientation – beyond the aforementioned convergence of boredom and entertainment. The cheerful mass-cultural nihilism of the consumer scene is no less clueless and without future than the high-cultural nihilism of affluent private persons who assemble art collections to attain personal significance. For the time being, 'high' and 'low' will follow the maxim '*Après nous le solaire.*'

After the end of the fossil-energetic regime, there may *de facto* be what geopoliticians of the present have referred to as a shift from the Atlantic to the Pacific space. This turn would primarily bring about the change from the rhythm of explosions to that of regenerations. The Pacific style would have to develop the cultural derivatives of transition to the techno-solar energy regime. Whether this will simultaneously fulfil expectations regarding worldwide peace processes, the even distribution of planetary wealth and the end of global apartheid remains to be seen.

39

The Exception: Anatomy
of a Temptation
Americanology 2

No one would seriously dispute that global capitalism – as polycentric as its structure might be – favours certain places, countries and populations. The United States of America is undoubtedly one of its preferred regions, not to say its main residence. It is the country in the modern that, more than any other, has given itself the constitution of a comfort sphere. One could almost say that in the case of the USA, the crystal palace presents itself as an immigration country. In keeping with this, most of its inhabitants have developed an inclination to view themselves not merely as agents of an economic system, but as carriers of a motivation that has long borne an irresistible name: the American Dream.[1] Its basic definition includes the postulation that the number of its definitions is virtually as high as the number of the country's inhabitants. If one reduces all the dreams dreamt on American soil about the meaning of existence in that country to their essentials, however, one will probably be left with no more than three irreducible motifs.

The first consists in the proposition that the USA is essentially the country where, in contrast to the numerous lethargocracies in the rest of the world, *anyone who wants to do something new can do something new*. Among the constitutional rights of US citizens, one outstanding element is the expectation of finding at all times a space favourably disposed towards advances and initiatives. One could call this the right to the West, in a more than solely geographical sense, as 'the West' – as we saw in the reflections above – is a symbol of impunity in the unilateral penetration of unexplored areas. Once they may have been called Wyoming and California; today they are genetic research, nanotechnology, the colonization of Mars or artificial life.

The second characteristic is tied to the term 'chosenness' – a word that moves through a multi-coloured spectrum of meanings, starting with the notion that it is the most natural thing in the world to be at the top in all respects and extending to the rarely voiced, but widely palpable idea that the deep purpose of this country is to be the venue for the Protestant outdoing of the Jewish exception. Chosenness is the Anglo-American declination of the subjectivity invented in continental Europe; it means that transatlantic being-subject denotes the possibility of being called from the midst of normal, non-moved life to be the agent of an intimately felt mission. Chosenness is the American password for the disinhibition of action and appearance on the world stage. Consequently the mission statement, the project creed, constitutes America's original contribution to the list of speech acts. The linguistic side of Americanism is expressed not only in the frequently derided superlatives of which the natives make such ample use; its most binding form is in the verbal gestures with which citizens of the United States pledge their 'commitments'. The oft-glossed religiosity of Americans, a source of bafflement to Europeans, very frequently implies the strongly pre-Christian notion – reformulated with great criminal energy by Calvin – that God is with the victors, whatever the angelic pipes of the New Testament might sing and say about the preference of the Almighty for the weak.[2]

The third and final attribute is connected to the psychodynamic social contract of the USA, which ensures the everlasting precedence of manias over depressions. One manifestation of this is the code of optimism that visitors from Europe find so cheering, albeit often baffling, and which constitutes the true national language (although self-critical idioms, even an indigenous version of negativism, can also be found). This gives rise to the zestful habit among ordinary Americans of formulating problems as challenges. The spontaneous consequence of this is that obstacles are met with programmes for eliminating them. Nowhere else in the world would it be conceivable that an initiative to intensify cancer research and other medical projects could take the external form of an appeal to increase the defence budget, as could be read in the *New York Times* of 3 May 1998: as defeat in the battle against previously unvanquished diseases is fundamentally un-American, the war against devious causes of death must be waged using the 'whole will of our nation'. (One can assume that echoes of the 'war on poverty' from the New Deal era influenced this language game.) The war against the invisible after 9/11 also had a much-noted, muddled second front, for it is equally un-American to be vulnerable to untraceable terrorists. The national mobilizations against illness and hidden enemies are direct products of an implicit manic amendment stating that no citizen of the United States should be expected to accept the existence of an internal or external reason for depression. US citizens profit from an additional human right that demands a subordination of discouraging affects to high spirits, and endorses the elimination of the causes for discouragement by any means. Anyone living in the USA will always enjoy the support of their cultural environment in consistently thinking away and clearing away all impediments to exhilaration. This leads to a collective habitus of forced emotional accounting fraud, as no one wants to be in the red in the balance of high and low. When connoisseurs of the scene stated after the Enron scandal that it was merely the tip of an iceberg of monstrous proportions, this may have been true in the realm of dollar transactions; but one should not overlook how far the dollar is itself based on an emotional economy where the entire motivation system is pervaded by the concealment of reasons for depression and the sugar-coated falsification of assets.

If one brings together these three primary characteristics, one reaches the following assessment: in its psychopolitical design, the United States of America is the country of actually existing escapism.[3] The home of every kind of escapee, it primarily harbours people who, faced with the hopelessness of their previous home situation, migrated to a wide space of second chances. An asylum for countless desperate and shipwrecked individuals, it took up many of the refugees who managed to save themselves from the floods of world history. An immigration country for unbound surplus drives, it offers a field of action most of all to those who believe in the precedence of initiative over inhibitions. As the Shining City on the Hill, it shows an endless crowd of emissaries from the gloomy yonder a plain wide enough to provide all enthusiasms with the right to settle and promulgate at a safe distance from one another. If one had to articulate the radiance and the paradox of the United States in a single sentence, it would be this: it allowed the forces of 'history' to withdraw from 'history'. A further sentence then explains the current temptation: the forces that have escaped 'history' are now in the process of rediscovering 'history' for themselves.

America's globally radiating charm thus comes from the psychopolitical constitution of its 'society'. From the eighteenth century to the present day, the inhabitants of the 'States' have succeeded in producing a non-Leibnizian version of optimism that could be repeatedly updated. Following this model, the given world can be considered the best, provided it looks sufficiently perfect from Ellis Island to be perfected infinitely in additional ways. This positioning on thoroughly positive ground is often taken for naïveté; in truth, it is a reformulation of the meaning of being from the perspective of participating in its improvement.[4] This does not imply scaling optimism down to meliorism, as some America-friendly Europeans believe, but rather ramping optimism up to overoptimism. This permits the historically unprecedented combination of harsh realism and boundless irreverence towards the real – prefigured, if anywhere, from a distance in the staid religiosity of the ancient Romans, who managed to reconcile sentimental reverence towards origin with mechanical cruelty in present-day matters. The imperial Romans too were able to bow their heads before a higher power before returning seamlessly to the everyday business of repression. That is why Benedict of Nursia found the most effective instruction for the New Human Being of a post-Roman Europe when he replaced the 'worship and kill' of Romanism with the 'pray and work' of Christian monastic civility.

One understands, then, why the philosophical and psychopolitical dictates of the American way of life produce the most perfect manifestation of a post-historical mode of existence. While the Europeans (like the Japanese, the Chinese, the Indians, the Russians and some others along with them) only entered the world of post-historical conditions step by step over the last fifty years as new arrivals, the Americans can be considered veterans of post-history owing to their special path. For them, the news of the end of 'history' lost its novelty long ago. For them, the liberation from old scripts took place as soon as their country was founded. The American 'Revolution' took place at the same time as the Declaration of Independence, which abandoned not so much the English motherland as the entire system of Old European measurements, weights and prejudices about the burden of the world. The term 'revolution', when meant politically and connected to the future, thus smacks of pointless excitement to Americans – as if one expected them to wage the war they won against the British Crown two hundred years ago all over again.

The only liberation movement that still has meaning for Americans is that in which one attempts to break free from the personal relics of historical life, one's origins in one's own family: every individual can repeat the secession from history in private by liberating the inner child from the dominance of the parental world. The immeasurable expanse of the American therapy landscapes testifies to the resolute rejection by the country's population of all that was once oppressive external reality. One should not forget that the ultimate aim of the liberation of the inner American child is the victor created before all time – the victor who enters the stage today with the features of a victim. Needless to say, the countless child-selves of the therapeutic archipelago known as the USA still embody the strongest bastion of post-history. Just as the immigrants could only become true Americans at the cost of leaving behind the identities they had brought with them,[5] their descendants are now also liquidating the mental rubble that was brought to the New World from the inner worlds of yesterday. American therapy consists in converting historical fracture into post-historical self-reliance.

Naturally the concept of work also lost its Old European meaning in the USA: it refers not simply to the participation in transforming material into a higher-value product through invested energy – until, at the vanishing point of value creation, workers emancipate themselves from work as such. American work is a performance whose meaning is to show how the subject can proceed from the abundance of opportunities to the superabundance of success. Where else would it be conceivable for people to move to the South and slave away even more than in their previous homes? And where else could people in an officially egalitarian culture look upon the increasingly gaping chasm between rich and poor with such equanimity? The relaxed shamelessness of the American oligarchy proves how far the coronas that surround every success in that country are perceived by the great majority of Americans as emanations of their own faith. In the meritocratic climate, even the exaggeratedly remunerated achievements of others serve to prove the validity of the shared dream. Hence the absence, so enviable for Europeans, of *ressentiments* towards those who have made it.

In the light of all this, one can understand why the figures are always deceptive when dealing with the United States of America. According to its deep economy, the land needs no balances. It lives in a world above numbers, for it never moves from a given value to a higher one, as in trivial growth, but rather from perfection to over-perfection. It is only when viewed superficially that the United States, like every nation in the capitalist system, depends on constant economic and demographic growth. It is not the economic figures that prove its greatness; on the contrary, its greatness radiates the figures.

The thorn in the side of the great escapist nation, however, is the fact that the USA has no longer had what today's patriots call 'energy independence' since the end of the Second World War. Since the encounter between President Franklin D. Roosevelt and King Ibn Saud aboard the USS *Quincy* near the Suez Canal (a few days before the Yalta Conference in February 1945), the strategic alliance between the earth's two great poles of escapism has become one of the constants of recent world politics. From that moment on, the narcissistic escapism of the USA was firmly tied to the narcotic escapism of the Arab rentier states. Because of its strong dependence on petroleum imports from the regions around the Persian Gulf, the American exception thus remains at the mercy of external circumstances in humiliating fashion – the Carter Doctrine, which stated that the USA would take all steps to maintain control over the Gulf's resources, puts this entanglement in a nutshell. It is not surprising, then, that the ugliness of the historical world trickled into the interior of the American sphere of idealization through this realistic bond.[6]

In the light of current events, it is apparent how, at the pinnacle of the unfolding of its power, the most thoroughly post-historically constituted country in the world is seized by the temptation to intervene in 'history' once again – this time not only in the role of the referee, however, who steps out of his reserve for short moments to settle the undignified quarrels between historical powers. The present American incursion into world events shows the hallmarks of a comprehensive restoration: it implies the transformation of the USA back into a historical power, which is inconceivable without the reinterpretation of the world as a scene where historical events are still, or once more, taking place. 'History', however – as explained above – is the successful phase of the unilateral style of action.

The turbulences surrounding the Iraq War, which was intensely desired by the Bush Administration, prepared long in advance and conducted with exemplary one-sidedness, had a mental side effect that could be felt worldwide, and which by far overshadowed the immediate consequences of the fighting: suddenly the USA was perceptible as a foreign body in the moral ecosystem of the post-historical world commune, as its government was displaying, more clearly than ever before, the will to play the part of the single remaining historical power – not only this time, but also in future. To explain what job the Americans were doing in Iraq, George W. Bush had to draw, as usual, on the Old Testament, for example Isaiah 61: 'He has sent me [. . .] to proclaim freedom for the captives and release from darkness for the prisoners.' He was even more emphatic, however, in his invocation of 'history', which alone can give meaning to the current drama: 'This call of history has come to the right country.'[7] 'We meet here during a crucial period in the history of our nation, and of the civilized world. Part of that history was written by others; the rest will be written by us.'[8] In this case, one must ascribe analytical qualities to buzzwords. Bush's America re-historicizes itself, unmistakably stepping out of its post-historical state by claiming for itself, before the whole world, the insignias of the history to be made. Five signs of sovereignty are necessary for this: the primacy of strength, nobility of motives, the privilege of one-sidedness, self-amnesia for past and future violence, and control over the words (and images) that follow the deeds. For this one-sidedly proclaimed re-historicization, America risks alienating its allies in Europe and the rest of the world, but more still breaking with its own best traditions. Moreover, it permits itself the provocation of demonstratively ignoring the choir of reasonable hinderers, including its closest friends on this side of the Atlantic – its worked-up ideologues went so far as to slur this group as a European band of cowards and adolescents, eaters of soft cheese and dubious innards. In their patriotic rage, some Americans even accused the French of being nothing but a horde of unwashed woman-sniffers. If words meant war, then numerous patriotic commentators in the USA would long have declared it upon the sceptics in the rest of the world.

The politics of the United States steps up to the podium like a culture of perpetrators from Europe's most virulent historical period, ready to embark, celebrating its own noble motives in thymotic euphoria, insisting on its national capacities, sure of victory even before the action has begun, remorseless and self-absorbed after the completed operation, always revising its own records of success, monotonously and summarily asserting the rightfulness of its strikes, and willing to bury American casualties with the usual ceremonial trappings, while leaving the very numerous casualties on the other side to their own people with a formal expression of regret at a sub-altern level. As if in some scene from the early Modern Age, the USA sends in its fleets to drive world-taking forward as a naval power; like a modern colonial power, it uses aerial and ethereal weapons to win out in asymmetrical warfare against hopelessly inferior opponents; like a neo-apostolic bringer power, it makes use of the right to invade that follows from the knowledge that they must bring God's gift to mankind – in the present case it is termed 'democracy' – to unwilling recipients, by force if necessary. Let us note that the word *damakrata* has recently come into modern Arabic usage, approximately meaning 'Western assault on a country for the purpose of turning it into a market economy'.[9]

The historico-philosophically decisive motive of the Iraq War lay in the explicit re-establishment of unilateralism as a style of practice; only now, in the light of action theory, is it becoming clear how much this was the central characteristic of the world-historical period. From a Spinozist point of view, the only justification for European world-taking would have been the fact that the powers for it were

available; as every ability has a specific sense of necessity attached to
it, the imperial Europeans in their time were simply proceeding along
the lines of force that were given through their ability. The Anglo-
American intervention in Iraq can be read in analogous fashion: it
proved spirit and strength by presenting itself as a simple imperial 'I
can' on the geopolitical stage. Those involved did what they did – in
Tony Blair's words – 'because we could'.

Naturally all observers, even those favourably disposed towards
the USA, are aware that American militarism has been condemned
for some time to stand out in the post-historical world as a parasite
of yesterday. By its nature and its origin, the American military is a
relic of the 'history' in which America allowed itself to become
involved like an armed moderator of sorts after 1916, without first
questioning its cheerful isolation. From their own planet, the
Americans placed a powerful tangent onto the historical world, where
unliberated souls rolled in the dust of their wars. Subsequently,
however, American armies had grown to a monstrous strength during
their deployments in Europe and the Pacific; they became almost
uncontrollably inflated during the arms race with the Soviet Union,
which spanned almost half a century and made enormous resources
available for so-called 'defence'. Finally, they stagnated at an excessive level when 'history' began to show signs of ending in a nuclear
stalemate.

The significance of the armament era for the post-historical learning cycle reveals itself retrospectively in the fact that here, the mutual
inhibition of the highest-ranking actors had become the primary
evidence of world politics. Once the generals too realized that attack
had lost its priority in the history of armed violence, the historical
institution of war itself seemed ripe for post-historicization. As one
can discern now, however, the age of stalemate left behind an ambigu-
ous legacy whose dark side manifests itself today in the view of the
American leadership that the experience of inhibition purely concerned the military domain, and could be laid aside after the disappearance of the East–West confrontation. With a blindness reminiscent
of classical heroes, American strategists and their consultants
overlook, thanks to their hereditary inability to recognize elementary
facts, that reciprocal inhibition is the modus operandi of the
postmodern world context as such, for this inevitably rests on
compaction, feedback and – to fall back on this tired word after all
– interconnection.

Since then, an unparalleled temptation has been afoot in the disu-
nited West: the temptation to write new scripts for the disinhibition
of the 'only world power'. Does this mean that the hour of the intel-

lectuals will strike again? Will we once more witness thinkers hurrying to stand by those willing to attack in the transition from illusion to practice? Must we brace ourselves for consultant analysts and publicists like Brzezinski, Kagan, Kaplan, Luttwak, Wolfowitz, Podhoretz, Fukuyama, Rice and many others delivering their onslaught on the corridors of power even more successfully than in previously known episodes of great politics? Are not the speechwriters of imperialism jostling one another everywhere to occupy key positions on the new semantic market?

The re-ideologization of the public space is indeed in full swing, with golden times ahead for self-appointed violence experts and for the realists who propagate a new harshness, or a return to the rules of old realpolitik. For the moment, admittedly, it seems that it is less the turn of the academic advisers than of the Islamist activists – and their Western exegetes, who wish to make themselves useful as dream-interpreters of the coming violence.[10] The significance of the Islamists for the re-historicization of the USA cannot be overestimated. They seem to be the men of the moment, addressing the 'call of history' to keen presidential ears – ears that are unexpectedly open to enemy advice. It is the criminal neo-unilaterals from the Middle East who, more clearly than all domestic consultants, call out the keywords to the actors in the Western centres of power for the disinhibition of their unilateral strikes.

We can now see how the foreign policy of the USA has unfolded the paradox of the American exception step by step. This paradox can be articulated in several synonymous turns of phrase: to save the American Dream, its defining actors are hurrying to wake up from it; to retain the privilege of having escaped from history, the political dramaturges are leading their country firmly back into history; to secure their splendid lightness of being, the leadership teams of the United States are steering towards severe overloads; to preserve their country's sources of optimism, its intellectual climate controllers are plunging it into the blackest realism.

The final paradox is shown most clearly in the astute violence handbooks of the war correspondent and polemologist Robert D. Kaplan: *Warrior Politics: Why Leadership Demands a Pagan Ethos* (2002) and *The Coming Anarchy: Shattering the Dreams of the Post Cold War* (2001), two books whose sole purpose is to get the country beneath the stars and stripes in shape for a Hobbesian world that is supposedly not subject to the law of civilized compaction, but rather at the mercy of a generalized hewing and stabbing in almost stateless spaces. Kaplan permits no doubt as to the only possible choice for the role of the planetary Leviathan in this scenario.

The *translatio historiae* into the USA is currently being undertaken with all the pomp and circumstance that befits an investiture. The ritual is opened with the transfer of the territorial zero point from which all mandates for neo-historical action will henceforth emanate: since the autumn of 2001 there has been an American Holy Sepulchre, 'Ground Zero', that gift of militant Islamism to the newly self-historicizing power, a gift that, moreover, gives new proof of the Adamitic power of all things American to imprint self-exclaiming names on the real. It continues with the transfer of innocence, the central figure of postmodern and victimological morality, without which, even in the scripts of neo-history, no lashing out is any longer conceivable; in future, the attack must take place in the victim's name. The ceremony is rounded off by the transfer of authorization to declare a state of emergency – not only with the voice of the political sovereign, who calls their opponent their enemy for the duration of the conflict, but also with that of the ontological sovereign, who establishes the fact of adversity in the world and declares eternal war upon it.

This would seem to initiate a complete remake of 'history'. The *translatio actionis* into the USA – starting with the demission of Europe before a *fait accompli* after 1945 – is joined by the *translatio passionis* that has constituted a new colour on the American flag since '9/11'. Since the potential super-perpetrator also proved able to pass itself off as the super-victim, there are no longer any obstacles to the country's mobilization for the new 'making of world history' – except for its own democratic-escapist tradition.

What now follows can, to the extent that it has so far become discernible, be summarized under the heading 'The Revenge of Post-History'. For, far from allowing themselves to be infected with the élan of the self-proclaimed historical power, a significant part of the remaining democratically committed world seems to have conspired to make life difficult for the last radiant perpetrator on earth. While the American army in Iraq swept Saddam Hussein's demoralized troops aside within a few days, marginally supported by Britons, Poles, Italians and other contenders for tips granted to waiters at the table of newly served 'history', the vast remainder of the unwarlike lined up all over the world with new self-confidence, as if they had only become fully aware of their own values when faced with this spectacle. The values are, of course, the same as those purveyed by the post-historical America of yesterday, values approached from all sides since 1945 on both straight and crooked paths. These critics of the Iraq War do not speak out against the USA's leaders with the voice of 'anti-Americanism' – a word that some agitators like to view as a secondary term for 'anti-Semitism' in order to reinforce the unseemliness of the objection all the more. They say what they see fit to say not out of immature contrariness but in unison with post-historical logic, which views the unilateral behaviour of the world power as a quotation from the golden days of Europeid inconsideration. What is expressed in the many-voiced reservations about the foreign-policy habitus of the USA is no more or less than a clarified anti-unilateralism. In a field of highly fed-back political practice, this has long constituted a natural mode of co-operative culture – which also includes presenting the necessary distinctions discreetly and indulgently as 'criticism among friends'. It is also clear why Israel, America's co-exceptional ally and co-defier of international opinion, is made to feel its share of the clarified anti-unilateral spirit. Those interested are free to misinterpret this as 'new anti-Semitism' – which, to complicate matters, does actually exist, although the term 'anti-Semitism', which referred to political racism and thus to a historically overcome intra-European matter, has long ceased to be appropriate in the old and new frictions between Israel and its Arab and Muslim haters.[11]

But why do a great many Americans, even those who cannot be suspected of Bushism, have so much difficulty rediscovering the authentic voice of America in the voices of the war-sceptical others from the Seine to the Ganges? Should the veterans of post-historical life not get on superbly with the recruits from other countries? Would it not be the most natural reaction for all self-aware Americans to welcome all latecomers who disavow the Old European vice of making history? How is it that, at the political level, the most mature culture of post-historicity withdraws with such aversion and contempt from the primary signs of the post-historical world – the laws of reciprocity, the return of deeds to their doer and the systemic feedback of operations? This contempt is expressed most brazenly in the USA's dealings with the United Nations, which it has meanwhile come to view merely as a machine for producing simultaneously translated paralysis and a breeding ground of mediocre diplomatic bohemianism. Yet even if these judgements were correct, one would still have to ask: why do those Americans on political duty show such a spectacular disinterest in becoming a member of a club that would immediately admit people like them?

The *moral* answer to these questions is that the USA identifies itself with its role as the key power in the maintenance of political order out of a sense of responsibility: this great country must therefore cultivate its benign unilateralism so that it can neutralize malign or incorrigible countries (which are given the 'rogue' label). A *pragmatic* answer, however, would state that the USA is condemned to an aggressive geopolitical calculation of interests in order to occupy as many key positions on the geopolitical chessboard as possible before new global players such as China and Europe gain strength – hence the checkmating of Europe through the integration of Turkey into the EU, which Washington desires. The *noopolitical* answer, which was recently suggested by the cyberwar experts Arquilla and Ronfeldt, is that the USA is rallying its ideational and communicative resources in the face of the unstoppable information revolution in order to assert its leadership in the noosphere of the twenty-first century to the fullest extent.[12] The *mythodynamic* answer, finally, can be recognized in the general motifs of the American Dream: anyone who defines themselves as its active carrier is unwilling to become involved in situations where everyone who wants to do something does not retain enough leeway to do what they envisage; they are, and will remain, unwilling to relinquish the seal of chosenness inextinguishably inscribed on the bodies and souls of those receptive to it; they are, and will remain, unwilling to give precedence to the objective reasons for being depressed over the special right to exhilaration.

The American secession from history thus came at a price that is gradually becoming estimable: in order to exit from history into post-history over two hundred years ago, the secessionists had to export and retain an Old European subject formation that now makes them immune to learning for generalized post-historicity. The combination of a post-historical exceptional situation and a strong perpetrator position was waiting to disintegrate explosively sooner or later – at the latest when the motivation surpluses of American potential could no longer be acted out in national projects (and in the hero cult of Hollywood scripts).[13] From that point on, it was in the air that actual 'history' would be demanded back by perpetrators ready to act – all the more so because the American psyche proved completely unable to contain the spirit of revenge after the attack of 9/11. Certainly numerous citizens of the United States had begun to suspect, since the Vietnam debacle at the latest, how much their dream was in jeopardy, as much through the internal course of the American experiment as through the external course of the world; but only a few still want to continue along the path that led the country into a phase of self-doubt and reconsideration after the lost and unjust war in East Asia.

The first re-historicization of America after 1968 was characterized by disappointment, narcissistic depression and self-reproach after the war crimes carried out in East Asia on Vietnamese soil; at that time, the task was to deal with the evidence that the country had lost its privileged status of being good. The first return to history (which was simultaneously a return to ugliness) was assisted by models of excessive cultural criticism from Germany and France, and led to a cult of ethnic and victimist particularity presented as 'history from below'. 'Critical theory' played an outstanding part in this as a ready-made of social criticism: it provided a demonstration of how easily criticism can be turned into kitsch; for just as kitsch functions in the art system as a short cut to grand emotions, critical kitsch acts as a short cut to outrage. It transforms the elevation of noble sentiment over ignoble facts into a mass-produced item. One need hardly explain why there had to be a market for this in the USA.

This market has now become saturated to such a degree that neither a further twist of the masochism spiral nor an additional radicalization of the already excessive suspicion towards the 'system' could offer any moral gains.[14] The second re-historicization, by contrast, was staged very much in the style of a manic restoration from the time of George H. W. Bush onwards. It seemed self-evident that it would deal once more with 'history' from above – or rather, from the very top. Where current 'history' is meant to flow directly from the highest sources, it must proceed as the present action of God through a chosen nation whose leaders, not unlike Protestant Jesuits, have found the most effective strategy for self-disinhibition. This return into history also installed a variety of kitsch, this time as a ready-made of political theology.

In 1993, Edward N. Luttwak published a book with the programmatic title *The Endangered American Dream: How to Stop the United States from Becoming a Third-World Country and How to Win the Geo-Economic Struggle for Industrial Supremacy* – a book that was welcomed by a sedate patriotic-masochistic press as shock therapy at the right time for their relegation-threatened nation. Luttwak had already made a name for himself as one of the leading exponents of contemporary strategic studies; since then he has also been considered an intelligent exegete of his country's latent political theology, in that he reformulated America's elitist imperative with the help of a secular sociology of competition. As an observer of global trends, Luttwak had naturally understood that the exceptional situation of America was unsustainable in the long term; as a declared exceptionalist, however, he showed clearly that for him, as for the great majority of his compatriots, accepting this fact without resistance was out of the question. His intervention combines these two aspects to arrive at a 'visionary' perspective. In the first phase, Luttwak brings up the warning signs of American 'decadence': the economies of Japan and Europe have largely caught up on the

American post-war lead; the publicly funded school system has been stagnating for years; the middle classes have been economically and culturally depleted since the Reagan era; capitalism is lacking the money after which it is named; drug dealers do their business in broad daylight, even near the government district of Washington – not forgetting that for some time, American prostitutes working in Japan have no longer been able to demand a 'US girl bonus', for when a country's star falls, the price of its people's flesh on the international market does the same.

For Luttwak, these are no less than indications of the USA's free fall into insignificance. What others would consider a return of America to the relative normality of a still enormously rich, yet also problem-ridden civilization is interpreted by the author as the descent of his country into near-nothingness; for his readers, the term 'third-world country' sounds sufficiently apocalyptic to make it clear what the USA must never become. For the chosen, mediocrity is forbidden. Consequently, in a second step, the author recommends a programme of mobilization for the imminent geo-economic world war, from which his country is meant to emerge once again as number one – before later, at the pinnacle of its success, initiating a disarmament on its own terms.

Luttwak's deeply symptomatic book shows that the American ideologues want to save their country's dream rather than interpret it, but cannot save it without turning it on its head. Here the performative constitution of the American project, the eternally vital battle for the soul of the country, changes into a dangerous auto-hypnotic programming towards neo-nationalist and ultra-narcissistic aims. On the American *Raft of the Medusa*, the existence of the depression group is for the most part simply denied. According to the puritanical code there are no losers in this country, only people who wallow in self-pity. Luttwak does, at least, manage a few references to the USA's explosively growing drug problem in his review of the 'endangered American Dream' – in the capital alone, 25,000 people are reportedly earning a living as professional or amateur drug dealers. Their clients are certainly not the children of the Woodstock generation, however, which was hungry for illuminating excursions to the archetypal realm; they are armies of frustrated individuals who have committed themselves to chemical salvation from American reality.

The psychopolitical accounting fraud that carries the system as a whole is primarily meant to render invisible the gigantic number of losers who had to stay behind in the gambling hall of the pursuit of happiness. Nonetheless, the data is in such plain sight that even admirers of the American model find it difficult to ignore. The number of hopelessly impoverished people in the USA is greater than the population of Iraq, there are more chronic consumers of psychophar-macological drugs than in any other country in the world, there is a higher rate of extreme obesity than anywhere else,[15] there are more politically unrepresented groups and non-voters than in any other democratic state, there are ten times as many prisoners per capita as in Europe and six to eight times more than in most other countries in the world. And yet all these problem collectives remain true to the American way of life by staying above water through an elaborated system of depression concealment and inner accounting fraud. They avert their eyes from the abyss that yawns beneath every hapless fortune-seeker in the country. One hears a melody drifting upwards from it, a well-known melody whose words one can only make out when listening closely. Once understood, they make the listener shudder: 'If I can't make it there, I won't make it anywhere.'

Nonetheless, it would mean doing an injustice to the American excep-tion if one did not take into account the role of the USA in world politics after 1918. In the present context, it has become evident that the term 'world politics' does not simply refer to a dimension of what we call international relations; it stands for the totality of political regulation tasks involved in the management of the great hothouse. Thus world politics is nothing other than the administration of the crystal palace – policing measures, security services and disposal methods included. If the United States is so often termed a form of world police on account of its foreign policy function, this is for the simple reason that the duty of the modern hegemon has undeniably fallen to US Americans: they have accepted the role of guaranteeing the political and military conditions for the running of the great comfort system. The moral premises of this commitment could be viewed as a self-transcending egotism: it is based on the assumption (confirmed on more than a few occasions) that what is good for the USA also holds advantages for both its Atlantic and its non-Atlantic partners. This is the objective reason for the reliable constant of Western European Americanophilia after 1945. It is, after all, a proven fact that the current world system – which, as we have seen, is by no means a sphere without an outside – is a patchwork of vary-ingly free market economies on the basis of nation-states whose outer borders are marked almost everywhere by the presence of American troops.

If one acknowledges these conditions, the liberal notion of the primacy of the economy appears in a new light: one must indeed assume the priority of economic facts within the capitalist world interior – but these facts have always had a world-political, or more precisely a geopolitical character, because the great hothouse cannot be run successfully without the securing of resources and management of its shell. In the militaristic style of US foreign policy (especially the increasing militarization of energy policy), then, we should see the regulatory component of Western consumption structures as a whole. From this perspective, the division in the Atlantic community provoked by Bushism takes on great civilization-political significance, for it must now be seen whether Europeans are capable of emancipating themselves from the status of a silent partner in the American politics of violence, without themselves re-militarizing their relations with the suppliers of energy and natural resources.

40

The Uncompressible, or:
The Rediscovery of the Extended

Once again: in the crystallized world system, everything is subject to the compulsion of movement. Wherever one looks in the great comfort structure, one finds each and every inhabitant being urged to constant mobilization; yet none of what changes and moves still has the quality of 'history'. Possibly the only addenda to the complex of events and narratives once known as world history will be a world climate protocol, a corresponding world energy codex and the creation of a global environmental police – desiderata whose realization is currently only foreseeable as a distant option, as the USA and other high-consumption countries will, for the time being, feel too strong to forego their prerogative of increased environmental exploitation.

In terms of the human spatial experience, the main result of terrestrial globalization for the populations of European nations was that the world became wonderfully large, though this was accompanied by shock at the sublime uninhabitability of the oceans. I have discussed the ambivalent anti-maritime undertone in the affective balance of most Modern Age Europeans – culminating philosophically in Kant's demand for things to comply with the human cognitive apparatus, especially those of philosophers with lifetime professorships. This was echoed in Heidegger's regionalism, which held that life in harbour towns, let alone on ships, was an aberration. For a long time, opening the mind towards the sea remained the province of minorities, and was only truly at home in the merchant subcultures of coastal towns and, if anywhere further inland, then only among itchy-footed dreamers and readers of discoverers' memoirs. Since then, however, the opposition between 'sea-churners' and

250 The Grand Interior

'land-treaders' so virulent for the entire Modern Age has lost its meaning almost entirely. Whether one is more maritime or terran in one's disposition, the rapid media of today have opened the horizon for new formats.

The caesura between modernity and postmodernity can be highlighted by referring to the spatial feelings of people within the comfortable installation. The sticky omnipresence of the news has ensured that countless numbers experience the once-wide world as a dirty little ball. Those born after the advent of television know nothing of the sweetness of life in the boundless world. The true feeling of the Modern Age, which blossomed here and there into the 1930s, presupposed slow media. Only seagoing vessels, earth globes and travel literature could give the mixture of awe and curiosity a form in which the seafaring peoples and reading persons on land could respond to the earth's newly explored dimensions. A contributing factor was that the slowness of long-distance traffic in the nautical age left the distances their dignity. The long routes kept the prices for access to foreign lands high; they contributed to the exotic veil still spread over the discovered world. Until the advent of mass tourism after the Second World War, first-hand knowledge of the world was costly, rare and seductive. We recall: Othello won Desdemona's love because he could relate how he suffered on his journeys to the wilderness.[1]

All this became one memory among many through the tachotechnologies of the twentieth century. Within two generations, telephone networks, radio systems and jet engines in air travel caused the overcoming of distance to be taken for granted to such a degree that space was perceived as an almost negligible factor. As it could not offer any appreciable resistance to its rapid traversals, it seemed to constitute the basic area of being-in-the-world, accommodating reduction, compression and annulment almost of its own accord. In 1848, speaking of the 'revolutionary' achievements of the bourgeois age in the second most famous passage of *The Communist Manifesto*, Marx and Engels stated that 'all that is solid melts into air'; to this, the sensibility of the twentieth century adds: all that is extended and demands space is compressed into a minimal inert block. Intercontinental telephone conversations are the most obvious manifestation of this; anyone who wants to see the myth of the disappearance of space confirmed need only reach for the telephone or perform a few mouse clicks.

The 'spatial revolution' of the present, of which Carl Schmitt wanted to give an account in his observations on the fading world-historical role of *Land and Sea*,[2] was actually concerned with spatial compression. What it brought about was the neutralization of distances. It negated the separating effect of interstices; it shortened the paths between here and yonder to a remainder that could not be compressed any further. The residual space could be bothersome, but it was no longer in a position to demand attention or reverence. Though the moderns do not possess the gift of bilocation reported of some medieval saints, that of translocation is very natural for them – and if they cannot be in two places simultaneously, they certainly can be in any number of successive ones.

Under these circumstances, space became a seemingly ignorable factor. It had been defeated as distance and barrier in practice, been scorned in theory as a dimension serving mastery, and become a silent background as a carrier of traffic and communication; in ideology-critical terms, it had a bad reputation as a centre of reification. From the perspective of those who demanded swiftness, the only good space was a dead space; its foremost virtue was the ability to make itself imperceptible. For the sake of rapid processes, it was meant to step back from all its former ontological purposes: creating discrete neighbourhoods, scattering particles, separating bodies, positioning agents, offering boundaries between the extended, making clusters more difficult, containing explosions and drawing multiplicities together into a unity. The only traditional quality of space that remained was its conductivity – or, more precisely, the aspect combination conductivity/connectivity/mediality, without which the endeavours of modernity to overcome space through compression would not lead to any meaningful results. The space of distance, separation and placement called nature was replaced by the space of gathering, connection and compaction that surrounds us as the technical environment. Here the removed can be called into the here and now physically or *in effigie* from any distance. Monitors show what spatiality means today: one calls up, one manipulates, one combines, one secures, one deletes. Thanks to the global networks, countless points on the earth's surface are transformed into reading rooms – assuming that a collection[3] is what Heidegger sought to show, namely the gathering of signs of being to a here-now-us collecting point for the truth. As we know, Heidegger held the bizarre view that there were only two authentic reading rooms for the great study of being: one among the pre-Socratics (or Aristotle), the other in Freiburg-Todtnauberg. Suffice it to say that on this point, as on many others, Heidegger scarcely had any followers. His view that language was the central collector is likewise not supported by the evidence in the current multimedia world.

The modern spatial compression (alias the spatial 'revolution') continues a cultural caesura that had originally taken place in ancient Greece through the addition of vowels to the Middle Eastern consonantal alphabets. As shown by McLuhan, Goody, Havelock and others, it was the advent of the Greek alphabet that enabled the development of Old European reader subjectivity, whose main characteristic was the ability to 'deal with texts' – that is, the situation-independent comprehension of meaning.[4] Greek poetry and prose render explicit an otherwise latent ability of the human intellect: to imagine persons, things and constellations in their absence. Written texts enable the intelligence to emancipate itself from the necessity of *in situ* attendance in varyingly understandable circumstances. This means that in order to deal with a situation cognitively, I no longer need to immerse myself in it as a participant and, in a sense, merge with it; reading a description of it is sufficient, and gives me the freedom to stay where I am and associate with it what I want. After the textual caesura, being-in-the-world explicitly split into experienced and imagined situations – or rather, the textualization of imagined situations enabled them to break the monopoly of understanding-by-being-in-the-situation. The Greek alphabet initiated the adventure of the de-contextualization of meaning. What that means becomes clear if one considers that until the medial turn in the nineteenth century, all higher culture in Europe – leaving aside the specialized developments of music and panel painting – had been written culture, the simulation of something absent, and that even musical and graphic culture were tied to writing systems. This corresponded to a politics born of the spirit of bureaucracy and imperial epics.

Old European textuality belongs to the prehistory of modern spatial compression because it enabled the revolt of the text against the context, the tearing-away of meaning from the lived situations. In so far as it rehearses de-contextualizing thought (usually termed reading), it emancipates the intellect from the obligation to participate in real constellation, unlocking for it the boundless expanse of non-*in situ* worlds. It creates the theoretical human being – exemplarily attacked by Nietzsche in the figure of Socrates. Its representative is the strong observer, that junior of the absolute which is elsewhere in any given situation. Even on the point of death, the wise man behaves as if he had already read the scene somewhere; Socrates even claims that in life, he is already in the place where death will take him: the other location, the place of eternal forms, the home of the immortal letter. Socrates was able to become the European wisdom hero par excellence because he lived his life in constant rejection of the authority held by that which was present; above all, he rejected the expectation that he would piously immerse himself in the situations manipulated by rhetoricians, politicians and windbags. He is the chief witness of the intelligence that 'drops out' in order to re-contextualize itself in ideational circumstances. Since Plato, this twofold operation – the intelligence's break with current situations and its resettlement in ideal ones – has been known as philosophy. Wherever it left its traces, one had to decide between a reading or a participating attitude towards life.[5]

One can recognize the success of this greatest European liberation movement in the fact that there were already anti-intellectual restorations in antiquity that turned against the supposedly false freedom of floating in an imaginative space purged of real-world ties. The Jesuan polemic against the Pharisees was one such reaction of the lived against the read, as was the laughter of the Thracian maid at the scatterbrained philosopher Thales in the well. Since the Stoics, ancient teachings of wisdom have been motivated primarily by the wish to re-embed thought in lived life, even when, with typical philosophical presumption, propagating the unity of the lifeworld and the universe. Diogenes is the comic hero of the un-comical return into the embodiable.

One could call these tendencies the first re-appropriation of the *in situ* principle: they articulate the protest by the participatory sense against the (allegedly or actually) excessive breaking-away of the reading-observing intelligence from shared situations. Diogenes, Jesus and the Thracian maid are thus reactionaries in the precise sense of the word, at least in the eyes of those who prefer reading to living. All three, as well as the Stoics and the Epicureans, would have accepted this label – if anything, they might have elucidated their position by pointing out that life, without ceasing to be a primary impulse of its own, must occasionally be a reaction: a pure opposition to all deforming constraints and pure resistance against unjustified compressions. In the language of maids: one shouldn't put up with everything; and in leftist rhymes: without defence, your life is a pretence.

Since then, such 'reactionary' impulses have been wandering through the ages in manifold variations; they return with the early socialists, the Situationists, the communitarians and the group therapists. They echo in the vitalists' criticism of the armchair theorists. They probably reached their most highly articulated level in Marshall MacLuhan's praise of audio culture, which he claimed restored to holistic, non-linear perception the rights that had been undermined by European writing culture. One response to this was Maurice Blanchot's book-romantic thesis that literature held the potential for a 'total experience'. This position is illustrative through its absurdity:

by celebrating reading as a total power of absorption, it seeks to make us forget that it is in the nature of reading to dissolve the totalitarianism of lived situations.[6]

A comparable development can be observed in current thought with reference to ignored space. The great return to the context now appears in the manifold reflections on 'embedding' as passive solidarity. Once distances are seemingly only there to be overcome, once national cultures only exist to mingle with other traditions, once all the earth's surfaces only represent the immobile counterparts to their elegant collections as geographical maps and aerial photographs, and once space as such means no more than the nothingness between two electronic workplaces – then we can predict the direction which the resistance against these de-realizations will take: sooner or later, the culture of presence will have to assert its rights once more against the culture of imagination and memory. The experience of the extended will defend itself against the effects of compressions, abbreviations and skimmings. Just as de-contextualized meaning has 'ultimately' always depended on being embedded into a non-omittable situation in order not to disappear entirely into abstractions, so too compressed space must be tied to the unspoilt experiences of extension if it is to avoid vanishing completely in secondary processes. This realization is articulated today by those who insist on the memory of the local against the de-contextualizing tendency of universalisms and tele-machines.

The new spatial thought is the revolt against the contracted world. The rediscovery of slowness is accompanied by that of local extension – but how? By suddenly ceasing to shrink our own existence to a scale of one to one hundred thousand, or one to ten million? By suddenly learning to read extended life in maps again?[7] By finding our way back from chronolatry to topophilic feelings? If, in a word, it were once again time to drive the shameless sellers from the temple of the present?

Yet, as plausible as these corrective movements may seem – could we be sure of hearing the pure voices of the place after expelling the traders? The re-emphasis of the local has its pitfalls, for the term 'local' is one of the most frequently misunderstood words in the language games of those journalists and sociologists who have chosen globalization as their field. Even 'reactionary' spatial thought must be learned. Usually 'local' is used as an antonym of 'global' or 'universal' – with 'global' and 'local' referring to the same homogeneous and continuous space. Homogeneous spaces are defined by the equipotency of points within them, and the connectivity of those points through direct lines.

This spatial conception made it possible to assert that 'The universal is the local without walls'[8] – a claim that sounds striking, yet could not be further from the truth. It seems appealing because it defines the world as a sum of provinces; so there is no universality, only inter-provincial relationships. It is symptomatic because it expresses the helpless common sense that one encounters wherever the spatial constitution of existence in the global age is brought up. It is naïve because it posits a symmetry where there can be none, and tears down walls where none stand. The hybrid terms 'glocal', 'glocalize' and 'glocalization' introduced by the world sociologist Roland Robertson are cut from the same cloth;[9] they too mirror the deceptions underlying current discourses on globalization.

The error, simply put, lies in relating the local and the global to each other in the same way as the point and the field. Wherever this occurs, the local is inevitably understood as if its nature were the same as the global, but the local residents simply refused to admit it; the local is envisaged like a spot in a regular spatial grid. Let us imagine an introverted nest on the edge of the Alps where a multinational corporation plans to set up a branch: if the managers explain to the natives why they have come, and the residents concede that there is no harm in letting the strangers in, the pragmatic union of 'us' and 'them' should be complete after a short time, and the large would soon feel at home in the small as much as the small in the large. One always assumes something unproven: that the relations between the strangers and the locals take place in a homogeneous locational space where positions are fundamentally reversible.

In reality, the meaning of 'local' lies in the re-emphasis of the asymmetrical with all its implications. This is an intellectual event of some consequence, as placing this weight on the place heralds a language for the non-compressible and non-abbreviated. The emphasis on the local asserts the autonomous rights of that which is extended in itself, despite the progress of de-contextualization, compression, mapping and the neutralization of space.

With localism, one could say, existentialism is reformulated in space-analytical terms. Now it is capable of saying with adequate explicitness what existence as a self-spatializing force means. It learns thoroughly how to articulate that, and why, being defined by embeddedness has *de facto* always been an unsuspendable factor. This gives rise to a general logic of participation, situatedness and indwelling – I refer again to the fact that contemporary art, with its turn towards installation, has achieved a significant headstart on philosophical analysis in this respect.[10] This reveals that there is no existence without participation in unabbreviated being-extended, being-connected, being-possessed, unless the ability to be embedded were undermined by a psychosis or by constant fleeing – but is psychosis in particular not a type of unauthorized building, and is fleeing not space-forming in a certain sense? The indwelling relationship – as shown by the central spatial thinkers of the twentieth century – is always connected to an interior-forming activity, a de-distancing practice (in Heidegger's sense) and a pacifying cultivation (in Schmitz's sense).[11] Where there is habitation, things, symbionts and persons are joined to form local solidary systems. Dwelling develops a practice of locational fidelity over an extended period – this is especially palpable, incidentally, among nomads, often misunderstood and cited as witnesses to cheerful infidelity, who usually seek out the same places in a rhythm of long-term cycles. Dwelling creates an immune system of repeatable gestures; through successful habitualization, it combines being-relieved with being-burdened by clear tasks.

For this reason, indwelling is the mother of asymmetry. It may be that social philosophers are right in teaching that humans are 'socialized' by learning to take over the role of the other; this does not mean taking over the dwelling of the other. The place held by the other can neither be stolen nor be rented. Indwelling transpires precisely as that which I can only do with myself and those close to me, and the other only with themselves and those close to them. The positions are ontologically inexchangeable, like the left and right hands of the bilateralized body. At most, we can enter a *synoikismós*, a communal residence, or a *koínos bios*, living together in a shared enclosure; these would give rise to a new focus of shared cultivations from whose wealth and quarrels other others are excluded. In this case, higher-level communal residences should in turn group us together with the other others; beyond a certain size, however, such syntheses would only be legal figures and rhetorical addresses.

Elementary foyer solidarity, if it can be so called, is a basic layer of the ability to say 'we': the first person plural pronoun is not the term for a group object, but rather the performative evocation of a collective constituted by self-excitation and self-spatialization. This does not rule out trans-local solidarity on the basis of empathy with absent strangers – the Christian churches, when not denying one another salvation, and the Buddhist *sanghas*, to name only these two, prove quite clearly that love can form a *res extensa* of its own kind as long-distance attention and coherence in the diaspora. Certainly, there is also the projective solidarity with which tele-sentimentality, the modern variation of hysteria, dons a 'we' costume. It is especially common among inhabitants of the crystal palace whom one shows images of disasters outside.

Whoever inhabits does not behave towards their dwelling, their environment or their social world as a cartographer or land surveyor. A geometrician who comes home stops measuring and reducing; they project themselves into the habitual at a scale of one to one. Indwelling is passive commitment to one's own situation, a suffering and co-producing of its vague and unmistakable extension; it is partisanship and a sense of self-inclusion in a regional pleroma. This can neither be reduced true to scale nor expanded beyond a certain degree.

One sees immediately that the extendedness of embedding situations is the natural accomplice of the lasting. It is the origin of cultivations that cannot be achieved without repetition and persisting with a single matter. One can, of course, move house and settle anew, one can divorce and remarry, one can emigrate and be naturalized somewhere else – as we know, the moderns do all this more often and more aggressively than the ancients. Even in new situations, however, the basic situation returns; one establishes oneself in a particular place and extends oneself by means of local resonances. Hölderlin's intuition probably articulated the *in situ* principle most clearly: 'Full of merit, but poetically, man dwells on this earth.' The phenomenologist Merleau-Ponty interprets the rooting of being in its own worldly voluminosity with the statement that 'our body is not primarily *in* space: it is of it', and Heidegger offered the most general formulation possible in his analytics of being-in-the-world: 'In Dasein there lies an essential tendency towards closeness.'[12] These claims converge in a space-theoretical perspective: they state that existence, as the positing of a symbolic and physical volume, means residing in the uncompressible. One could even say that existence and self-extension converge. Dwelling implies the principle of 'occasional sealing', which means that even those who change their residence frequently cannot avoid developing a habitus of dwelling on their way. Psychologists have observed that people who travel a great deal show behavioural patterns which they interpret as a mobile cocooning; the models for this are the aforementioned nomads, for they, quaintly put, are at home on their travels, or, less quaintly put, they use deterritorialization itself to reterritorialize themselves.[13] This is a different way of pointing out that nomadic cultures, for all the flexibility one attributes to them, constitute the most conservative, 'domestic', closed systems that have appeared in the spectrum of social evolutions.

41

In Praise of Asymmetry

It is thus hyperbolically true, but objectively false, that all things solid melt into air. The great mobilization through capital has to leave alone whatever resists liquidation. It cannot shift local cultures by foreign money transfer; it can modify the generative processes, but not replace them. Nor does everything extended simply disappear through compression. The theses of Marx and Engels, and those of the current sophists of spatial elimination, prove rather that the world's capitalist compaction is mirrored in a great many arrogant exaggerations that one cannot expect to retain their aesthetic and moral acceptability in the long term. Apart from all its factual characteristics, 'globalization' is a topos that attracts populist ghost lights in droves: it serves as a collecting point for unfounded claims about the course of the world. Alongside its complex real-world operation, it has generated a superstructure of simplificatory fantasies and panics for household and state use – most of them sociological versions of flying dreams or phobic and thrilling visions of the loss of employment, body weight and local identity. They invoke the devaluation of local competencies, proclaim invasion and foreign infiltration; but most of all they speak of being forced to compete with invisible people who have no scruples about doing most things better and more cheaply – like those shameless dentists from Hungary and Poland who replace the teeth of Western Europeans for half the usual price.

Political publicists who ride the wave of such sentiment fly kites over the heads of the audience, and for a while one watches them with fascination. But if one traces the popular phantasms and exag-

gerations back to objective factors, one finds structures and procedures that speak a different language. Even in the midst of the
long-distance delirium of 'globalization', the great majority of services and transactions are inevitably local; not only do local telephone
calls far outnumber long-distance calls, but economic transactions
also take place mostly locally and between neighbours, albeit not
necessarily in face-to-face situations. Even the German export
economy, proportionally the largest in the world, does most of its
business with partners in the European Union, primarily those behind
the next fence – France and the Netherlands. Even if long-distance
commodity trading is a massive reality, as gigantic fleets of oil tankers
and container vessels testify, to say nothing of the speculative flair of
the money markets, most purchases and sales of real goods are essentially changes of ownership on an expanded weekly market, and in
many branches the talk of competition is no more than a rumour.
Domestic demand remains the soul of the real economy everywhere;
the American automobile industry, to name a well-known example,
has long ceased even to attempt selling its products abroad. The
majority of French citizens still spend their holidays in the south of
their own country, be they sovereigntists or Atlanticists, and whether
they say *mondialisation* or 'globalization'.

Such remarks on economic facts, admittedly, only approach the
meaning of localism indirectly, as the decisive dimensions of local
becoming are entirely unaffected by such oppositions as local market/
global market or village/city. Lived extendednesses are not products
that can be sold, either in the immediate vicinity or overseas. The
contrast between the urban and the rural too plays a very indirect
part in the existential-topological interpretation of being-in-the-place.
Procreation, for example – to confront the reader with the most
heightened case of asymmetry – is a process that no one would object
to terming local. It is subject to peculiar spatial laws, starting with
the increasing rotundity of the mothers, to which one cannot truly
do justice either in the phrases of the anti-globalists or in those of
the neo-liberals. Involuntary, invasive habitation in the first niche
does not express an equal relationship between the visitor and the
maternal host; from the child's point of view, it is the most one-sided
operation it will ever perform in its existence, even if it should later
become a dictator. That it can nonetheless be welcomed proves the
resilience of the asymmetry we call life.

Next to biological procreation, it is the growth and training of
children, the cultural passing-on and adoption of this offering by the
recipient generations, that offer the most powerful paradigms for the
incompressible which develops in obstinately asymmetrical processes.

Learning to live means learning to be in places; places are essentially unabbreviable spheric extensions surrounded by a ring of things that are omitted and stay away.[1] Being-in-the-world will always retain the basic feature that it leaves out everything in which it cannot itself be present. Thus the school of existence implies learning extension as learning navigation in uncompressible time-space fabrics.

In procreation and child-rearing, the asymmetry of transmission makes itself felt in all successful processes of generations or 'traditions'. So far, there has never been a culture that did not expect its children to be on the taking side in the passing on of cultural knowledge. Language is inevitably there before those who will learn it; its internal might is so spacious that there was good reason to view it as the 'house of being'. This characterization only stands out as romantic hyperbole in the modern media world, as it no longer sufficiently acknowledges the marginalization of linguistic practices. This makes it all the clearer why natural languages are a nuisance for those who propagate the view that we all have to move far more: they are offended by these sluggish symbolic systems, as they do not readily submit to the demand for compression and acceleration. In the realm of signs, they are what real estate is in the realm of things – with the difference that the latter can be brought into circulation as commodities, whereas languages can neither be bought nor sold, only learned. For members of the fast classes, learning a language is one of the worst ordeals; it is like the Chinese water torture, where slowness is the soul of cruelty. From the liberal perspective, natural languages are the greatest obstacles to modernization in the world, and prove only the regressiveness and self-satisfaction of the speakers. Whoever seriously believes that French, Polish, German, Korean and other similar vessels of lethargy will get them through the twenty-first century evidently considers themselves part of a losers' collective. There is only one way to be fit for the future: monoglossia, that is to say holding on to the natal idiom. According to the modernizers, the world should be such that all permissible situations can be expressed in basic English; this has proved highly successful at airports and board meetings, so why not in other circumstances too? It is for related reasons – because of the resistance to extension in more developed cultural practices – that positivistic training planners object to the humanities in general, and the concept of literary and artistic education in particular. They see clearly that reading *Faust* costs entire days, while *War and Peace* delays the reader for several weeks; and anyone who wants to become familiar with all of Beethoven's piano sonatas and Rihm's string quartets will have to invest months.

The principle of asymmetrical extension is not only characteristic of micro-sociological phenomena or the development of languages and high-culture competencies. It also pervades the core area of the political sphere – starting with the right to citizenship, which splits living, featherless, two-legged creatures into sharply asymmetrical groups: the members and non-members of the nation. The same 'us and them' difference is nestled in the heart of the great solidary-communal structures, especially the pension systems, where the correspondence between entitlement to benefits and appropriate contributions from those involved must be guarded with legitimate jealousy. Here everything depends on the system's ability to establish successfully an asymmetry between contributors and non-contributors and to limit its subversion by 'social parasites'.

That localism is not reactive in its nature, but must rather be understood as an affirmation of creative extension-in-the-place, is evident in the main business of democratic life, namely recruiting citizens for 'public duties' via their citizenship. What has summoned city-dwellers to participate in the community since the return of cities in late medieval Europe is the local force field, where the most agile pursuers of personal interests suddenly discover themselves as *cittadini*, as *citizens*, as *Bürger*, as *citoyens* – that is, as carriers of a shared interest and an exaggerated animation. The local force field is not political, in so far as collective affects circulate within it; otherwise politics would merely be the emanation of local disturbances and perfidies. And it is political, in so far as the community, the city or the nation (and perhaps the group of nations) constitutes the realization of a will embodied in that place to solve problems recognized through voiced differences of opinion and passions, and to re-examine found solutions. This only succeeds when the political place simultaneously projects itself into the future with local egotism and local enthusiasm – that is, when the place is stronger than the ideologies and the civil commune remains more attractive than the multinational sects that grasp for the state. If I am unable to have provincial feelings, politics is not a suitable profession for me. The *res publica* can only function as a parliament of local spirits. Civil societies soon decay if they fall into the hands of ideologues and sect leaders who are passing through (Hitler was the prototype of the stranger who gains power among weakened natives with slogans – which Hermann Broch noted and described in his 'mountain novel' *The Spell*, still one of the most far-reaching works of fascism theory).

The totalitarian concept politicians of the twentieth century demonstrated where the seizure of power through phantom programmes at the expense of polis-based immune forces and local civic spirits can lead within a few years.

As far as speculative capitalism as an abstract, invasive programme of success is concerned, one will have to call upon its current exegetes to prove that they are not followers of a globally operating sect; the suspicion towards 'capitalism as religion' has been voiced, and awaits resolution.[2] The life form known as the 'democratic nation' can only survive if it balances out the semantics of self-interest and self-preference with the semantics of freedom for other things and of having something to give.

42

The Heavenly and the Earthly Left

Thus, from the elaborated concept of the local, a group of characteristics emerges that makes abstract progressives blush. What comes
into view under the pressure of muddled universalism, clarified
through counterpressure – twentieth-century thinkers furthered these
clarifications – is the extended component of successfully lived life,
which does not become what it can without being immune, self-
preferential, exclusive, selective, asymmetrical, protectionist, uncompressible and irreversible. This catalogue may sound like the summary
of a far right party manifesto; in reality, however, it lists the characteristics that inhere in the infrastructure of becoming in real human
spheres. They belong to the attributes of finite, concrete, embedded
and transmittable existence. To draw one more time on the phraseol-
ogy of ontology, being extended in one's own place is the good habit
of being.

As long as the left intends to remain or become an earthly left, it
will, for all its love of symmetry, have to take up contact with these
definitions, unless it would prefer to have an affair with the infinite
– which one could certainly understand, as earthly social democracy
is philosophically boring and aesthetically unrewarding.

A few of the values in the alternative list – more precisely, the
demands for a meta-life whose relation to the world is neglectful of
immunity, preferential towards the foreign, inclusive, unselective,
symmetrical, duty-free, as well as compressible and reversible at will
– can be realized in practice from time to time, but only those that
are supported by the first list. If the second list did not exist, we could
never breathe the 'air from other planets' without which the cultural

carriers of the West would view existence as constant suffocation. Indeed, perhaps the hallmark of high culture is that it abets the implantation of the impossible in the real. It projects the dowry of the prenatal world into the public sphere. From an immanence-philosophical perspective, this means that higher and more improbable states emanate from the current one: active nature drives its own luxurious tendencies to ever higher levels. The opening up of the first list towards the second in certain aspects indicates the élan of civilization, which preserves itself by expanding, heightening and further differentiating itself – only by attentively tying the second back to the first, however, can a reign of ghosts be avoided.

The fact that the age of globalizations brought effective increases of improbability proves that souls take part in the growth of the horizons. Under the duress of growth, they learned to express themselves in general ontological terms two and a half thousand years ago. Thinking in universal values provides inner support while the horizon drifts. Thus abstract universalism is not *only* the devious nonsense that pragmatists, Nietzscheans and all possible forms of realists wish to see in it (to quote Carl Schmitt: 'Whoever says "humanity" seeks to deceive'); it is *also* the semantic reflection of the world growing large in the time of the burgeoning world system. Universalism: a stage of maturity. Falling for reflections is the occupational hazard of enlighteners; they too are entitled to support. Even they, whose teaching profession acts as a learning disability, will concede the necessity of further training sooner or later.

That souls grow with the world forms, however, in the steppes, the cities and the empires, is one of the facts from which philosophy began; it could still point it in the right direction during the metamorphosis necessitated by the global situation. At the time of the polis, Aristotle held the view that only someone to whom 'greatness of soul' (*megalopsychía*) had become second nature could be a citizen. Why should this no longer apply to the contemporaries of the global and nation-state era, simply because they now speak of 'creativity' rather than 'greatness of soul'? The creative people, one hears now and again, are those who prevent the whole from being bogged down by harmful routines. Perhaps the time has come to take the catch-phrase at its word.

Notes

Chapter 1 Of Grand Narratives

1 Immanuel Kant, 'What Does It Mean to Orient Oneself in Thinking?', in *Religion Within the Boundaries of Mere Reason and Other Writings*, ed. & trans. Allen Wood & George di Giovanni (Cambridge University Press, 1998), pp. 3–14.

2 Gilles Deleuze & Félix Guattari, *What Is Philosophy?*, trans. Graham Burchell & Hugh Tomlinson (London & New York: Verso, 1994), p. 208.

3 See *Sphären I, Blasen, Mikrosphärologie* (Frankfurt: Suhrkamp, 1998); *Sphären II, Globen, Makrosphärologie* (Frankfurt: Suhrkamp, 1999); and *Sphären III, Schäume. Plurale Sphärologie* (Frankfurt: Suhrkamp, 2004). In English so far: *Bubbles, Spheres I: Microspherology*, trans. Wieland Hoban (Los Angeles: Semiotext(e), 2011).

4 See Michel-Pierre Lerner, *Le monde des sphères*, 2 vols. (Paris: Les Belles Lettres, 1996/7).

5 See *Sphären III, Schäume*, ch. 2, 'Indoors', section A, 'Worin wir leben, weben und sind', esp. pp. 501–34, as well as ch. 3, section 9, 'Das Empire – oder: Das Komforttreibhaus; die nach oben offene Skala der Verwöhnung', pp. 801f.

6 Aristotle, *Physics*, 212b.

7 See the classic study by Dietrich Mahnke, *Unendliche Sphäre und Allmittelpunkt* (Halle: Niemeyer, 1937).

8 See *Sphären II, Globen*.

9 See Martin Albrow, *The Global Age: State and Society Beyond Modernity* (Palo Alto: Stanford University Press, 1996). With the half-descriptive, half-programmatic phrase he chooses as his title, Albrow expresses the idea that after the half-millennium between Columbus's

expedition and the Second World War, which stood under the sign of world synthesis by Europeans, a new quality or level of globality has been reached to which one must react with a new epochal concept, or a meaningful name for the current age; see also pp. 141f below.

10 *Sphären II, Globen*, ch. 8, 'Die letzte Kugel' [The Last Orb], pp. 801–1004.
11 See Hans Freyer, *Weltgeschichte Europas*, third edition (Stuttgart: Deutsche Verlags-Anstalt, 1954); necessary corrections of the Eurocentric view of terrestrial globalization can be found in, among other works, A. G. Hopkins (ed.), *Globalization in World History* (London: Pimlico, 2002).

Chapter 2 The Wandering Star

1 Friedrich Hölderlin, *Hyperion and Selected Poems*, ed. Eric L. Santner (New York: Continuum, 1990), p. 41.
2 See Helmut Pape, *Die Unsichtbarkeit der Welt* (Frankfurt: Suhrkamp, 1997).
3 See Rémi Brague, 'Geozentrismus als Demütigung des Menschen', in *Internationale Zeitschrift für Philosophie*, 1/1994, pp. 2–25.
4 Karl Rosenkranz, *Ästhetik des Hässlichen* (Leipzig: Reclam, 1990), p. 20.
5 The poet gave the negative hero Philoctetes the most insubordinate words in antiquity: 'I find the gods evil' (Sophocles, *Philoctetes*, l. 452).

Chapter 3 Return to Earth

1 Alexander von Humboldt, *Cosmos: Sketch of a Physical Description of the Universe*, trans. Edward Sabine (Cambridge University Press, 2010), p. 68.
2 Ibid., p. 73.
3 See Immanuel Kant, *Critique of the Power of Judgement*, trans. Eric Matthews (Cambridge University Press, 2001), §26, 'On the estimation of the magnitude of things of nature that is requisite for the idea of the sublime' (pp. 134ff) and §28, 'On nature as a power' (pp. 143ff).
4 Humboldt goes much further in this than his colleague and rival Charles Darwin, who had only brought back a few manifestly sublime 'pictures' from his journey around the world on board the *Beagle* from 1831 to 1836, including this: 'Among the scenes which are deeply impressed on my mind, none exceed in sublimity the primeval forests undefaced by the hand of man; whether those of Brazil, where the powers of Life are predominant, or those of Tierra del Fuego, where Death and Decay prevail. Both are temples filled with the varied productions of the God of Nature: no one can stand in these solitudes unmoved, and not feel

that there is more in man than the mere breath of his body' (*Charles Darwin's Beagle Diary*, ed. R. D. Keynes [Cambridge University Press, 2001], p. 443). Darwin likewise knew that one who studied the earth could no longer get far with an aesthetic of the beautiful; in the spirit of the times, it had to be augmented by that of the (quantitatively and dynamically) sublime: 'Lastly, of natural scenery, the views from lofty mountains, though certainly in one sense not beautiful, are very memorable. When looking down from the highest crest of the Cordillera, the mind, undisturbed by minute details, was filled with the stupendous dimensions of the surrounding masses' (ibid.).

5 Walter Benjamin, 'Paris, Capital of the Nineteenth Century', in *Reflections*, ed. Peter Demetz & trans. Edmund Jephcott (New York: Schocken, 1986), p. 154.

6 This was expressly noted, some generations after Humboldt, by such authors as Nietzsche, Husserl and Merleau-Ponty; see Stephan Günzel, 'Nietzsches Geophilosophie und die "gemässigte Klimazone" im Denken des Abendlandes', in *Dialektik*, 1/2001, pp. 17f.

7 Edwin 'Buzz' Aldrin, *Return to Earth* (New York: Random House, 1973).

Chapter 4 Globe Time, World Picture Time

1 See the phenomenological clarifications of Hermann Schmitz in *System der Philosophie*, vol. 3: *Der Raum*, part 1: *Der leibliche Raum* (Bonn: Bouvier, 1967), §119, 'Der Richtungsraum' (as well as §§219–31) and §120, 'Der Ortsraum' (likewise §§132–5).

2 Rilke, to whom we owe the term 'world interior' [*Weltinnenraum*], attempted to overcome the basic experience of modernity that things and people, in a purely position-spatial sense, die out from atmosphere withdrawal, by seeking to revive the world through his own experiential power with a form of poetic animism. The result of this could no longer be a Platonic world soul, but rather an individual-cosmological intensity corresponding to the mode of contemporary 'poetic dwelling'.

3 The success of the three-dimensional globe, however, had already been relativized by the planispheric representations of the earth that had been ubiquitous since the late sixteenth century, and had the advantage of being reproducible in atlases.

4 Martin Heidegger, 'The Age of the World Picture' (1938), in *Off the Beaten Track*, ed. & trans. Julian Young & Kenneth Haynes (Cambridge University Press, 2002), p. 71. TN: although the translation has been left unmodified here, Heidegger's use of the verb *vorstellen* is rather more idiosyncratic than the gerund 'representing' suggests, as it invokes its literal sense of placing (*stellen*) something before (*vor*) the self, giving the act of imagining or mentally representing a quasi-physical character; this also applies to the related words *herstellen*,

bestellen or *Gestell*, which all bear connotations of placing. More generally, although the convention of translating *Vorstellung* as 'representation', particularly in the works of Kant and Schopenhauer, is justified in those contexts, it is also slightly misleading, in that the representation taking place there is a mental, not an external one – a mental image; in everyday usage, the verb *sich (etwas) vorstellen* means 'to imagine (something)' or 'to envisage (something)', while its non-reflexive form *vorstellen* means 'to present', 'to introduce' or 'to perform'. Though the use of a word like 'representation' is necessary to achieve adequate terminological distinctions in Schopenhauer, it would be mistaken simply to assume that it is the natural cognate of *Vorstellung*, as it would normally correspond far more to *Darstellung*. In the present text, as Sloterdijk often means a more active, shaping process than mere mental representation when he speaks of *Vorstellung* and its related forms, I have tended to use such words as 'imagine' or 'envisage'.

5   Concerning the late medieval premises of this shift, see Alfred W. Crosby, *The Measure of Reality: Quantification and Western Society, 1250–1600* (Cambridge University Press, 1997).

6   It is a banality that commodity and money are states of capital; that texts, images and celebrities likewise are gradually being understood by the agents of the modern cultural sector, despite traditional intellectually conservative reservations. The way in which this applies to texts and images can be learned from, among other sources, the reflections of Georg Franck in *Ökonomie der Aufmerksamkeit. Ein Entwurf* (Munich: Hanser, 1998). An illuminating description of the economy of celebrity can be found in Thomas Macho, 'Von der Elite zur Prominenz. Zum Strukturwandel politischer Herrschaft', in *Merkur*, 534–5/1993, pp. 762–9, as well as Macho, 'Das prominente Gesicht. Notizen zur Politisierung der Sichtbarkeit', in Sabine R. Arnold, Cristian Fuhrmeister & Dietmar Schiller (eds.), *Politische Inszenierungen im 20. Jahrhundert. Zur Sinnlichkeit der Macht* (Vienna: Böhlau, 1998), pp. 171–84.

7   See Elly Decker, 'Der Himmelsglobus – eine Welt für sich', in *Focus Behaim Globus*, vol. 1 (Nuremberg: Germanisches Nationalmuseum, 1992), pp. 89–100.

8   One significant exception is Barthold Hinrich Brockes's poem 'Das Firmament' (in *Irdisches Vergnügen in Gott, bestehend in Physicalisch- und Moralischen Gedichten*, part 1 [Hamburg: Grund, 1723]), which can be read as an escalating response to Pascal's dictum on the eternal silence of infinite spaces. Admittedly, the title of Brockes's poem is misleading, as its point is precisely that there is *no longer any* firmament that could provide cosmic stability, only a non-spatial location of the soul in God: 'As a thick flood from the bottomless sea / Engulfs sinking iron, the space of the abyss / Closed in around my spirit in an instant. / The tremendous crypt, filled with invisible light, / A bright darkness with no beginning nor limits, / Swallowed up the entire world, burying even my thoughts; / My whole being became dust, a speck, a nothing, /

And I lost myself. Suddenly it struck me down; / Despair threatened my breast, filled with confusion: / And yet, o healing nothingness! O blissful loss! / Omnipresent God, in you I found myself again.'

These verses show three things clearly: firstly, the poet no longer understands the original cosmographic meaning of the term 'firmament'. Secondly, in analogy to the ocean, he imagines the heavens as something by which one can be engulfed. Thirdly, the only force that can save us from the shipwreck of the imagination in the bottomless is a God with an 'essential tendency towards closeness'.

The idea of the firmament enjoyed an afterlife not only in poetry, but also in delirium. Daniel Paul Schreber notes in ch. 6 of *Memoirs of My Nervous Illness* (New York Review Books, 2000 [originally published in German in 1903]) that a number of the souls of the departed haunting him name 'the firmament' as their place of origin.

Chapter 5 Turn from the East, Entrance into the Homogeneous Space

1 Eugen Rosenstock-Huessy, *Die europäischen Revolutionen und der Charakter der Nationen* (Moers: Brendow, 1987), p. 264.
2 This note on the tendency towards 'western passage' is taken up in Giacomo Marramao, *The Passage West: Philosophy After the Age of the Nation State*, trans. Matteo Mandarini (London & New York: Verso, 2012).
3 Schmitz, *System der Philosophie*, vol. 3, p. 441.
4 See Armand Mattelart, *The Invention of Communication*, trans. Susan Emanuel (Minneapolis: Minnesota University Press, 1996), pp. 47f.

Chapter 6 Jules Verne and Hegel

1 Jules Verne, *Around the World in Eighty Days*, trans. William Butcher (Oxford & New York: Oxford University Press, 1999), p. 19.
2 In praise of pure movement, see Karl Marx & Friedrich Engels, *The Communist Manifesto* (1848), ed. Gareth Stedman Jones (London: Penguin, 2002), and Thomas de Quincey, 'The English Mail-Coach, or The Glory of Motion' (1849), in *The Confessions of an English Opium-Eater and Other Writings* (Oxford & New York: Oxford University Press, 1998), pp. 183–233.
3 Hermann Graf Keyserling, *Reisetagebuch eines Philosophen* (1918) (Munich: Langen-Müller, 1980).

Chapter 7 Waterworld: On the Change of the Central Element in the Modern Age

1 Antonio Pigafetta, *The First Voyage Around the World, 1519–1522: An Account of Magellan's Expedition*, ed. Theodore J. Cachey (University of Toronto Press, 2007), p. 25.
2 Edward W. Said, *Culture and Imperialism* (New York: Vintage, 1994), p. xv. Said's ironic formulation reflects the cynicism of the British deportation system, in which first the Caribbean, then New England and finally Australia served as destinations for a utilitarian export of criminals.
3 Herman Melville, *Moby Dick* (Oxford & New York: Oxford University Press, 1998), p. 248.
4 Ibid., p. 99 (end of ch. 24). It is one of the central facts of modern theory culture that these seaborne studies led to the rise of nautical empiricism against university scholasticism (until the universities reabsorbed the experience-based attitude and countered sedentary empiricism with the mobile kind). One of those who made a principle of travelling and seeing for himself early on was Fernández de Oviedo, who tirelessly repeats in his *Historia general y natural de las Indias* that 'what I have said cannot be learned in Salamanca, in Bologna, or Paris'. Quoted in Kathleen Ann Myers, *Fernández de Oviedo's Chronicle of America: A New History for a New World* (Austin: University of Texas Press, 2007), p. 26.
5 Pigafetta, *The First Voyage Around the World*, p. xix.
6 See Immanuel Wallerstein, *The Modern World-System I: Capitalist Agriculture and the Origins of the European World-Economy in the Sixteenth Century* (Berkeley and Los Angeles: University of California Press, 2011) and *The Modern World-System II: Mercantilism and the Consolidation of the European World-Economy, 1600–1750* (Berkeley & Los Angeles: University of California Press, 2011). For Wallerstein, the term 'world-system' certainly does not refer to the inclusion of all countries and cultures in the new relationships; it does, however, indicate that the economic transaction space now developing goes beyond local markets, countries and empires.
7 Adam Smith, *The Wealth of Nations, Books I–III* (London: Penguin, 1999), p. 519.
8 Oswald Spengler made this the axiom of civilizatory epochs preceding the death of advanced civilizations. See *The Decline of the West*, trans. Charles Francis Atkinson, vol. 1 (New York: Knopf, 1950), p. 37: 'Expansion is a doom, something daemonic and immense, which grips, forces into service, and uses up the late mankind of the world-city stage [. . .].'
9 Until the late eighteenth century, the logbooks from expeditions of discovery remained secret affairs of the seafaring states; see the observations of Georg Forster on the second of Captain Cook's expeditions, in

A *Voyage Round the World*, ed. Nicholas Thomas & Oliver Berghof, 2 vols. (Honolulu: University of Hawai'i Press, 2000).

10 The definition of the entrepreneur as 'debtor-producer' comes from Gunnar Heinsohn and Otto Steiger, whose book *Eigentum, Zins und Geld. Ungelöste Rätsel der Wirtschaftstheorie* (Reinbek: Rowohlt, 1996) presents a suggestive model for the explanation of the dynamic of innovation in modern economy as a *property economy*.

Chapter 8 Fortuna, or: The Metaphysics of Chance

1 Boethius, *The Consolation of Philosophy*, trans. P. G. Walsh (Oxford & New York: Oxford University Press, 2000), p. 22.
2 Conversely, the late eighteenth century also discovered the human who, in an absolute sense, has bad luck – or, as Malthus would say, the poor man who is 'born into a world already possessed' and whose parents cannot feed him. Such an unfortunate, according to Malthus, 'has no business to be where he is. At nature's mighty feast there is no vacant cover for him' (Thomas Robert Malthus, *An Essay on the Principle of Population*, ed. Donald Winch [Cambridge University Press, 1992], p. 249).
3 Friedrich Nietzsche, *Thus Spoke Zarathustra: A Book for Everyone and Nobody*, trans. Graham Parkes (Oxford & New York: Oxford University Press, 2005), p. 143.
4 Ibid.

Chapter 9 Risk-Taking

1 See Jochen Hörisch, *Heads or Tails: The Poetics of Money*, trans. Amy Horning Marschall (Detroit: Wayne State University Press, 2000). TN: as the original title uses the word *Poesie*, not *Poetik*, it would be more accurately translated as *The Poetry of Money*.
2 Daniel Defoe, *An Essay Upon Projects* (1697).
3 Concerning the typology of the entrepreneur prince, see Werner Sombart, *Der Bourgeois. Zur Geistesgeschichte des modernen Wirtschaftsmenschen* (Munich & Leipzig: Duncker & Humblot, 1923 [reprint: 1987]), pp. 102f.

Chapter 10 Delusion and Time: On Capitalism and Telepathy

1 The fundamental shift of mood becomes apparent if one compares the triumphant timbres that predominated at the celebrations on the 400th

anniversary of Columbus's voyage in 1892 with the atmosphere of self-flagellation on the 500th anniversary in 1992.

2 One can gain insight into the meaning of this blindness if one takes into account that another keyword of the highest order is missing from the same dictionary: media. See Jochen Hörisch, 'Der blinde Fleck der Philosophie: Medien', in *Deutsche Zeitschrift für Philosophie*, 5/2003, pp. 889f. The crux of the matter is clear: a philosophy that understands its dependence on discoveries and media could probably no longer be philosophy in the ordinary sense.

3 See Bent Flyvberg, Nils Bruzelius & Werner Rothengatter, *Megaprojects and Risk: An Anatomy of Ambition* (Cambridge University Press, 2003).

4 In a letter to Doña Juana de Torres, Columbus wrote: 'Our Lord made me the messenger of the new heaven and the new earth, of which he spoke in the Book of Revelation by St John, after having spoken of it by the mouth of Isaiah', quoted in Kay Brigham, *Christopher Columbus: His Life and Discovery in the Light of His Prophecies* (Barcelona: Editorial Clie, 1990), p. 50.

5 See Lyndal Roper, *Oedipus and the Devil: Witchcraft, Sexuality and Religion in Early Modern Europe* (London & New York: Routledge, 1994), ch. 6, 'Stealing Manhood: Capitalism and Magic in Early Modern Germany', pp. 126–31. The same essay also illustrates the problem of transmission techniques in these early telecommunications: according to Anna Megerler, the souls of two criminals had been locked in Anton Fugger's crystal ball, condemned to wander through the air – could there be any faster, yet also more unreliable informants?

6 For an impression of the later state of her consultancy approach, see her book *Herzschlag der Sieger. Die EQ-Revolution* (Munich: Econ, 1997). Note the fascinating double meaning of 'heartbeat' [*Herzschlag*]. The heartbeat of the losers [TN: *Sieger* means 'winners'] is examined, more in the tone of a depressive counter-consultation, by Richard Sennett in his book *The Corrosion of Character: The Personal Consequences of Work in the New Capitalism* (New York: Norton, 1998).

7 See Felix Alfred Plattner, *Jesuits Go East*, trans. Lord Sudley & Oscar Blobel (Westminster, MD: Newman, 1952).

Chapter 11 The Invention of Subjectivity – Primary Disinhibition and Its Advisers

1 This must even take precedence over the frequently mentioned motif of self-familiarity.

2 See Boris Groys, *Unter Verdacht. Eine Phänomenologie der Medien* (Munich: Hanser, 2001). In the more methodologically benign terminology of Heinz von Foerster, one would speak of the willingness to be surprised by the other (and by oneself).

3   For an overview of European and French disputes over the subject from a language-analytical perspective, see Vincent Descombes, *Le complément de sujet. Enquête sur le fait d'agir de soi-même* (Paris: Gallimard, 2004).

4   Concerning subjectivity as a machine figure, see Anson Rabinbach, *The Human Motor: Energy, Fatigue and the Origins of Modernity* (Berkeley & Los Angeles: University of California Press, 1992).

5   In the era of German Idealism, this fourfold complex was augmented by officialdom and geniusdom. See Friedrich Kittler, 'Das Subjekt als Beamter', in Manfred Frank, Gérard Raulet & Willem van Reijen (eds.), *Die Frage nach dem Subjekt* (Frankfurt: Suhrkamp), pp. 401–20.

6   'They dogmatize like infallible popes.' See *The Writings of William James: A Comprehensive Edition*, ed. John J. McDermott (Chicago & London: University of Chicago Press, 1977), p. 724.

7   See Wolf Lepenies, *Melancholy and Society* (Cambridge, MA: Harvard University Press, 1992), pp. 179ff.

8   In his notes on Dostoyevsky, Lukács indirectly pinpointed the principle of disinhibition when he spoke of a 'Second Ethics': while the first prohibits murder, the second makes it a commandment. See Norbert Bolz, *Auszug aus der entzauberten Welt. Philosophischer Extremismus zwischen den Weltkriegen* (Munich: Fink, 1989), pp. 13–20. In his Poznan speech, Himmler said: 'The only commissar we have must be our own conscience. [. . .] The commissar who orders us to attack must be our only bravery [. . .].' The reference to the commissars reveals the moral scenario in which the SS men believed they were operating: a competition in brutality with the Soviet exterminators.

9   See Thomas Mann, *Reflections of a Nonpolitical Man* (1918), trans. Walter D. Morris (New York: Frederick Ungar, 1983), p. 427: 'The intellectual who becomes convinced he must act is immediately at the point of political *murder* – or, if not this, then the morality of his action is always such that political murder would be the consequence of his way of acting.'

10 Regarding the older mantic aids to disinhibition and control over one's actions, we will say here only that the revival of the classical arts and authors inevitably occasioned the return of frowned-on practices such as the reading of omens – with consequences that extend into the oracle industries of today. Concerning the use of astrology in early Protestantism, see Claudia Brosseder, *Im Bann der Sterne: Caspar Peucer, Philipp Melanchthon und andere Wittenberger Astrologen* (Berlin: Akademie, 2004).

11 See Thomas Mann's letter to Karl Kerényi from 7 September 1941, in *Mythology and Humanism: The Correspondence of Thomas Mann and Karl Kerényi*, trans. Alexander Gelley (Ithaca, NY: Cornell University Press, 1975), p. 103: 'It is essential that the myth be taken away from intellectual fascism and transmuted for humane ends. I have for a long time done nothing else.'

Chapter 12 Irreflexive Energies: The Ontology of the Headstart

1 Heinrich Mann, *Geist und Tat. Essays* (Munich: dtv, 1963), pp. 125f.
2 For the origin of this comparison, see Heiner Mühlmann, *The Nature of Cultures: A Blueprint for a Theory of Culture Genetics*, trans. R. Payne (Vienna & New York: Springer, 1996), p. 115.
3 Fyodor Dostoyevsky, *Crime and Punishment*, trans. David McDuff (London: Penguin, 1991), p. 309.
4 Ibid., p. 310. George Lukács clearly followed on from Raskolnikov's theses in his left-fascist phase.
5 Dostoyevsky's analysis is foreshadowed by the fragments of Hegel's *Jenaer Realphilosophie* on crime, which is interpreted there as the secret assertion of an exceptional right against the formally recognized general laws (as the gesture of a 'single will to power', p. 225), while the law that demands concrete validity sets itself in motion as an antithetical impulse of the general, i.e. as an injury of the injurer. See G. W. F. Hegel, *Jenaer Systementwürfe III. Naturphilosophie und Philosophie des Geistes*, ed. Rolf-Peter Horstmann (Hamburg: Meiner, 1987), pp. 212f.
6 Nietzsche, *Thus Spoke Zarathustra*, p. 143.
7 TN: there is a play on words here between *Ursprung* [origin] and *Vorsprung* [headstart].
8 Schopenhauer attributes the words 'du sublime au ridicule il n'y a qu'un pas' to Thomas Paine; see Arthur Schopenhauer, *The World as Will and Representation*, trans. Judith Norman, Alistair Welchman & Christopher Janaway, vol. 1 (Cambridge University Press, 2010), p. 202.
9 Friedrich Hölderlin, *Odes and Elegies*, ed. & trans. Nick Hoff (Middleton, CT: Wesleyan University Press, 2008), p. 113.

Chapter 13 Nautical Ecstasies

1 Melville, *Moby Dick*, p. 1.
2 See Dirk Baecker, 'Die Unruhe des Geldes, der Einbruch der Frist', in *Wozu Soziologie?* (Berlin: Kadmos, 2004), pp. 109–24.
3 Victor Hugo, *The Toilers of the Sea*, trans. James Hogarth (New York: Modern Library, 2002), p. 77.
4 Conrad Ferdinand Meyer, *The Tempting of Pescara*, trans. Clara Bell (New York: Fertig, 1975), p. 135.

Chapter 14 'Corporate Identity' on the High Seas, Parting of Minds

1 Bloch's well-known description of the geographical utopias of the Modern Age as expressions of 'horizontal treasure-hunting' (*The*

Principle of Hope, trans. Neville Plaice, Stephen Plaice & Paul Knight [Cambridge, MA: MIT Press, 1995], p. 755) clearly shows a certain bias towards the aforementioned model. In fact, such treasure-hunter socialism assumed that nature always comes for free. Taken as a whole, Bloch's work displays a very pronounced Saint-Simonist trait, expressed in the conviction that the 'exploitation of man by man' should be replaced by the exploitation of the globe by humans. Concerning Bloch's extension of the treasure hunt to the world history of bringing forth, see *Sphären III, Schäume*, pp. 774f.

2   See Anon., *An Historical Account of the Circumnavigation of the Globe, and of the Progress of Discovery in the Pacific Ocean* (Edinburgh: Oliver & Boyd, 1836), pp. 45f.

3   Christopher Columbus & Bartolomé de las Cases, *The Diario of Christopher Columbus's First Voyage to America, 1492–1493*, ed. & trans. Oliver Dunn & James E. Kelley (Norman: University of Oklahoma Press, 1991), p. 29.

4   See Klaus Heinrich, *Floss der Medusa. 3 Studien zur Faszinationsgeschichte mir mehreren Beilagen und einem Anhang* (Basel & Frankfurt: Stroemfeld, 1995), pp. 9–45.

5   Concerning the motif 'Stop history!', see Eric Voegelin, *Order and History*, vol. 4: *The Ecumenic Age* (Baton Rouge: Louisiana State University Press, 1974), pp. 329–33. We shall explain why this imperative became obsolete after the completion of terrestrial globalization (1945/1974) in the section on post-history.

Chapter 15   The Basic Movement: Money Returns

1   Her cult was founded in Rome after the return of Augustus from his expedition to the Orient in 19 BC.

2   Marx too pointed out the 'return of the point of departure into itself' as a feature of the incipient movement of capital: 'At first sight, circulation appears as a simply infinite process. The commodity is exchanged for money, money is exchanged for the commodity, and this is repeated endlessly' (Karl Marx, *Grundrisse (Introduction to the Critique of Political Economy)*, trans. Martin Nicolaus [New York: Vintage, 1973], p. 197). Marx's aim, however, is to show two things: firstly, that in the money–commodity–money metamorphosis the initially mysterious phenomenon of added value can appear, which stimulates the accumulation process, and secondly, that the competition between capitals must lead to crises of utilization, and thus to social crises that obstruct the happy return of money to itself as capital.

3   William Shakespeare, *The Merchant of Venice*, act 1, scene 1.

4   See Peter L. Bernstein, *Against the Gods: The Remarkable Story of Risk* (New York: John Wiley & Sons, 1998) and François Ewald, *Der Vorsorgestaat* (Frankfurt: Suhrkamp, 1993), section II, 'Vom Risiko', pp. 171–275.

Chapter 16 Between Justifications and Assurances: On Terran and Maritime Thought

1 In political-sociological terms, the British philosophy of common sense mirrors the fact that in England, the historic compromise between (civil) trade and (aristocratic) property was made earlier, and in more solid forms, than in the territorial states on the continent. This encouraged a climate in which untragic and convivial social philosophies could thrive, while on the continent – especially the German princedoms – tragic and authoritarian state philosophies gained the upper hand.

2 Some inattentive histories of philosophy describe the ships on the title page of Bacon's book as departing.

3 *Historia ventorum*, 1622, the first section of Bacon's *Historia naturalis et experimentalis ad condendam philosophiam*, published as the third part of his *Instauratio Magna*.

4 Edmund Husserl, *Experience and Judgement: Investigations in a Genealogy of Logic*, trans. James S. Churchill & Karl Ameriks (Evanston: Northwestern University Press, 1973), p. 30. TN: the German word translated as 'ground' in the quoted passage is the same as the one translated directly before it as 'soil', namely *Boden*.

5 TN: 'reason' and 'foundation' are both translations of *Grund*.

6 TN: here the author plays with yet another semantic shading of *Grund*.

7 Johann Gottfried Herder, *Journal meiner Reise im Jahr 1769*, in *Schriften. Eine Auswahl aus dem Gesamtwerk* (Munich: Wilhelm Goldmann, 1960).

8 Immanuel Kant, *Critique of Pure Reason*, ed. & trans. Paul Guyer & Allen Wood (Cambridge University Press, 1998), p. 339 ('On the ground of the distinction of all objects in general into *phenomena* and *noumena*').

9 Johann Wolfgang von Goethe, *Italian Journey, 1786–1788*, trans. Elizabeth Mayer (London: Penguin, 1992), p. 228.

10 G. W. F. Hegel, *Philosophy of Right*, trans. S. W. Dyde (New York: Cosimo, 2008), p. 128.

11 The paragraph is famous not least because Carl Schmitt invoked it as a basis for his own geopolitical doctrines: just as, in Schmitt's interpretation, Marxism was merely a world-historical realization of the preceding §§243–6 of Hegel's *Philosophy of Right*, Schmittism was to bring about the corresponding fulfilment of §247. This remained a hollow ambition, however, both because of the inadequacy of Hegel's contributions to political oceanology and because the element-theoretical narrowness of Schmitt's fundamental geopolitical theorem, the dogma of the power-constitutive role of dominion over earth, sea, air and fire, caused him to miss the decisive dimension of a modern doctrine of power, namely the media-theoretical one.

12 'The Roman conquers by sitting.' The central principle of the agrometaphysical-imperial age: this is the epoch in which commands, administra-

tion and exploitation of resources take precedence over flows, circulations and investments. One must admit that the territorial states of the seventeenth and eighteenth centuries, as long as they strove for modernization, were still dealing primarily with internal disclosure work; the establishment of 'infrastructures' and internal markets of communication for commodities and news (channels, roads, bridges, land registers, publishing, post, telecommunications, standards for measurements and weights, orthography, grammar, schools, banking, courts, currencies, taxes, statistics etc.) absorbed the majority of state energies, relegating questions of world connections to the outside to secondary status. This is evident in virtually all philosophical discourses that remain trapped in a terran, 'physiocratic', agrosophical horizon based on immovables.

13 'To be free means to calculate the moves of your competitors while remaining securely impervious to such calculability oneself.' Terry Eagleton, *The Ideology of the Aesthetic* (Oxford: Blackwell, 1990), p. 74.
14 Schopenhauer, *The World as Will and Representation*, p. 25.
15 See Cornel West, *The American Evasion of Philosophy: A Genealogy of Pragmatism* (Madison: University of Wisconsin Press, 1989).
16 See Dorothea Waley Singer, *Giordano Bruno: His Life and Thought, with Annotated Translation of the Work*, On The Infinite Universe and Worlds (New York: Greenwood, 1968), p. 245. Bruno also wished to create an exact analogy between Columbus's voyage and his own mental exploration of outer space and breaching of the 'outermost celestial sphere' to enter the infinite space. See Giordano Bruno, *The Ash Wednesday Supper*, ed. & trans. Edward A. Gosselin & Lawrence S. Lerner (University of Toronto Press, 1977), pp. 88ff.
17 See Bruno, *The Ash Wednesday Supper*, First Dialogue (pp. 79–106).
18 Ralph Waldo Emerson, 'Circles', in *The Portable Emerson*, ed. Carl Bode & Malcolm Cowley (New York: Penguin, 1981), pp. 228 & 230.
19 See Francis Fukuyama, 'The End of History', in *The National Interest*, 16/1989, p. 7.
20 See Boris Groys, 'Warten auf die grossen Ameisen, Gespräch mit Barbara Kuon', in *Der Geist ist ein Knochen. Zur Aktualität von Hegel's Ästhetik*, ed. Kulturamt-Stadtarchiv Stuttgart (Stuttgart: Klett-Cotta, 1997), pp. 8–39.
21 See Gerhard Gamm, *Die Flucht aus der Kategorie. Die Positivierung des Unbestimmten im Ausgang der Moderne* (Frankfurt: Suhrkamp, 1994).

Chapter 17 Expedition and Truth

1 See Michael Walzer, *Exodus and Revolution* (New York: Basic, 1986).
2 Heidegger, 'The Age of the World Picture', p. 68.

3 Ibid., p. 70.
4 Ibid., p. 69.
5 See Henry Hobhouse, *Seeds of Change: Six Plants That Transformed Mankind* (Washington, DC: Shoemaker & Hoard, 2005); Sidney W. Mintz, *Sweetness and Power: The Place of Sugar in Modern History* (New York: Penguin, 1986); Alfred W. Crosby, *Ecological Imperialism: The Biological Expansion of Europe, 900–1900* (Cambridge University Press, 1986). Concerning the role of hothouses in the resettlement of plants, see also *Sphären III, Schäume*, section 'Atmosphärische Inseln', pp. 338f.
6 Martin Heidegger, 'The Question Concerning Technology', in *The Question Concerning Technology, and Other Essays*, trans. William Lovitt (New York: Garland, 1977), p. 13.

Chapter 18 The Signs of the Explorers: On Cartography and Imperial Name Magic

1 Hans Freyer, *Weltgeschichte Europas*, p. 480; this ability to strike out directly, however, as Freyer implicitly knows, is the hallmark of historical action as such. It is clear that one would forbid it from a post-historical perspective (technologically primitive, logically daring, legally uninsurable). The 'wrong question' thus arises from projecting categories of post-history (insurance age) backwards onto history (pre-insurance age).
2 See Bruno Latour, 'No Globe, but Plenty of Blogs', in *Domus*, April 2004.
3 See Karl Schlögel, *Im Raume lesen wir die Zeit. Über Zivilisationsgeschichte und Geopolitik* (Munich: Hanser, 2003).
4 Carl Schmitt, *The Nomos of the Earth in the International Law of the Jus Publicum Europaeum*, trans. G. L. Ulmen (New York: Telos, 2003), pp. 86–100.
5 Concerning the legal formalism and discourse-theoretically questionable nature of Columbus's conquistadorian speech acts, see Stephen Greenblatt, *Marvellous Possessions: The Wonder of the New World* (Oxford & New York: Oxford University Press, 1991), pp. 86–118. The journalist and Africa-explorer Henry Morton Stanley made at least 400 'contracts' for Leopold II of Belgium with African chieftains, which were mostly interpreted by the latter as friendly alliances and by the Europeans as subjugation agreements and exploitation licences. A comparable collector of 'contracts' was Carl Peters (1856–1918), who laid the foundations of German East Africa with over 120 'contracts'.
6 Melville, *Moby Dick*, pp. 356f.
7 See Peter Sloterdijk, *Tau von den Bermudas. Über einige Regime der Einbildungskraft* (Frankfurt: Suhrkamp, 2001), pp. 27–40.

8   'You were the first to go around me'; it is notable that the decisive verb of globalization, *circumdare*, initially meant 'to surround' rather than 'to go around'; this reminds us that even then, people still imagined the earth as something that can be 'surrounded', namely by celestial domes, whose circumnavigation was admittedly inconceivable. When the deed is done, the encircler appears as the encloser: if one takes the tendency to its logical conclusion, circumnavigation transpires as the new enclosing. The circumnavigating traffic replaces the enclosure of the domes, and the active subject becomes the true 'encompassing' entity.

9   We lack a synoptic description of the ethnic, culture-nationalistic and religion-communal ideas of chosenness in Modern Age Europe. See, to an extent, *The Collected Works of Eric Voegelin*, vol. 22: *History of Political Ideas*, vol. IV: *Renaissance and Reformation*, ed. David L. Morse & William M. Thompson (Columbia: University of Missouri Press, 1998), part four, ch. 3, 'The People of God'.

10 TN: 'Whose map, his realm' – an adaptation of the phrase *Cuius regio, eius religio* [Whose realm, his religion].

11 Schmitt, *The Nomos of the Earth in the International Law of the Jus Publicum Europaeum*, p. 132.

12 Ibid.

13 Ibid., p. 133.

14 See John Goss, *The Mapmaker's Art: An Illustrated History of Cartography* (Chicago: Rand McNally, 1993).

15 See ibid. Waldseemüller's map is halfway between the new heart maps and the older mantle maps, where the outlines of countries and oceans were projected onto a liturgical mantle, especially that of the emperor.

16 See Rodney Broome, *Terra Incognita: The True Story of How America Got Its Name* (Seattle: Educare, 2001).

17 See Ludger Lütkehaus (ed.), *Tiefenphilosophie. Texte zur Entdeckung des Unbewussten vor Freud* (Hamburg: Europäische Verlags-Anstalt, 1995) (originally published in 1989 under the title *Dieses wahre innere Afrika*); concerning Freud's intimate relationship with the 'dark continent', see pp. 2–7. The formulation 'wahres inneres Afrika' comes from Jean Paul's posthumous novel *Selina* (1827).

18 Sigmund Freud, *The Ego and the Id*, trans. James Strachey (New York: Norton, 1990), p. 58. That this land was already densely populated did not bother the conquistador Freud, any more than it bothered other land-takers of the imperial age; for him, the magnetizers of the nineteenth century became the Indians of the unconscious, and the hypnotists his Palestinians.

Chapter 19   The Pure Outside

1   Sigmund Freud, *The Question of Lay Analysis*, trans. James Strachey (New York: Norton, 1990), p. 38.

2   Christoph Ransmayr, *The Terrors of Ice and Darkness*, trans. John E. Woods (New York: Grove, 1996).

3   Martin Heidegger, *Being and Time*, trans. John Macquarrie & Edward Robinson (Oxford: Blackwell, 1978), p. 140.

4   Maurice Merleau-Ponty, *Phenomenology of Perception*, trans. Colin Smith (London & New York: Routledge, 2002), p. 171.

5   Maurice Merleau-Ponty, 'Eye and Mind', trans. Carleton Dallery, in *The Primacy of Perception and Other Essays on Phenomenological Psychology, the Philosophy of Art, History, and Politics* (Evanston: Northwestern University Press, 1964), p. 159.

6   Ibid., p. 166.

7   Deleuze & Guattari, *What Is Philosophy?*, p. 179.

8   See Gert Raeithel, *'Go West': Ein psychohistorischer Versuch über die Amerikaner* (Frankfurt: Syndikat, 1981).

9   See Rosa Amelia Plumell-Uribe, *La férocité blanche: des non-blancs aux non-Aryens: génocides occultés de 1492 à nos jours* (Paris: Albin Michel, 2001).

10 Schmitt, *The Nomos of the Earth*, pp. 92–9; see also Jacques Derrida, *The Politics of Friendship*, trans. George Collins (London & New York: Verso, 1997). It was Nietzsche, incidentally, who sketched the first outlines for a theory of moral decompensation in externality: 'the question which should be asked is rather: who is actually "evil" according to the morality of ressentiment? In all strictness, the answer is: none other than the "good man" of the other morality, none other than the noble, powerful, dominating man, but only once he has been given a new colour, interpretation, and aspect by the poisonous eye of ressentiment. [. . .] these same men, who are *inter pares* so strictly restrained by custom, respect, usage, gratitude, even more by circumspection and jealousy, and who in their relations with one another prove so inventive in matters of consideration, self-control, tenderness, fidelity, pride and friendship – these same men behave towards the outside world – where the foreign, the foreigners, are to be found – in a manner not much better than predators on the rampage. There they enjoy freedom from all social constraint, in the wilderness they make up for the tension built up over a long period of confinement and enclosure within a peaceful community' (*On The Genealogy of Morals*, trans. Douglas Smith [Oxford & New York: Oxford University Press, 1996], pp. 25f).

Chapter 20 Theory of the Pirate: The White Terror

1   See Charles Glass, 'The New Piracy', in *London Review of Books*, 24/2003; also William Langewiesche, *The Outlaw Sea: A World of Freedom, Chaos and Crime* (New York: Farrar, Straus and Giroux, 2004).

2 *Goethe's Faust, Parts I and II*, trans. Louis MacNeice & Ernest Ludwig Stahl (London: Faber and Faber, 1965), p. 273 (l. 11185–11188).
3 Melville, *Moby Dick*, p. xli.
4 Ibid., p. 175.
5 Ibid.
6 Ibid.
7 See Vilém Flusser, *From Subject to Project: On Becoming Human* (London: Free Association Books, 2001).

Chapter 21 The Modern Age and the New Land Syndrome

1 Adam Smith noted in his *Inquiry* that in England's North American colonies, as soon as a workman has earned a small surplus, he will tend to invest this in land acquisition and become a settler or planter: 'He feels that an artificer is the servant of his customers, from whom he derives his subsistence; but that a planter who cultivates his own land [. . .] is really a master, and independent of all the world' (*The Wealth of Nations, Books I–III*, p. 482).
2 Melville, *Moby Dick*, p. 356.
3 The condemnation of Israel at the conference on colonialism held in Durban, South Africa, in 2001 is just one recent episode of the triumphalist tribunalization of past and present historical events.

Chapter 23 The Poetics of the Ship's Hold

1 See *Sphären II, Globen*, ch. 3, 'Archen, Stadtmauern, Weltgrenzen, Immunsysteme. Zur Ontologie des ummauerten Raums'.
2 TN: the correspondence is even clearer in the German, as the word for 'nave' is *Kirchenschiff*, literally 'church ship'.

Chapter 24 Onboard Clerics: The Religious Network

1 This was also documented by Melville in *Moby Dick*. In the Whaleman's Chapel in New Bedford, before leaving for Nantucket, the narrator notices a series of marble tablets in memory of all the sailors who died at sea: 'What deadly voids and unbidden infidelities in the lines that seem to gnaw upon all Faith, and refuse resurrection to the beings who have placelessly perished without a grave' (p. 32).
2 Horst Gründer, *Welteroberung und Christentum. Ein Handbuch zur Geschichte der Neuzeit* (Gütersloh: Gütersloher Verlagshaus G. Mohn, 1992), p. 87. TN: the phrase 'great commission' refers to Christ's command to spread his teachings.

3 A liturgical symbol of this planetary self-elevation is the tiara, which, though it had already assumed its shape as a three-tiered hyper-crown in the fourteenth century, was adapted to the globalized situation in the sixteenth by the addition of a monde (globe) at the tip of the crown. See *Sphären II, Globen*, excursus 6, 'Die Entkrönung Europas. Anekdote über die Tiara', pp. 788ff.

4 Concerning the assembling performance of sport arenas and other 'collectors' in mass culture, see *Sphären III, Schäume*, ch. 2, 'Indoors. Architekturen des Schaums', pp. 626f. There it is emphasized that instances of total effect can only come about through a combination of collectors (large-scale interiors) and connectors (mass media).

Chapter 25 The Book of Vice-Kings

1 Some Princes of Wales at least visited India, though as far as we know it was always *before* they were crowned rulers of Great Britain.

Chapter 26 The Library of Globalization

1 See Georg Forster, *Entdeckungsreise nach Tahiti und in die Südsee 1772–1775*, ed. Hermann Homann (Tübingen & Basel: Erdmann, 1979), p. 419.

Chapter 27 The Translators

1 Concerning the world of creole languages, see Hans Joachim Störig, *Abenteuer Sprache. Ein Streifzug durch die Sprachen der Erde* (Munich: dtv, 1992), pp. 345ff; on the number of languages, see David Crystal, *The Cambridge Encyclopedia of Language* (Cambridge University Press, 2005).

Chapter 28 Synchronous World

1 See Peter Sloterdijk, 'The Time of the Crime of the Monstrous: On the Philosophical Justification of the Artificial', trans. Wieland Hoban, in *Sloterdijk Now*, ed. Stuart Elden (Cambridge: Polity, 2012), pp. 165–81. Martin Albrow's aforementioned suggestion is interesting in this context: to consider the period between 1492 and 1945 (or until the climate conference in Rio de Janeiro) 'modernity' or the 'age of globalization' with equal validity, setting this apart from the 'global age' of the incipient transnational world form, for which the heroic phase

of globalization created the necessary conditions. If one understands globality in this way as a result and *fait accompli* of globalization, the 'post-historical' structure of this 'global age' we have entered stands out – that is, a shift of emphasis from history to news, and from a reliance on regional pasts to a reliance on trans-regional futures. Only then does Albrow's playful motto – 'Forget modernity!' – become understandable, if not quite acceptable. See Albrow, *The Global Age.*

2 François Laplatine & Alexis Nouss, *Métissages. De Arcimboldo à Zombi* (Paris: Pauvert, 2001).

3 See Gilles Deleuze & Félix Guattari, *Anti-Oedipus*, trans. Robert Hurley, Mark Seem & Helen R. Lane (London & New York: Continuum, 2004), p. 244: 'The only universal history is a history of contingency.'

Chapter 29 The Second Ecumene

1 See Peter Sloterdijk, *Der starke Grund, zusammen zu sein. Erinnerungen an die Erfindung des Volkes* (Frankfurt: Suhrkamp, 1998). In our opinion, Heiner Mühlmann has undertaken the most stimulating attempt to derive a general theory of culture from an analysis of stressory and post-stressory mechanisms in *The Nature of Cultures.*

2 See Voegelin, *Order and History*, vol. 4: *The Ecumenic Age*, ch. 6, pp. 272–99.

3 Ibid., pp. 376f.

4 See Voegelin, *Order and History*, vol. 3: *Plato and Aristotle* (Baton Rouge: Louisiana State University Press, 1957). We refer to Voegelin's monumental work because, although its impact has remained negligible, it can be considered an exemplary self-penetration of philosophical Catholicism; it also shows especially clearly that defences of *philosophia perennis* in the twentieth century frequently become involuntary obituaries instead.

5 See Johann Figl, *Die Mitte der Religionen. Idee und Praxis universalreligiöser Bewegungen* (Darmstadt: Wissenschaftliche Buchgesellschaft, 1993).

6 See Deleuze & Guattari, *What Is Philosophy?*, p. 100.

7 In terms of its deep structure, this was the intellectual task to which *philosophia perennis* devoted itself, and whose impossibility occasioned its failure. See *Sphären II, Globen*, ch. 5, 'Deus sive sphaera oder: Das explodierende All-Eine', pp. 465–581.

8 Marshall McLuhan & Bruce R. Powers, *The Global Village: Transformations in World Life and Media in the 21st Century* (Oxford & New York: Oxford University Press, 1992), p. 93.

Chapter 30 The Immunological Transformation: On the Way to Thin-Walled 'Societies'

1 See Albrow, The Global Age, and Jürgen Habermas, The Postnational Constellation: Political Essays, trans. Max Pensky (Cambridge: Polity, 2001).

2 I use this term to encompass the reflections with which the theory of intimate spheres (microspherology) is 'elevated' to the level of a theory of large immune structures (states, realms, 'worlds'). See Bubbles, Spheres I: Microspherology and Sphären II, Globen, Makrosphärologie.

3 Concerning the imaginative complex of the 'portable God', see Régis Debray, God: An Itinerary, trans. Jeffrey Mehlman (London & New York: Verso, 2007), pp. 83f.

4 For an elaboration on this phrase, see Bubbles, pp. 59f.

5 See Arjun Appadurai, 'Global Ethnoscapes – Notes and Queries for a Transnational Anthropology', in Richard G. Fox (ed.), Recapturing Anthropology: Working in the Present (Santa Fe: School of American Research Press, 1991), pp. 191–210.

6 For the anthropological explanation of deeper layers of the feeling of belonging via the concepts of the 'uterotope' (or sphere of election) and the 'thermotope' (or sphere of pampering), see Sphären III, Schäume, pp. 386–405.

7 Roland Robertson, Globalization: Social Theory and Global Culture (London, Thousand Oaks & New Delhi: Sage, 1992), p. 182.

8 Walter Lippmann, admittedly, had already pointed out similar abstinence rates among the (non-)voters damned to passivity and incompetence in 1927 in his democracy-sceptical masterpiece The Phantom Public.

9 TN: in referring to height, the author invokes the original implication of the word 'decadence' (from Lat. decadere, 'to fall away').

Chapter 31 Believing and Knowing: In hoc signo (sc. globi) vinces

1 See Oskar Halecki, The Millennium of Europe (Notre Dame, IN: University of Notre Dame Press, 1963).

2 See Wolfgang Reinhard, Geschichte der europäischen Expansion, 4 vols. (Stuttgart: Kohlhammer, 1983–90).

3 Concerning the term 'collector', see Sphären III, Schäume, ch. 2, 'Indoors: Architectures of Foam', section C, 'Foam City. Makro-Interieurs und urbane Versammlungsbauten explizieren die symbiotischen Situationen der Menge', pp. 604f.

4 This insight forms the basis of the recent universal-historical study by J. R. McNeill and William H. McNeill, The Human Web: A Bird's-Eye

View of World History (New York: Norton, 2003), which describes world history as a process of network-tightening. Unfortunately, the McNeills' birds flew too high to see that they had been fooled by an optical illusion, and had projected the only phase of effective world-forming network-tightening, namely the period between 1492 and 1974, onto the complete duration of the anthropic adventure.

5 Columbus & de las Cases, *The Diario of Christopher Columbus's First Voyage to America, 1492–1493*, p. 21.
6 For a defence of Friday, see Hugo, *The Toilers of the Sea*, p. 234.
7 Cristóbal Colón, *Textos y documentos completes*, ed. Consuelo Varela (Madrid: Alianza, 1982), pp. 230–4.
8 Concerning the figure of Christophorus, see *Sphären II, Globen*, introduction, section III, 'Gott tragen', pp. 96–117.
9 TN: 'In this sign you will conquer.'
10 Oliver Morton, 'Geoscience on Parade', in *prospect magazine*, January 2004.
11 Schopenhauer, *The World as Will and Representation*, p. 3.
12 Wallerstein, *The Modern World-System I*, p. 357.

Chapter 32 Post-History

1 This limitation of the concept of history is, in my opinion, the only way to leave behind the dogmas of Eurocentrism, evolutionism and imperial universalism without denying or reducing the role and function of Europe; whoever wants to 'provincialize Europe' can only do so by measuring the real dimensions of world-production during the European episode of 1492–1945. See Dipesh Chakrabarty, *Provincializing Europe: Postcolonial Thought and Historical Difference* (Princeton & Oxford: Princeton University Press, 2000).
2 See Jeremy Rifkin, *The European Dream: How Europe's Vision of the Future is Quietly Eclipsing the American Dream* (Cambridge: Polity, 2004), as well as Ulrich Beck & Edgar Grande, *Cosmopolitan Europe*, trans. Ciaran Cronin (Cambridge: Polity, 2007).
3 TN: 'Gauck Office' refers to the office of the Federal Commissioner of the Stasi Archives, a government agency holding all records concerning the monitoring activities of the secret police (*Ministerium für Staatssicherheit*, commonly known as *Stasi*) in the GDR. The commissioner from 1990 to 2000 was the former pastor Joachim Gauck, who, at the time of translating (2012), is Federal President of Germany.
4 The series of true historians (after philosophical preludes in Voltaire, Herder, Condorcet and Hegel) was formally opened by Jacob Burckhardt, whose study *The Civilization of the Renaissance in Italy* (1860) moulded the early European age of world-taking and world-founding into a luminous tableau. Of those who foretold its end, Oswald Spengler still stands out: his studies on the 'decline of the West' are a

historico-morphological farewell to 'Faustian' culture as the only one capable of thinking the idea of history, and the only one that produced, experienced and reflected on 'history' in the stricter sense. Halfway between Burckhardt and Spengler stands the young Nietzsche, who (from the viewpoint of 'the disadvantage of history for life') took a stance against historicism's tendency towards silliness. Arnold J. Toynbee worked his way towards a post-historical perspective in his late work *Mankind and Mother Earth: A Narrative History of the World* (1976).

5 See Gründer, *Welteroberung und Christentum*, and Karl Hammer, *Weltmission und Kolonialismus. Sendungsideen des 19. Jahrhunderts im Konflikt* (Munich: Kösel, 1978). See also ch. 24, 'Onboard Clerics: The Religious Network'.

Chapter 33 The Crystal Palace

1 For more on this, see *Sphären II, Schäume*, pp. 344–50. The literary reactions to Dostoyevsky's London trip can be found in his travel account *Winter Notes on Summer Impressions* (1863), a text in which the author makes fun of, among other things, the 'sergeants of civilization' and the hothouse character of 'highly cultivated progressives', and also articulates his fear of the Baalesque triumphalism of the exhibition pavilion. Dostoyevsky sees the post-historical equation of being human with possessing spending power in the French bourgeoisie: 'money is the highest virtue and human obligation'.

2 Concerning the building's history, see Chup Friemert, *Die gläserne Arche. Kristallpalast London 1851 und 1854* (Munich: Prestel, 1984).

3 See Michael Musgrave, *The Musical Life of the Crystal Palace* (Cambridge University Press, 1995).

4 Concerning an interpretation of Heidegger's theory of boredom in connection with the development of modern irony and relaxation, see *Sphären III, Schäume*, pp. 728ff.

5 See Benedict de Spinoza, *Ethics*, ed. & trans. Edwin Curley (London: Penguin, 1996), p. 173: 'The more we understand singular things, the more we understand God' (part V, XXIV).

6 See the section 'Absolute Inseln' in *Sphären III, Schäume*, pp. 317–38.

7 Walter Benjamin, *The Arcades Project*, ed. Rolf Tiedemann, trans. Howard Eiland & Kevin McLaughlin (Cambridge, MA: Harvard University Press, 1999), pp. 37 & 42.

8 Concerning the motif of 'cosy' [*gemütlich*] and 'uncosy' [*ungemütlich*] capitalism, see Dieter & Karin Claessens, *Kapitalismus als Kultur: Enstehung und Grundlagen der bürgerlichen Gesellschaft* (Frankfurt: Büchergilde Gutenberg, 1973).

9 'Capitalism as Religion' (1921), trans. Rodney Livingstone, in *Selected Writings*, vol. 1: *1913–1926* (Cambridge, MA: Harvard University Press, 1996), pp. 288–91.

10 Concerning the problem of perception and representation posed by the capitalist context of life as a whole, see *Sphären III, Schäume*, ch. 3, section 9, 'Das Empire – oder: Das Komforttreibhaus; die nach oben offene Skala der Verwöhnung', pp. 803–33.

Chapter 34 The Dense World and Secondary Disinhibition: Terrorism as the Romanticism of the Pure Attack

1 See Emmanuel Lévinas, *Otherwise Than Being, Or, Beyond Essence*, trans. Alphonso Lingis (Dodrecht: Kluwer Academic, 1991), ch. III, 'Sensibility and Proximity', section 6, 'Proximity', pp. 81–98.
2 See Norbert Bolz, 'Warum es intelligent ist, nett zu sein', in *Blindflug mit Zuschauer* (Munich: Fink, 2005), pp. 59–68.
3 Paul Berman draws a comparison with 'fleabites'; unfortunately, the author scratches himself so vigorously that he over-interprets Islamist terror as a new totalitarianism. See *Terror and Liberalism* (New York: Norton, 2004), p. 13. Unconcerned about skewed images, he adds: 'The United States in its bovine stupidity failed to recognize those fleabites as war.' Consequently, we find insect warfare once again being praised as great politics.
4 See Boris Groys, 'Terror als Beruf', in *Ausbruch der Kunst. Politik und Verbrechen II*, ed. Carl Hegemann (Berlin: Alexander, 2003), pp. 125–48.
5 See Frank Lentricchia & Jody McAuliffe, *Crimes of Art + Terror* (Chicago & London: University of Chicago Press, 2003), pp. 6–17.
6 See Ralf Dahrendorf, *Der Wiederbeginn der Geschichte. Vom Fall der Mauer zum Krieg im Irak. Reden und Aufsätze* (Munich: C. H. Beck, 2004).
7 See *Sphären III, Schäume*, ch. 3, section 9, 'Das Empire – oder: Das Komforttreibhaus; die nach oben offene Skala der Verwöhnung', pp. 801f, as well as James L. Nolan, *The Therapeutic State: Justifying Government at Century's End* (New York & London: New York University Press, 1998).
8 See Norman Podhoretz, 'World War IV: How It Started, What it Means, and Why We Have to Win', in *Commentary*, September 2004.

Chapter 35 Twilight of the Perpetrators and the Ethics of Responsibility: The Cybernetic Erinyes

1 Kurt Bayertz, 'Eine kurze Geschichte der Herkunft der Verantwortung', in *Verantwortung. Prinzip oder Problem?*, ed. Kurt Bayertz (Darmstadt: Wissenschaftliche Buchgesellschaft, 1995), pp. 3–71.

2 See Klaus Briegleb, *Mephistos 'Faust'. Textbuch. Essay* (Deutsches Schauspielhaus Hamburg, 1999).
3 See Ulrich Gaier, *Fausts Modernität. Essays* (Stuttgart: Reclam, 2000), pp. 7–56.

Chapter 36 The Capitalist World Interior: Rainer Maria Rilke Almost Meets Adam Smith

1 Negri and Hardt have, therefore, rightly abandoned the mole as the totem animal of the radical left and proclaimed the snake its successor – a well-chosen symbol for the gnosticizing left following the failure of the dream of proletarian revolutions.
2 See Chen Guidi & Wu Chuntao, *Will the Boat Sink the Water? The Life of China's Peasants*, trans. Zhu Hong (New York: Public Affairs, 2007).
3 See Pablo Gaytán Santiago, *Apartheid social en la ciudad de la esperanza cero* (Mexico City: Interneta/Glocal, 2004).
4 See Jacques Attali, *L'homme nomade* (Paris: Fayard, 2003).
5 See Romain Rolland's letter to Sigmund Freud in response to the latter's 1927 book *The Future of an Illusion*. It should also be noted that the word *Weltinnenraum* has sometimes been misunderstood as a kind of place name: in his essay 'Weltinnenraum und Technologie', Peter Demetz goes so far as to state that certain Rilke readers, following the author, 'fled' to the world interior, as if it were some refuge rather than a mode of experience. See Demetz, 'In Sachen Rainer Maria Rilke und Thomas Mann', in *Sprache im technischen Zeitalter*, 17–18/1966, pp. 4–11.
6 Gaston Bachelard, *The Poetics of Space*, trans. Maria Jolas (Boston: Beacon Press, 1994), pp. 183–210. For an examination of Bachelard's theory of space in the context of a history of the tension between locationality and spatiality, see Edward S. Casey, *The Fate of Place: A Philosophical History* (Berkeley & Los Angeles: University of California Press, 1997), pp. 287–96.
7 TN: though it is actually her father's shroud that Penelope is weaving in the *Odyssey*, its description as a 'bridal dress' points to its expected role in precipitating the wedding desired by the suitors, as she had promised to marry one of them following its completion.
8 See David Simpson, *Situatedness, Or, Why We Keep Saying Where We're Coming from* (Durham, NC: Duke University Press, 2002) and David W. Winnicott, *Home Is Where We Start from: Essays by a Psychoanalyst* (New York: Norton, 1986).
9 Melville's Bartleby, of course, responds to every suggestion with the words 'I would prefer not to.'

Chapter 37 Mutations in the Pampering Space

1 This thesis is supported at greater length in the third chapter of *Sphären III, Schäume*, 'Auftrieb und Verwöhnung. Zur Kritik der reinen Laune', pp. 671–859.
2 *Sphären III, Schäume*, p. 398.
3 TN: the phrase *Unbehagen in der Entspannung* is almost certainly meant to recall Freud's *Das Unbehagen in der Kultur*, which, though published in English as *Civilization and Its Discontents*, would be more accurately translated as 'Unease in Culture'.
4 See *Sphären III, Schäume*, pp. 838f.
5 Concerning the contrasting phenomenon of passionate fetching by the traditional collector, see Manfred Sommer, *Sammeln. Ein philosophischer Versuch* (Frankfurt: Suhrkamp, 1999), pp. 392ff.
6 Julien Benda had already pointed out the dangers of a 'romanticism of harshness' in his 1927 text *The Treason of the Intellectuals*.

Chapter 38 Revaluation of all Values: The Principle of Abundance

1 For an examination of this concept, see *Sphären III, Schäume*, ch. 3, section 2, 'Die Mängelwesen-Fiktion', pp. 699f. There I show that because of his institutionalistic interests, Gehlen only drew the illiberal line of conclusions from the concept.
2 See Rolf Peter Sieferle, 'Gesellschaft im Übergang', in *Archäologie der Arbeit*, ed. Dirk Baecker (Berlin: Kadmos, 2002), pp. 117–54.
3 See Peter Sloterdijk & Hans-Jürgen Heinrichs, *Neither Sun Nor Death*, trans. Steve Corcoran (Los Angeles: Semiotext(e), 2010).
4 See Ulrich Bröckling, article 'Unternehmer', in *Glossar der Gegenwart*, ed. Ulrich Böckling, Susanne Krasmann & Thomas Lemke (Frankfurt: Suhrkamp, 2004), p. 275.
5 See Dante Alighieri, *De Monarchia*, book I, ch. XIV: 'every superfluity is displeasing to God and Nature, and everything displeasing to God and Nature is evil' (*The De Monarchia of Dante Alighieri*, ed. & trans. Aurelia Henry [Boston & New York: Houghton Mifflin, 1904], p. 50).
6 Smith, *The Wealth of Nations, Books I–III*, p. 441.
7 See Sieferle, 'Gesellschaft im Übergang', pp. 139f: 'The current demand for "social justice" aims to confiscate property from the productive sector and redirect it "socially" into the unproductive sector. As those without property (and perhaps even the unproductive or unemployed) could tend towards being in the social majority, we could be faced with a notable change: the democratic state becoming an agency of extra-economic constraint and attempting to tax the productive capitalist economy in order to support the unproductive, parasitic poor.'
8 Ibid., p. 125.

9 The life story of an exemplary unsettler on this front is told in Peter Singer, *Ethics into Action: Henry Spira and the Animal Rights Movement* (Lanham, MD: Rowman & Littlefield, 1998).
10 See Hermann Scheer, *The Solar Economy: Renewable Energy for a Sustainable Global Future*, trans. Andrew Ketley (London: Earthscan, 2002).
11 TN: in Germany, these colours represent the main Conservative Party (CDU) and the Green Party (Bündnis 90/Die Grünen) respectively.

Chapter 39 The Exception: Anatomy of a Temptation

1 Concerning the interpretation of this dream, which was at times also termed the 'American Creed', by Israel Zangwill (the originator of the 'melting pot' metaphor), see Arthur M. Schlesinger Jr., *The Disuniting of America: Reflections on a Multicultural Society*, revised and enlarged edition (New York: Norton, 1998), pp. 38f.
2 Harold Bloom attempts to show that a post-Christian, syncretistic religion is already dominant in the USA in his book *The American Religion: The Emergence of the Post-Christian Nation* (New York: Simon & Schuster, 1992). See also Craig Venter & Peter Sloterdijk, 'Wir erleben eine Fusion zwischen Börse und Bio-Illusion', in *Frankfurter Allgemeine Zeitung*, 21 February 2001, pp. 51f.
3 See Yi-Fu Tuan, *Escapism* (Baltimore: Johns Hopkins University Press, 1998), p. 9. For outlines of a general escapology, see *Sphären III*, *Schäume*, pp. 748f.
4 The metaphysics and ethics of improvement partly go back to older British sources, especially in the field of Gladstonian liberals; see Ian Bradley, *The Optimists: Themes and Personalities in Victorian Liberalism* (London: Faber & Faber, 1980), pp. 200–21.
5 See Schlesinger, *The Disuniting of America*, pp. 23–44.
6 The current slogan of the American Far Right, 'Let's blow up the Middle East', expresses how the elimination of this troublesome dependency is imagined in the narcissistic heartland. See also Robert Baer, *Sleeping with the Devil: How Washington Sold Our Soul for Saudi Crude* (New York: Three Rivers, 2004). It is also a logical assumption that 9/11 was intended to destroy the *entente cordiale* between the escapist systems: hence Bin Laden's choice of mostly Saudi Arabian perpetrators for the fatal flights.
7 From the State of the Union Address on 28 January 2003, reproduced (abridged) in George W. Bush, *We Will Prevail: President George W. Bush on War, Terrorism and Freedom* (New York: Continuum, 2003), p. 220.
8 From the speech to the American Enterprise Institute in Washington on 26 February 2003, reproduced in Bush, *We Will Prevail*, p. 225.
9 I am indebted to Gilles Kepel for this information.

10   For an extremely symptomatic example of this role, see Paul Berman, *Terror and Liberalism* (New York: Norton, 2003) – a book in which the term 'totalitarianism', which already explained little in Hannah Arendt's day, is employed to draw a parallel between the current hate-fuelled worldviews of Islamists and earlier Western anti-modernists. The approach has certain merits, but fails in Berman's case on account of half-educated analogies.

11   Concerning the idea-historical derivation of traditional Islamic anti-Judaism, see Jean Lacarrière, *L'Orient et l'Occident. Les origins d'un conflit* (Paris: Gallimard, 2003). See also *Neuer Antisemitismus? Eine globale Debatte*, ed. Doron Rabinovici, Ulrich Speek & Natan Sznaider (Frankfurt: Suhrkamp, 2004), as well as Pierre-André Taguieff, *Rising from the Muck: The New Anti-Semitism in Europe*, trans. Patrick Camiller (Chicago: Ivan R. Dee, 2004). One notable thing about the last of these is that it replaces the historical term 'anti-Semitism' with the more adequate 'Judeophobia'.

12   See John Arquilla & David Ronfeldt, *The Emergence of Noopolitik: Toward an American Information Strategy* (Santa Monica: RAND, 1999).

13   See Groys, 'Warten auf die grossen Ameisen'.

14   See Paul Mann, *Masocriticism* (Albany: SUNY Press, 1999).

15   This is evidenced by a unique national debate on fat, indeed a profound hermeneutics of fat; see, among others, Jedediah Purdy, 'Jeder ein König. Amerikaner sind dick. Auch ihre Politik hat ein Problem – da gibt es Zusammenhänge', in *Die Zeit*, 44/2004, p. 44.

Chapter 40   The Uncompressible, or: The Rediscovery of the Extended

1   See Sloterdijk, *Tau von den Bermudas*, pp. 27–40.

2   Carl Schmitt, *Land and Sea*, trans. Simona Draghici (Washington: Plutarch, 1997).

3   TN: Heidegger's play on words, taken up here by Sloterdijk, is between the verb *lesen*, 'to read' (or, less commonly, 'to gather') and the noun *Lese*, 'collection' (normally in the sense of a vintage). Thus the reading room [*Lesesaal*] also becomes a collection room.

4   More recently, see also Derrick de Kerckhove & Claude de Vos, *Le monde de l'alphabet*, manuscript (2004).

5   See the letter by Husserl to Hugo von Hoffmannsthal from 12 January 1907: an invocation of the alliance between art and phenomenology based on a shared passion for 'purely aesthetic' seeing and a 'purely philosophical' intellectual attitude (the word 'purely' [*rein*] appears thirteen times on three pages), as well as a shared rejection of confinement to mere living.

6   See Maurice Blanchot, *Le livre à venir* (Paris: Gallimard, 1959).

7 See Karl Schlögel, *Im Raume lesen wir die Zeit. Über Zvilisationsge-schichte und Geopolitik* (Munich: Hanser, 2003), a book that càn be read as a key work of a new culture of geography, or of a historical existential topographics.

8 Miguel Torga, *The Creation of the World*, quoted in T. N. Harper, 'Empire, Diaspora and the Languages of Globalism, 1850–1914', in Hopkins, *Globalization in World History*, p. 141.

9 See Robertson, *Globalization: Social Theory and Global Culture*, p. 193. These terms, according to Robertson, imitate the Japanese word *dochakuka*, which approximately expresses the idea that Japanese products for the global market have to be adapted to the circumstances in their place of consumption.

10 See *Sphären III, Schäume*, pp. 523ff.

11 See Heidegger, *Being and Time*, pp. 138f and Schmitz, *System der Philosophie, Der Raum*, vol. 4 (Bonn: Bouvier, 1995), §218 (pp. 258–308). TN: the translation of *Sein und Zeit* quoted here renders *Ent-fernung* as 'de-severance', but 'de-distancing' is perhaps a more natural choice.

12 Heidegger, *Being and Time*, p. 140.

13 Gilles Deleuze & Félix Guattari, *A Thousand Plateaus*, trans. Brian Massumi (London & New York: Continuum, 2004), pp. 559f.

Chapter 41 In Praise of Asymmetry

1 In his remarks on the world-poverty of the animal, Heidegger notes that it is locked in a ring of disinhibiting (i.e. behaviour-triggering) factors; with reference to humans, who are 'world-forming', it is more accurate to say that they are surrounded by a ring of things and relationships which they leave as they are: this leads to soft exclusion, exclusion through not-specifically-getting-and-including. Needless to say, this leaving outside – through no fault of one's own – of what is outside will forever remain a fundamental trait of human world-having and being-had by other things. Niklas Luhmann expresses this in his own way: 'initially, it (the world) is the wilderness of that which happens simultaneously, and hence by definition uncontrollably' (Niklas Luhmann, *Die Gesellschaft der Gesellschaft* [Frankfurt: Suhrkamp, 1998], p. 527).

2 See Dirk Baecker (ed.), *Kapitalismus als Religion* (Berlin: Kadmos, 2003).

Index

mythodynamics 167, 244
mythology 121, 215–16

naming practices 104–5
Napoleon 67, 68, 75
narcissism 197, 228, 238, 246
narrative, grand 3–5
NASA 21
National Socialism 64
nationalism 106, 121, 122–3,
    128–30, 168, 246, 261
nation-states 139, 143, 149, 150,
    152, 157, 178, 185, 225, 247
Nautilus (*Moby Dick*) 78
negativity 172, 234
Negri, Antonio 7, 193, 288n1
neighbourhood 31, 141, 177, 259
neo-Cynicism 209
neo-liberalism 182, 183
neo-Marxism 64–5
Netherlands 106, 126, 129, 168, 259
New Amsterdam 106
New Deal 234
New England 106
New Helvetia 106
new land syndrome 116–19
New Mythology 63
New Netherlands 106
New South Wales 106
New Testament 135
New World *see* America
Nicholas of Cusa 10
Nietzsche, Friedrich 49, 70, 75, 76,
    90, 92, 209, 221, 252, 280n10
  historicism 167, 285–6n4
nihilism 209, 232
nobility 48–9, 68, 154
'noetic epiphany' 145
noopolitics 244
North America 35, 72, 106
North Pole 107, 108
Northern Sea Route 77
Northwest Passage 77

numerals, Arabic 45
Nuremberg Rally 158

obedience 58, 59–60, 71
obesity 247
observation 67, 87, 98, 132, 198
obstruction 11–12
Occident 33–4
Odysseus 202
offensivity 66, 67–8, 69, 70, 74–5
officialdom 48, 273n5
oil 195, 214, 226, 238, 290n6
Old Testament 116, 238
Olympic Games 126
one-sidedness *see* unilateralism
'opportunities, society of' 61
optimism 82, 83, 171, 234–6, 241
orb motif 5–6, 8–10, 12–14, 19–20,
    21, 23–8, 31–2, 147–8
  in philosophy 15, 91, 92, 100–1
  in religion 6, 282n3
  symbolism 48, 102, 103, 106, 125,
    161
  see also globes
Orient 33–4
originality 74, 190, 192
other, inclusion of 179
other, real 187
outrage 19
outside 27, 29, 50–1, 109–11,
    114–15, 147, 152, 194,
    280n10
  see also externalization
Oviedo, Fernández de 270n4
ownership 101–4, 107, 117–18,
    214–15, 278n5

Pacific space 117, 232
pacifism 216–17
Pakistan 166
pampering 211–22, 223, 226
papacy 59–60, 61, 125–6, 129–30,
    168